William Dinwiddie

Puerto Rico

Its Conditions and Possibilities

William Dinwiddie
Puerto Rico
Its Conditions and Possibilities
ISBN/EAN: 9783337379179

Printed in Europe, USA, Canada, Australia, Japan

Cover: Foto ©Suzi / pixelio.de

More available books at **www.hansebooks.com**

PUERTO RICO
Its Conditions and Possibilities

By

WILLIAM DINWIDDIE

With Illustrations from
Photographs by the Author

NEW YORK AND LONDON
HARPER & BROTHERS PUBLISHERS
1899

INTRODUCTION

IT has been the writer's earnest desire, in the accompanying pages, which relate exclusively to our new possession, Puerto Rico, to place before the reader as complete a presentation as possible of the industrial, commercial, political, and social conditions existing on that island today; together with sufficient facts, figures, and comparisons of past institutions to give those personally interested in the future development of the fertile isle a comprehensive grasp of the administrative problems which confront us, and the possibilities for the embarking of American business enterprises.

Under the direction of Messrs. Harper & Brothers, the author spent the two months immediately following the Spanish evacuation of the island, constantly in touch with the leading Spanish citizens and native Puertoriqueños, who were importers, manufacturers, shopkeepers, estate-owners, lawyers, and politicians, and he has, by the aid of the varying opinions elicited, attempted to embody in this work a crystallization of the most profound and valuable ideas expressed.

He feels a deep appreciation of the courtesies extended to him by army officers—whereby he was enabled readily to traverse the island from end to end and make careful studies of agricultural and manufacturing interests—and wishes to tender special thanks to General Guy V. Henry and General John R. Brooke, who assisted him in gaining access to Spanish records.

INTRODUCTION

To the late Librarian of Congress, Honorable John Russell Young, he is particularly indebted for opportunity to study Puerto Rican literature in the archives of that library and elsewhere.

WILLIAM DINWIDDIE.

NEW YORK, March, 1899.

CONTENTS

CHAPTER	PAGE
I. The Evacuation of Puerto Rico	3
II. General Characteristics	9
III. Prevalent Diseases in the Island and Hygienic Precautions	22
IV. Geology	27
V. The Military Road	32
VI. Over the Trails	41
VII. The Great Caves	56
VIII. Industrial Possibilities	65
IX. Coffee Culture	85
X. Sugar Culture	101
XI. Tobacco Culture	115
XII. Fruit-Raising, Market-Gardening and Floriculture	128
XIII. Home Life	145
XIV. Life Among the Peasants	155
XV. Burden-Bearing	167
XVI. Cock-Fighting	175
XVII. The Principal Cities	180
XVIII. Schools, Churches, and Charitable Institutions	198
XIX. Burials and Cemeteries	209
XX. The Money of the Islands	214
XXI. Revenues and Taxes	225
XXII. Courts	232
XXIII. Political Methods	238
XXIV. Historical Sketch	250
APPENDIX	253

ILLUSTRATIONS

"THE FIRST FLASH OF FIRE AND SMOKE"	*Frontispiece*	
SAN JUAN HARBOR — VESSELS DECORATED IN HONOR OF THE DAY	*Facing p.*	4
SPANISH SOLDIERS IN SAN CRISTOBAL BARRACKS .		
RAISING THE FLAG OVER SAN JUAN, OCTOBER 18TH, 1898.	"	6
UNITED STATES TROOPS TAKING POSSESSION OF THE ARMORY OF THE FIRST SPANISH INFANTRY, SAN JUAN	"	8
THE FOOT-HILLS NEAR THE COAST OF PONCE.	"	12
THE MOUNTAINS OF CENTRAL PUERTO RICO	"	16
CORAL FORMATIONS ON THE TRAIL BETWEEN UTUADO AND LARES	"	28
THE MILITARY ROAD NEAR JUANA DIAZ	"	32
PICTURESQUE BRIDGE ON MILITARY ROAD, NORTH OF CAGUAS	"	34
CLIMBING THE MOUNTAIN ON THE GREAT MILITARY ROAD, NORTH OF AYBONITO.	"	36
THE TOWN OF AYBONITO, FROM THE SOUTH—THE HIGHEST POINT ON THE MILITARY ROAD	"	38
TREE FERNS ON THE ROAD	"	42
HALF WAY TO UTUADO	"	44
A BIT OF NARROW TRAIL OUT OF UTUADO	"	48
A SIDE TRAIL ON THE ADJUNTAS—UTUADO TRAIL	"	50
ON THE WAY TO THE CAVES	"	58
DAILY TRAIN ON THE SAN JUAN-CAROLINA RAILROAD	"	68
BEEF CATTLE OF PUERTO RICO	"	72
THE HOT SPRINGS AT COAMO	"	82
HAULING THE CROP OVER A HEAVY TRAIL	"	86
PACK-TRAIN CARRYING COFFEE TO MARKET		
COFFEE AND TOBACCO LANDS, NEAR CAYEY	"	90

ILLUSTRATIONS

PUBLIC SQUARE OF LARES	*Facing p.* 94
A COFFEE-PLANTER'S HOME, LARES, LOS MARIAS TRAIL	" 96
SUGAR-CANE FIELDS AT VIEQUES, OR CRAB, ISLAND	" 104
OLD SINGLE-STICK PLOUGH }	
PRIMITIVE METHOD OF REMOVING THE "BAGASSE" }	" 106
TYPICAL SUGAR-MILL NEAR PONCE—ANTIQUATED AND MODERN MACHINERY COMBINED	" 110
GIRLS STRIPPING THE LEAF TOBACCO	" 116
FINE TOBACCO LAND—CLEARED TO THE HILL-TOPS, CAYEY DISTRICT	" 120
CIGAR MAKING IN THE LARGEST FACTORY, CAYEY	" 124
A DATE-PALM	" 136
THE PAWPAW-TREE, WITH EDIBLE FRUIT	" 138
YAUTIA—LILY WITH EDIBLE TUBERS	" 142
COUNTRY HOUSE OF A WELL-TO-DO PUERTORIQUEÑO }	
GUAVA-TREE—FROM THE FRUIT OF WHICH GUAVA JELLY IS MADE }	" 146
THE DRAWING-ROOM OF A PUERTO RICO HOME	" 150
NATIVE TYPES—A MOTHER AND CHILDREN IN STREET COSTUME	" 158
A PEON VILLAGE NEAR CAGUAS	" 164
THE BREAD-WAGON OF CAGUAS	" 168
OXEN—THE PRINCIPAL DRAFT ANIMALS ON THE ISLAND	" 172
COCK-FIGHTING AT CAGUAS	" 176
THE STREET OF THE HOLY CROSS, SAN JUAN	" 182
A MARKET SCENE AT PONCE	" 188
AT THE INDUSTRIAL SCHOOL, SAN JUAN	" 198
THE TUNGILLO CHURCH, NEAR CAROLINA, BUILT IN 1813	" 200
THE CHURCH AT LARES	" 204
THE CATHEDRAL AT HORMIGUERO	" 206
A CEMETRY IN PUERTO RICO	" 208
A PAUPER BURIAL	" 210
MORTUARY DECORATIONS AT PONCE	" 212

PUERTO RICO

PUERTO RICO

CHAPTER I

THE EVACUATION

SPAIN formally released Puerto Rico from her sovereignty at twelve o'clock on Tuesday, October 18, 1898, by the withdrawal of her troops from the capital city of San Juan. It was the breaking of the last tie which has bound the easternmost fertile isle of the western hemisphere to a galling yoke of tyranny and taxation for nearly four hundred years.

The dawn of this memorable day in Puerto Rican history came clear, colorless, and hot; not a cloud dotted the sky, and, as the sun rose toward the zenith, the narrow, brick-paved streets of San Juan quivered with moist heat, and, in the breathless air, the surging crowds elbowed one another for positions of vantage within the narrow shadows of noonday.

Two days before the ceremony, every hotel in the town was crowded to its utmost capacity, and, on the night before the evacuation, strangers slept three and four together in the tiny, dark rooms, whose only source of light was the stained-glass doors opening into a central rotunda, suffering all night long from an infestation of humming, insatiable mosquitoes.

PUERTO RICO

In the harbor lay a Spanish transport, ready to carry home the soldiers, while outside, on a calm ocean, lay our ships loaded with blue-uniformed men, waiting for the moment when the booming of the midday gun was to sound the death-knell of Spanish supremacy and give Puerto Rico to the American government.

At daylight on Tuesday, the last callings of the Spanish bugles rang through the town from the quartels of San Cristobal and Morro, and sixteen hundred Spanish soldiers prepared to march through the massive-walled portals, down the narrow streets of the town, and out to the westward suburban town of Santurce, where they were to camp temporarily until the arrival of a second Spanish steamer; but, through the courtesy of General John R. Brooke, commanding our forces, they were granted permission to remain in their barracks until all the Spanish transports arrived.

A surrender of the conquered to the conqueror is a sad function from its very nature, but in this instance it was far more than sad; it was the acme of human misery, arising, however, not from the hurt done to martial spirit, but from the annihilation of happy homes. The Spanish soldiers and Guardia Civil have married largely among Puerto Rican women, and have become factors in the domestic life of the island. The evacuation program did not provide for a condition like this, so the Spaniard went back to his own country—though only for a time, perhaps—and his wife and children must weep and go hungry until his return.

As if in answer to the shrill blasts of Spanish bugles, came the deeper notes of our own, echoing back from without the city limits, and soon the steady, sturdy tramp of our own stalwart men resounded between the low walls of the city streets. *We* were going to cheer our country's

SAN JUAN HARBOR—VESSELS DECORATED IN HONOR OF THE DAY

SPANISH SOLDIERS IN SAN CRISTOBAL BARRACKS

THE EVACUATION

flag and glory in our new possessions; *they*—well, no one knows what the Spanish soldiers felt; a mixture, perhaps, of pleasure in going back to their hillside vineyards, of heartache at leaving their loved ones, and of well-masked hatred for those who had broken Spain's arrogant power.

As the hour of twelve drew near, American soldiers stood before the white front of the balconied home of past Spanish Governor-Generals, and in the Plaza before the Chamber of Deputies and the City Hall, and again at the gates of the castles of Morro and San Cristobal, patiently awaiting the coming of the hour. Around them, at all these places, were gathered queer, interesting, and withal motley crowds of American tourists and newspapermen, of well-dressed Spanish and Puerto Rican merchants and landholders, and of the dark-colored, ragged, and tattered natives. Little talk was indulged in, and enthusiasm, if there was any, was withheld from active expression. The minutes were passed in hushed waiting, a straining of eyes toward the bare flag-poles, and a nervous consultation of watches.

Now it was coming, and a long-drawn breath sighed through the packed crowds, followed by the first uneasy shuffling of feet. The cry of "Attention!" caused every soldier to straighten rigidly on his heels, except a few poor fellows who had dropped, weak and sweltering, under the fierce heat of the sun, and lay uncaring beneath the shaded walls. The newsmen craned their necks in eager expectancy, and the click of adjusted camera shutters could be heard from every point of elevation.

At each flagstaff a shoulder-strapped man stood grasping the flag-halyards, trying them now and again in fear lest they might fail at the critical moment, and, from their high-perched positions, they watched the clock-towers or looked seaward toward the bold, rugged, fortified castles for the first flash of fire and smoke from the great black guns.

Ding! and the little, sweet-toned bell of a near-by cathedral sang the first stroke of twelve; it was overpowered in its first vibrations by the deep-bellowing clang of the great bell on the City Hall. They answered each other in rhythmic chime, the ponderous and the weak, one after another, until the last echoing thrill of twelve made Puerto Rico ours.

The stars and stripes rose gently over every building, and were wafted by a new-born breeze, as if in sympathy with the rousing cheers of the surging Americans beneath, and as if in salutation to the roaring guns which belched their smoke far to seaward, as they boomed out the twenty-one shots of honor and of freedom.

It was a deeply impressive ceremony—done without ostentatious display, done without gold-laced uniforms or martial panoply, but well done. The very simplicity of the celebration appeals to American hearts. Our attitude was not that of the dictator, but of the protector. No bombastic speeches wounded the still sensitive Spanish pride, no great military pomp caused the teeth of a vanquished enemy to grind in hidden rage; we raised our flag softly, proudly, if you like, but we raised it with an outstretched hand of friendship.

With the floating of our flag over Spain's provincial capital of San Juan, the United States became, not only the master of a veritable Garden of Eden, but the possessor of a vast amount of government property. In the cities of the whole island permanent structures have been erected, in the nature of buildings for officials, barracks for soldiers, many hospitals, and, on the seacoast, massive stone forts. In San Juan, itself, our prizes include two wonderful stone forts, whose grey, moss-covered walls

RAISING THE FLAG OVER SAN JUAN, OCTOBER 18, 1898

THE EVACUATION

tell a story of antiquated defenses, which would, however, even now offer a very material protection against modern projectiles. On them were mounted fifty-six guns, new and old, twenty-eight of which are fairly modern, six-inch, breech-loading, rifled guns, and four modern mortars. In the magazines were stored immense quantities of powder and ammunition; in fact, shortly before war was declared, an entire shipload of the most approved projectiles was landed at San Juan, and now belongs to our government. Again, in this city, we now own a five-storied infantry barracks, which has been constructed during the last five years and will hold 100,000 men. It was damaged badly, but not beyond repair, during the three hours' naval bombardment of the city, when it was believed that Cervera's fleet lay in hiding in the harbor. There are two other immense barracks, but they are of old Spanish architecture—the quartel San Cristobal and the Marine barracks. The United States also owns a new city hall and a great public building, the "Intendencia," both facing the plaza of the city. The value of our entire acquisitions runs up into millions of money, which have been expended by Spain in furnishing homes for her soldiers and her officials, and in the vain attempt to protect and hold her colonial possessions, even though, in years gone by, she has valiantly and successfully repelled all assailants.

The American officers who had the honor of raising the flags at San Juan were Major J. T. Dean at the Governor's palace; Colonel Goethals, of the Engineer Corps, over the "Intendencia"; Major Carson, of the Quartermaster's Department, at the City Hall; and Major Day, in command of a battery of the Fifth Artillery, over Morro castle. Major Day also raised the first American flag floated at Ponce.

PUERTO RICO

Few troops took active part in the ceremony: two battalions of the Eleventh Infantry at different points; troop A of the Sixth Cavalry at the palace, and the Fifth Heavy Artillery at Morro and San Cristobal. All the afternoon, however, the soldiers were marching from camps without the city's limits, until at nightfall several thousand men were scattered through the town. On Monday night at every street corner stood the Spanish Guardia Civil, the official tyrant of the island, while sentries of the Spanish army were posted near all government buildings; when Tuesday's sunset came, our armed soldiers paced back and forth over the selfsame posts, while the Spanish soldiers—without guns, though armed with bayonets—wandered through the town as aliens, or gathered in clusters, in animated discussion. It was a curious metamorphosis.

Almost at the moment that the brilliant planet Venus shone faintly in the waning light of evening, a great gun on Morro castle, manned by men in blue, belched forth a farewell salute to day. The long white curls of smoke were wafted eastward slowly out to sea, and, as its billows ascended high in the air, the sinking sun tinted their topmost crest with rosy light, an omen, it was said, that the black cloud of Spanish cruelty had passed away, and in its stead had dawned the pearl- and rose-colored promise of future happiness for Puerto Rico.

UNITED STATES TROOPS TAKING POSSESSION OF THE ARMORY OF THE FIRST SPANISH INFANTRY, SAN JUAN

CHAPTER II

GENERAL CHARACTERISTICS

Physical Features

THE first impressions one receives of the island of Puerto Rico from the water, as the steamer churns through a placid sea as blue as the beautiful Mediterranean, are rather disappointing. These impressions depend largely upon how novel to the traveler are the expanses of limpid azure, with the distant highlands gradually rising from the flat earth near the sea to rough foothills, and then to sharp-pointed, irregular peaks, piled high behind each other, all clothed in the same unvarying, intense green, the entire landscape being wonderfully crowned with low-hanging, vaporous clouds, which roll forever into new, fantastic, nebulous forms.

If one has not seen the giant mountain-ranges of the southeastern coast of Cuba, lifted seven thousand feet in air, or those of the heart of the Antillean chain in Santo Domingo, which rise twelve thousand feet, in pinnacled peaks of verdure, from bases bound in coral and washed by the waves of a summer sea, then one will be tempted to exclaim, "What a paradise!" Comparison, the invidious mental enemy, alone can detract from the loveliness of this "Isle of the Gate of Gold."

Puerto Rican mountain-ranges rise massively only two thousand feet above the level of the sea, with here and there a peak gaining gradual elevation to three thousand, or, in the case of El Yunque in the northeast, thirty-seven hundred feet, but there are no great heights which hold the eye entranced. Neither do they make an effective showing from the sea, as the most marked elevations are far inland; in fact the mountainous backbone traverses almost the center of the island, beginning at a point near San German in the southwest corner, and crossing diagonally to El Yunque, the highest land near the northeast.

In circumnavigating the island, the western end has few suggestions of scenic beauty. The isle of Desecheo, like a partially-submerged cone,—the home of sea-birds only,—guards the northwest corner like a lonely sentinel. Looking toward Aguadilla, on the mainland, the country is slightly rolling, backed by a single low range of carved, ancient-coral formation in the middle ground, while in the misty distance there are suggestions of greater mountains. Mayaguez, the great western shipping port, is almost invisible from the sea, lying low down on the shoreline, and fronting an open harbor which is a dangerous one in heavy southwesterly or westerly weather. Still farther to the south, one looks into apparently better-protected, landlocked harbors, while the distant view carries the eye from the near-by, rolling foothills along the axes of heavy ranges.

The western end of the southern coast is monotonous in the extreme, and nothing breaks the weariness of the view except the dashing of waves on coral reefs, whose tireless builders have thrust their castellated homes upward through the foam and spray. The ancient and almost-deserted port of Guanica, foreshortened from the water into a mere dent in the coast-line, develops into as fine and beautiful a harbor as any on the island—excepting, perhaps, the sea-sheltered havens near Fajardo on the

GENERAL CHARACTERISTICS

east. It is surprising that cities should have sprung up near almost useless ports, while at this point—offering as it does a fine deep-water harbor, too narrow for much maneuvering at its mouth—a town once recognized as a point of ocean trade has not only failed to expand commercially, but has lost its old-time prestige. Its deterioration could probably be traced to political discrimination in San Juan.

Ponce, to the west of the center of the southern coast-line and two miles from the ocean, can just be seen with a field-glass, cradled in palms and green trees among the first of the rolling foothills, while the Playa, its port-town, stands, with flat roofs and whitened walls, on the disintegrated coral of the shore. The harbor is very open and shallow, though protected somewhat on the east by a spur of land, and slightly on the west by a little island reef, made a gem of beauty by the simple architecture of its white lighthouse.

From Ponce westward the landscape from the sea grows more pleasing, and one realizes the beauty of the mountain-ranges, each rising higher behind the other, the effect enhanced by the great spur from the main series which breaks away and follows the seacoast not many miles inland. At Jobos, on this portion of the shore-line, occurs another fine harbor with ample sea-room, which is used only by a few coasting vessels; the thriving city of Guayama, but five miles away to the westward, uses—curiously enough—the open roadstead of Arroyo, four miles on the other side, for shipping purposes, in preference to the fine, landlocked body of water at Jobos.

From the island of Vieques, on the southeast corner, to San Juan, on the northern coast, the landscape is broken by islets and islands, and the mainland shows jutting, rocky promontories, producing kaleidoscopic vistas of which one never tires.

PUERTO RICO

The islands of Vieques and Culebra, which lie off the east coast and belong to Puerto Rico, are low in contour, with little running water, though they are fertile in the extreme, and the waving cane-fields of Vieques, which stretch over hill and dale, are far more lovely, in their undulating, silken tassels, than those of the mainland, covering flat, unrelieved plains.

The thousand small islands which form the Lesser Antilles and curve off in a great arc to the southward from Puerto Rico, together with the innumerable coral islets shooting out from the northeast corner of the island, constitute a sea-screen which protects all the harbors of the eastern side; and it is quite probable that, under the impetus of American development, this side of the island—instead of being almost wholly deserted commercially—will become in time the most favored and sought after, for it undoubtedly offers natural advantages in a marked degree, in the shape of protected sea-room, with deep waters close inshore, such as are not possessed by the other three sides. It should be stated, however, that coral reefs and shoals abound, among which navigation is highly dangerous at present, owing to the lack of accurate charts; but when the Coast Survey shall have carefully mapped the submarine pathways, these difficulties will be overcome, for, between these submerged reefs, which act as sea-walls, are ample passageways of deep water.

It is said that this is the less fertile end of the island, but the opinion has gained credence from the fact that hitherto this region has contributed less in commercial products, and hence has attracted less attention in business centers, rather than because the soil possesses any inherent sterility, for it is beyond question quite as rich and productive as any other section of the land, and—

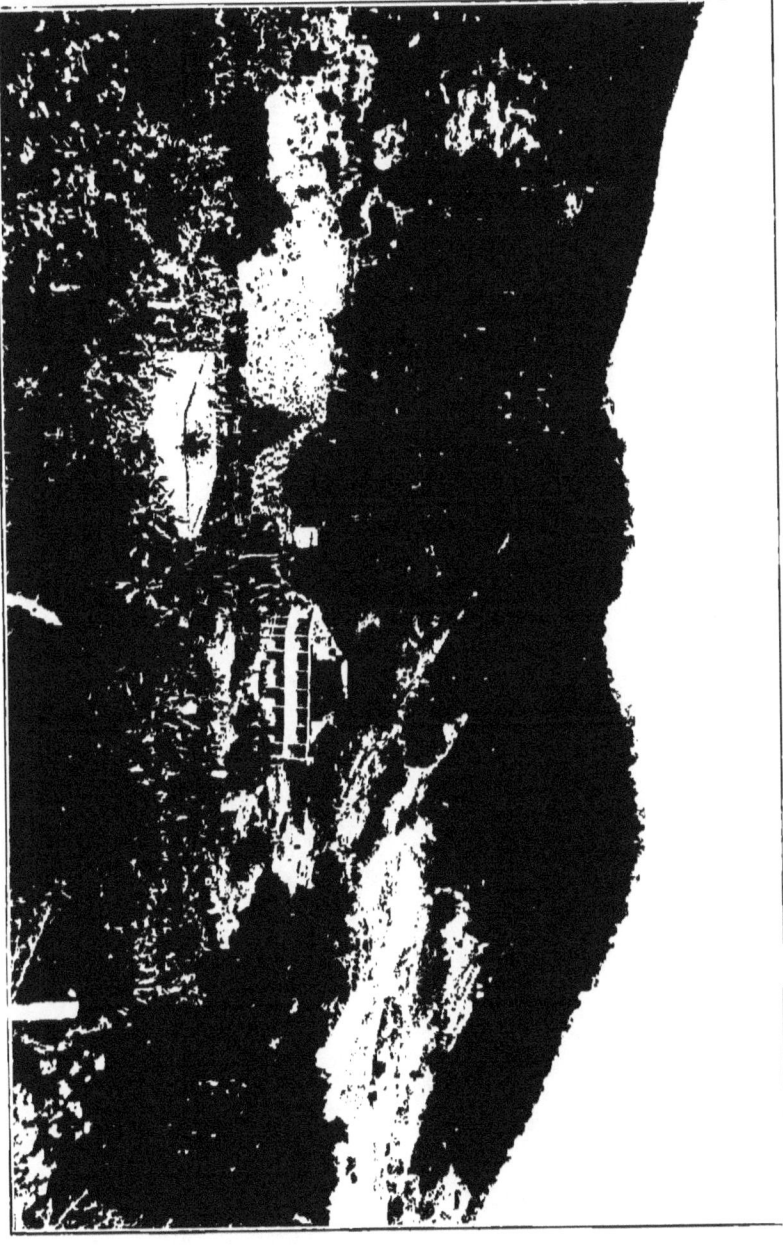

THE FOOT-HILLS NEAR THE COAST OF PONCE

given population and land and sea transportation facilities—it should outstrip other regions tributary to the less-favored harbors on the open coasts.

The northern side of the island has no good ports, with the exception of the embayed harbor of San Juan, and the landscape from afar is almost a dreary one. Arecibo is the only city—after the capital—which attracts the eye landward. Its cathedral seems to rise from a veritable city of thatched huts, though in reality these only hang upon the skirts of the main city, which is well built. Past its doors flows the second largest river on the island, Rio Grande de Arecibo.

San Juan is a city of delight to the vision. Its massive, high-walled, grey-grown forts may be seen far out at sea, their battlements crowning every bold salient of the shoreline. Across its harbor entrance, in heavy northern weather, the white-crested billows pile high on each other in a frenzied race toward shore ; this, viewed as a picture in nature, fills the heart with rapture, but, seen with the eye of the mariner, causes the face of the stoutest navigator to pale.

The deep, fast-flowing rivers, which fall into the sea from this side, are all spoken of by previous writers as being navigable for several miles inland, but mention is made, at the same time, of sand-bars and spits which close them effectually to shipping. From a commercial standpoint they would be of little use, even if their mouths were opened by dredging, as they flow between banks quite too close for the handling of anything but small fishing smacks, and, during a receding tide, the out-speeding current whips the water's surface into eddying whirlpools, which would be dangerous even for moored vessels.

On the whole it must be admitted that Puerto Rico,

from the water, is not an impressive sight; that it has few good harbors, and that the best of them appeal neither to the artistic nor technical eye; but it should be remembered that this little island has less than three hundred and fifty miles of coast-line, all told—or, roughly speaking, about as much as the coast of Massachusetts—and in this short distance it lays claim to fourteen harbors, though, in point of real commercial utility, it has not more than six. In an island which averages but ninety-five miles in length by thirty-five in breadth, half a dozen good ports will feel the strain of competition severely, when the time shall come that railroad transportation and good roads bind the agricultural country closely to the business centers.

Once on shore, the traveler through the island realizes for the first time what a wealth of artistic loveliness and fertile possibilities lies in this land clothed with a livery of tropical vegetation. Almost every foot of ground is steep and rolling, except along the coast-lines and in a few narrow valleys of the interior, where the earth lies seemingly as flat as a floor, from the banks of the wandering rivers to the very foot of the mountains, which rise abruptly to sharp, curved crests, a thousand feet above.

Table-lands there are none; the mountain uplifts are flexed into razor-backed ridges, and time and weather have fought against the form-preserving vegetation with sufficient success to mold their sides into soft erosional shapes, steep-sided and high, but covered to their very tops with rich, fertile, and cultivatable soil.

While there are no flat-topped mountain-ranges in the interior, the few narrow valleys, found mainly on the northern side east of the center, are elevated above the sea as much as a thousand feet, and no more delightful place of abode for white men can be imagined: per-

GENERAL CHARACTERISTICS

fect landscapes, a soil in which almost everything under heaven will grow, cool nights, bearable days, and the whole of this idealistic conception set off with a filigree-work of heaving clouds, wonderful rainbows overhanging the green of stately palms, waving, broad-leaved banana plantations, food- and fruit-trees, and jungle forests whose odd shapes and queer foliage lend a never-tiring charm to the scene. It is a tropic Elysium, and will become the winter Mecca of America.

Climate

Ask the average man who formed an integral part of the Army of Invasion which went to Puerto Rico what he thinks of the climate, and his opinion will most likely be forcibly expressed by the word " damnable." His judgment is a biased one, however, for it should be remembered that he bore all the hardships of a severe campaign. With a system weakened by life in fever-infected camps, and after a prolonged interval aboard cramped, foul-smelling transports, he was forced out, during the heat of summer, into torrid suns, chilling rains, and bottomless mud in tangled trails, subsisting, meantime, on a diet unknown to him in his own comfortable home—a mixture of " government straight " and tropical fruits. It is little wonder that his plaintive song voiced itself in the words of " God's Countrie." The fact is patent, however, that the army of Puerto Rico returned, in spite of necessary exposure, with few men left behind in lonely graves, and with a small percentage of sickness in its ranks, as compared with the men who were forced into the death-trap of Santiago, while those who have remained on the island, quartered in barracks, show a less percentage of illness in their forces than they did before leaving the United States.

PUERTO RICO

In spite of various and contrary opinions, the climate of Puerto Rico is not a difficult one for North Americans to hold their own in the year around, though it is most enjoyable in the middle of winter, when our own broad United States is clothed in ice and snow, chilled by sullen rains, or frozen by the biting winds of bitter blizzards.

The island lies within the torrid zone, between latitudes 17° 54′ and 18° 30′ N. On the mainland of North America at this latitude, the climate is quite unbearable to the unacclimated during the entire year—unless it be perhaps in sections where the altitude is five thousand feet or over—but, owing to Puerto Rico's position far out on the ocean to the eastward (longitude west from Greenwich 65° 35′–67° 15′), away from the warm waters of the Gulf Stream, together with the comparatively small area, which permits it to be swept by the prevailing trade-winds from end to end, the climate is one in which those of temperate regions may safely live, provided some care be taken of the health for the first few months until physical adjustment has taken place.

In the heat of summer, the temperature never rises above 95° Fahrenheit on the seacoast, and the nights are usually cool. Whatever unpleasantness pertains to the climate is the outcome of the excessive humidity of the atmosphere during the rainy season, and the clammy dampness of clear, dew-laden nights. Unquestionably the rainy season is a trial to the constitution, for the wet air, heated by sudden sunbursts, is difficult to breathe, and exposure to the chilly damp of night is apt to bring on pernicious and malarial fevers; however, with anything like proper care of the person and a fair diet of quinine, the summer season may be safely tided over.

In winter—or rather during the " dry season " of November, December, January, and February—the upper

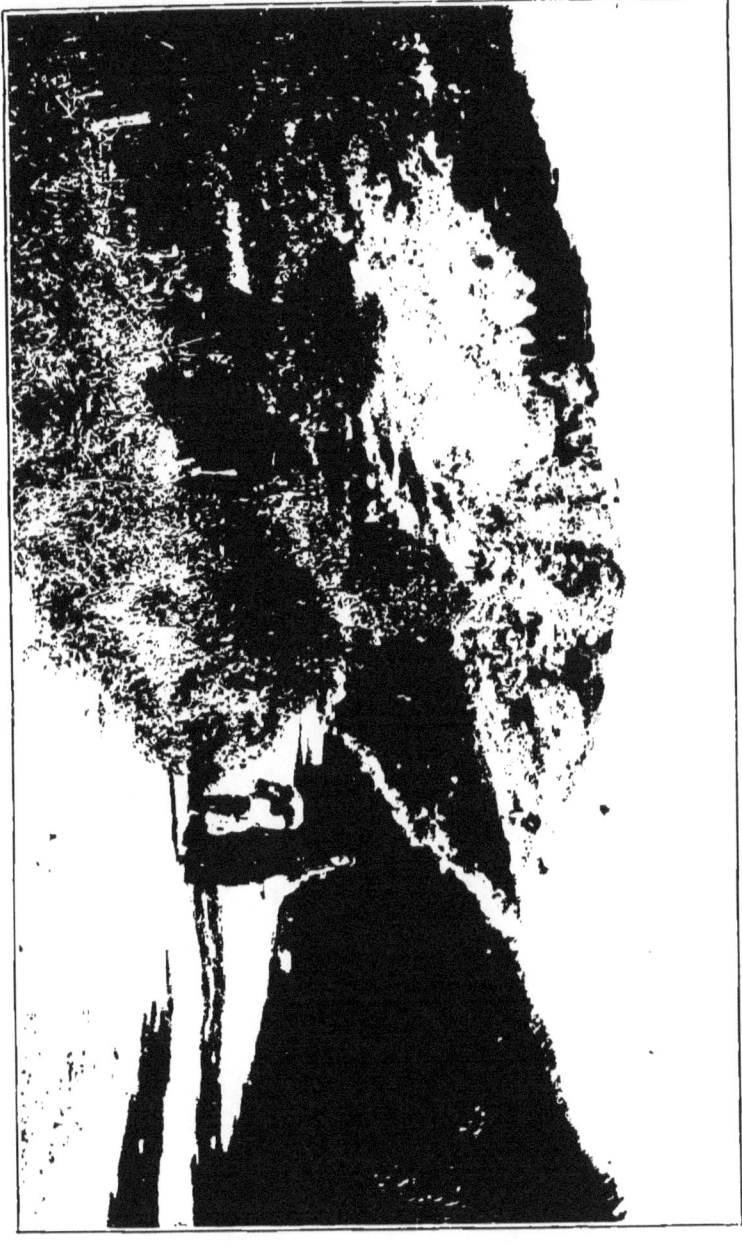

THE MOUNTAINS OF CENTRAL PUERTO RICO

GENERAL CHARACTERISTICS

limit of the mercury is about 80° on the coast and ten degrees less in the mountains, dropping lowest in January. There is a greater range in temperature between day and night at this season than in summer, the mercury sometimes falling, during darkness, to 65° on the coast and ten degrees lower in the highest altitudes. Sixty-five degrees means really cold weather to the Puertoriqueño, and the American who has lived on the island for a few months does not disdain to envelop his linen-clad person in a light overcoat.

The difference between the temperature in open sunlight and dense shade is so marked that it is actually dangerous to seek shelter from the sun, when overheated, in the shade of tree or jungle. Pneumonia is commonly produced in this way, and many of the pulmonary complaints arising in the island may be traced to injudicious cooling off beneath umbrageous natural arbors. A bit of superstition exists in the minds of the untutored natives to the effect that certain large trees, which form bowers of shade, exhale poisonous, noxious vapors, and that those who unwittingly or foolishly rest beneath them die with frightful pains in the chest and back; the true explanation being, of course, that acute congestion is superinduced.

The rainfall of Puerto Rico is very copious, estimated in its annual quantity, but the amount at any specific point varies greatly from year to year and month to month; also, some portions of the island are better watered by the dews of heaven than others.

In April and May the spring rains begin to drop their moisture from the sky, and it is no uncommon thing for it to pour down in heavy torrents almost constantly for two or three weeks, this incessant rain usually occurring on the northern half of the island, well up in the mountains. During such periods the roads are impassable for saddle or pack animals, and it is almost impossible for human beings to travel on foot over the trails.

During the interval from May to September, there is little rain—that is, comparatively little rain for a tropical country; it must be understood that in Puerto Rico a day never passes without rain falling somewhere in the mountain country, but, between the scheduled rainy seasons, it does not pour down for hours and days, but comes in quick, driving showers of a few minutes, usually late in the afternoon, and clears up with the dying sun, when one is almost paid for the discomforts of a drenching by the rare effects of a sky filled with glorious, crimsoned clouds and double rainbows.

The alarming stories of months of constant precipitation and deluge have no foundation in fact. It is known that the average annual rainfall at Havana is but a few inches more than in New York; though these statistics will not serve as a basis for judging the rainfall of the interior or mountainous regions, where the total annual precipitation is much greater. It is not probable that the yearly fall of rain, measured in inches, varies greatly in Puerto Rico from that in Cuba. Rains come more quickly and fall harder in a given time in the tropics than in more temperate climes, but there is the comforting compensation of their seldom lasting for more than a few minutes at a time. If these tropical countries had the same firm soils and as good roadways, complaints would never be advanced against the watery weather.

The northern half of the island—that is, the portion which lies to the northward of the great mountain watershed—has never known a drought, though near the coastline several weeks have occasionally passed without rain, during the dry season. The southern half, on the contrary—particularly the southeastern section—has at times

GENERAL CHARACTERISTICS

been without a drop of moisture on its coast-skirting soil for over three months, and it is related by the inhabitants of Vieques that a score of years ago the population had to bring fresh drinking-water from the main island, so general and lasting was the dried-up condition of their own.

During the summer interval, the weather is very stifling and oppressive on the coast, though in the high mountain regions it is quite pleasant. The morning hours are usually without a breath of air, and the heat is relieved only when the sea-breezes set in, about twelve o'clock, growing constantly stronger until five or six o'clock in the afternoon. Another period of breathless quiet occurs from this time until eight or nine in the evening, when the cool, dew-laden land-breezes flowing down the mountain-sides make it necessary to close the doors against the chilling dampness. The motionless hours of dusk are the most trying portion of the day, for small, blood-letting mosquitoes fill the air with humming wings, and it is utterly impossible to protect oneself from their poisonous lances.

The early historians record frightful devastation by hurricanes in the months of July and August; during the years 1825 and 1837, the general destruction of property and crops was so great that one writer was inclined to believe that these dire visitations would always be a great "deduction" from the value of West Indian property. It is true that during the hot weather of July and August cyclonic winds arise, accompanied by thunder and lightning, but it has been many years since a storm of any far-reaching violence has visited Puerto Rico. From personal inquiry among many men on the island, in respect to the frequency and strength of these hurricanes, it may be safely stated that their winds are usually puny affairs, as compared to our own cyclones of the broad prairies, and, as a generation may elapse between those of the roaring, death-dealing type, much sensationalism need hardly be developed.

In September and a portion of October, the autumnal deluges begin, and after some of the terrific cloudbursts, the whole face of the earth is actually covered with a quickly-disappearing lake—the tiny streams become raging torrents and the rivers vast floods which overflow the bottom-lands for miles on either side.

In October, the prevailing north and northeast winds release the population from the thraldom of heat and rain. From this time on until the spring rains supervene, Puerto Rico possesses a lovely climate.

The dryness of the southern side of the island may here be accounted for by pointing out that the persistent winds from the north have their moisture stolen from them on the northern side of the high mountains, which act as a screen to prevent the rain from being carried to the south. A double range of mountains in the western half of the island still more effectually prevents the equal distribution of rainfall; hence the greater dryness of the section toward the southeast.

Much of the salubriousness of the Puerto Rican climate, as compared with Cuba and the other neighboring islands, arises from the fact that the island has a remarkable number of fast-flowing rivers. Its exceptional fertility is due, in a measure, to the same cause. It is estimated that there are fifty-one large rivers and over twelve hundred small streams, creeks, and rivulets which find their way through the interlacing mountains, down deep gorges, and across fertile bottom-lands to the encircling ocean. One is simply amazed by the number of small, rapid streams which seem to gush out of the very mountain crests. There is hardly an area of a square mile which might not, if necessary, be irrigated, with small expense, from mountain streams. In the western half of the island, amid the mountain fastnesses, one sees, from dizzy mountain trails, exquisite, sunlit falls, dropping in silver threads for two hundred feet over steep rock-precipices, hidden at places in their descent by giant ferns and clusters of flowering plants. From the depths of the huge ravines rises the sound of tumbling waters, but the rivers are hidden from sight by the mass of tropical growth. By toiling down the steep-sided hills, clinging to the thick-growing coffee-bushes, step by step, one is at last rewarded by a vision of curling falls and boiling waters, embowered in arches of unfamiliar trees and pendent vines, which fills the soul of a lover of nature with thrills of joy. These streams give to the rural inhabitants an abundance of fresh, potable water, so essential to the maintenance of good health; from them, also, might be derived much power for running machinery; for, while they do at times become raging torrents, they never fall below a certain normal level. Again, much of the wonderful fertility of the lowlands is directly attributable to overflowing freshets, which, several times a year, deposit a mountain-gathered load of rich silt. This one factor, alone, of innumerable streams which vivify the air and land alike, makes Puerto Rico a place of habitation preferable to any of the other islands of the West Indies.

CHAPTER III

PREVALENT DISEASES IN THE ISLAND, AND HYGIENIC PRECAUTIONS

IT is customary to suggest hygienic rules and regulations by which the traveler in the tropics should be governed, but in practice he seldom lives up to the strict limitations of these formulæ; the army in Cuba and Puerto Rico—even where it was possible—never did, and, further, it is feared it never will.

The most common physical ailments which overtake the unacclimated, as well as the native population, are— first, dysentery, sometimes of so persistent a type as to cause death ; second, malarial and pernicious fevers, which take intermittent or malignant forms; and third, colds, catarrhs, pneumonia, and consumption.

Dysenteries, mucous-membrane affections, and lung troubles may usually be, in large measure, prevented by simple methods of taking care of the person. Never eat fresh fruits with which you are unfamiliar, is one rule, if dysentery is to be averted; this rule is broken by nine out of every ten persons who are of an inquiring turn of mind, the rare and delicious fruits being a sore temptation to the appetite. Mangoes, bananas, and nisperos, while fine-flavored and tempting, produce great distress in the average stomach by fermentation. Lemons (sweet and sour), limes, and oranges are considered safe, though the natives will never eat an orange after meals, nor for

DISEASES AND PRECAUTIONS

an hour after using alcoholic beverages of any kind. The too constant or frequent use of lemon or lime juice is not beneficial to some systems, as it brings on a chronic acidity of the stomach. Dysenteries which arise from malarial or bacterial poisoning of the intestinal tract may be alleviated by strict dieting, but not prevented. Such diseases can be overcome by medical aid only.

Malarial affections are universal, and those who make their homes in tropical countries are never immune, for long periods, against the visitations of this stealthy foe.

The germs of malaria are no doubt oftenest carried into the system by drinking-water, though the exact method or means of transmission is a much-mooted question with the medical fraternity. Residence near swamps, morasses, or cesspools, and in streets where sanitation is poor, where decaying garbage is carelessly thrown and effluvial emanations are constantly rising, produces malarial affections, even where boiled or distilled water is used for drinking purposes. Prevention, to a large extent, lies in using boiled drinking-water, in never living near marshy ground, in sleeping elevated above the earth (second-story rooms being preferable), and in keeping away from contact with the great unwashed and their homes.

After the system has started a malarial culture, exposure to draughts, chilling of the body, eating of fermented or fermentable foods, excessive exercise, overheating, or, in fact, any act which may suddenly disarrange the functional system, will, in a few hours, manifest itself in an attack of malarial fever, which will be more or less severe, depending upon the type and the strength of the culture preying upon the body.

Cognizance should be immediately taken of the slightest fever; and faith may be placed in the ability of the average native doctor, for if there is one thing he well understands it is the treatment of fever troubles. It is not wise to suggest personal medical treatment to the reader, though the writer has found, in practice, that a diet of one grain of red pepper and two of quinine, in capsules, taken at his limit of twelve grains a day, will hold a system filled with malaria at the normal. Quinine is the only known antidote which will finally kill and eradicate the malarial germs from the system, and its use becomes almost habitual to the dweller in tropical countries.

It is believed that no one is proof against malarial poisoning, and sooner or later—excessive care delaying, not preventing—the man of temperate climes will be overcome with fever.

The " tropic liver," or chronic enlargement of this organ, is an outcome of many attacks of fever, and is not only distressing, but a constant source of menace in after-life, for its possession means a chronic unbalancing of the abdominal functions. It can best be relieved by a lengthy sojourn in more northern regions.

The worst foe of equatorial countries is undoubtedly malaria, and its after-effects show themselves in a generally broken-down condition of the constitution. Anæmia is the direct result of a severe attack of malaria, for the red corpuscles of the blood are destroyed by the malarial plasmodia. Once in the clutches of this arch-enemy to health, the best remedy, again, is to leave the country temporarily; the next is carefully to diet the system and restore the blood by known medical remedies and nutritious food.

It makes the heart heavy to see the hundreds—nay, thousands—of native poor struggling through their daily avocations, with transparent flesh and white, bleached faces—victims of malarial diseases, which might be eased by better diet than plantains and sweet potatoes, and

DISEASES AND PRECAUTIONS

cured if quinine and other medicines were not, through excessive tariff, placed beyond the reach of their slender pocketbooks.

Colds and allied diseases are so easily induced in a hot climate, which keeps the pores of the skin constantly open, that few people escape being afflicted for many weeks at a time by some form of these distressing attacks; and once having contracted cold in the head, sore throat, or inflamed lungs, it is difficult to assuage the trouble. The hot, moist air in sunshine changing to a subtle chilliness under a heavy shower, or to positive dankness during the clear nights, constantly adds to the inflammation of the membranes, unless the utmost caution is exercised. A susceptible person or a victim to colds must take prompt measures to alleviate the simple trouble, or it may be followed by pneumonia, or by the far worse and more invidious disease, consumption. Woolen abdominal bandages are advocated as a means of reducing the danger of rapid changes in the surface temperature of the body, and are undoubtedly worthy of consideration. The writer, however, prefers to dress with a fair degree of warmth, generally wearing thin cotton underclothes, protected by light woolen overclothes. While in this way one may become overheated, the cooling-off process is not nearly so dangerous, with a complete covering of non-conducting woolen materials, as it is with the thin cotton and linen clothes affected by the native population. It is a good plan always to put on heavier clothes at night. If you feel the slightest chilliness, exercise, or put on a light overcoat. By following these suggestions, the grave afflictions of local congestion may be largely prevented.

Yellow fever need hardly be dreaded in Puerto Rico. It has never taken the form of an epidemic, and but few cases are reported from year to year. It has made itself more apparent, perhaps, in the barracks of the Spanish soldiers and in the prisons than elsewhere. It has been confined mainly to the coast towns, and is not heard of in the interior towns of high altitude. It is well to remember, however, that yellow fever is a disease of night, and that, by taking the precaution of not going out until after the sun is well up in the morning, and being in the house when the shades of evening fall, and living in upper-story rooms if possible, one runs little risk of being smitten by this dread disease. Yet no rule holds good during an epidemic, and avoidance of the fever-infected districts is the only safe recourse. Always keep away from sections of a coast town in the tropics where the poor, degraded, and vicious live; keep the person clean, change the clothing often, and live among cleanly surroundings.

On the whole, Puerto Rico has the most salubrious climate and engenders the smallest number of physical ailments among the unacclimated of all the regions of the western hemisphere within the torrid zone. In any country where vegetation grows rank and luxuriant, where the suns are hot and the rainfalls frequent, disease is necessarily more prevalent, but Puerto Rico has been remarkably free from the scourges which afflict the people of adjacent isles; moreover, it should be remembered, in summing up the situation, that this fair condition exists on an island where the population is, and has been for centuries, more dense than that of almost any other purely agricultural section of the New World.

CHAPTER IV

GEOLOGY

THE great Antillean mountain-range embraces Cuba, Haiti, Santo Domingo, Puerto Rico, Jamaica, and the smaller islands to the eastward, and includes a great submerged mountain-chain connecting the islands and extending westward toward the isthmian region of North America. It is, in general characteristics, the most wonderful on the earth. It rises at Brownson Deep, a little north of the shore of Puerto Rico, almost vertically from the depths of ocean, 27,000 feet to sea-level, its highest elevation above the surface of the water being 11,300 feet in Mount Tina of Santo Domingo. In other words, the West Indian islands are only the protruding tips of the mightiest and most precipitous mountain-range in the world. If it could be pushed up above the surface of the water, it would reach heavenward nearly ten thousand feet higher than Mount Everest in the Himalayas.

The immense depths of water on either side of this wonderful range are the greatest known in the Atlantic. The islands which rear their crests above the surface rise abruptly from the sea, with only scanty flood-plains on their margins, formed chiefly of terraces of coral rock of late geologic time.

The history of the geologic oscillations of this region is best told by Robert T. Hill, an eminent geologist of the United States Geological Survey, who has devoted many years to the unraveling of earth-problems relating to the West Indies. The submergence of the original land-area

—thought by some writers to be the lost Atlantis—took place in early geologic time, and while the waves of ocean rolled for ages over this sunken land, it was heavily laden with a calcareous deposit of shells and sea animals. Again, in the upheavings of the earth, it was reared high above the pounding surf—much higher than it is today—so that the solid land possibly extended from the present limits of southeastern United States to the mainland of South America, though there is much difference of opinion among geologists regarding this phase. Scientists who favor this idea have called the large area of land then exposed and connecting the two continents, the Windward Bridge. The Isthmus of Panama may have had no existence at that time, and the broad Pacific possibly surged freely against the steep shores of the eastward land.

Then came a second period of subsidence, until the largest islands were but tiny pinnacles above the deep; following this was another long period of calcareous deposition, and the ultimate uplifting of the islands known to us today.

During the first great uplift the wonderfully-folded mountain-ranges, encased in massive fossiliferous limestones, were formed, and, from the crumpled crests of the giant peaks, craters poured forth tuff and liquid lava, and the great subterranean caldrons filled every crack and fissure with melted igneous material.

The secondary sinking encrusted the entire surface with another layer of heavy limestones, thought to be somewhat softer, and filled with much later fossils.

At a late period of the last uplifting, the coral polyps made their appearance, and, skirting every shore-line, zealously built their rocky homes, even reaching out and throwing up their stony fortresses on the tops of sunken ridges. The elevation, still continuing, has created a

CORAL FORMATIONS ON THE TRAIL BETWEEN UTUADO AND LARES

GEOLOGY

series of coral terraces which gird the major portion of all West Indian islands, and reach for a considerable distance inland.

This is at best but a crude and rough outline of the wonderful past history of the Antillean range.

Puerto Rico has no known extinct craters, and it is unlikely that it was ever the seat of active volcanic disturbance.

The geology of the island is practically unknown, for it has almost always been neglected by students of nature and scientific men, whose attention has been given, with considerable care, to the geologic features of the other and larger islands of the group. There is little reason to believe that it materially differs, either in stratigraphy or mineral constituents, from those known in Cuba, Haiti, Santo Domingo, and Jamaica, as Puerto Rico is merely an extension of the same mountain-range which—with lowering elevation—extends eastward, and finally sinks into the blue ocean beyond the island of St. Thomas.

Massive limestones, deeply carved by rivulets and rivers, cover the mountains to their very tops. At a few points are seen the older basic rocks from which primeval land was derived. Near Lares, running east and west, is a beautiful castellated ridge, some thirty miles in length, of this older conglomerate and metamorphic rock, capped, apparently, by remnants of the harder limestones; but beyond these there are few indications of the original superstructure upon which the later island deposits were laid down.

The limestones vary greatly in quality and somewhat in color, changing from soft white, with almost straight fractures, to a cold grey and blue-steel coloring, with a hard, fine-grained texture and a highly conchoidal fracture. All varieties seem to make fine building-stone, produce macadam roads cemented almost as hard as the original rock itself, and burn in kilns to lime of great beauty and strength.

The mineral possibilities of the island are yet unsolved problems, but the known factors do not hold forth great promise to the speculator or investor. Viewed in the light of scanty discoveries made on the other islands, where the earth-disturbances took place on a more gigantic scale, and where—if at any point in this great range—valuable minerals should have formed in nature's crucible, the possible resources in rare minerals are not promising.

Iron ore of good quality has been found at several places on the island. It may be that asphaltum will be discovered in paying quantities. Coal is said to occur in the western ranges, but closer scrutiny will very likely prove it to be lignite. A mineral fuel—it may be said incidentally—located in this region would be a great industrial blessing, for the scanty supply of wood at the prevailing high price will make it necessary to import coal in great quantities, if the present industries are to make much expansion in the future.

Gold has been found in many of the mountain streams, notably in the Loquillo mountains in the northeast, under the towering peak of El Yunque. In the seventies a French company secured privileges from the Spanish government to wash gold from the streams near Rio Grande, but the work was soon abandoned—it is said, because of failure to find placer gold in paying quantities. No mother-lode has so far been located in this range, which may yet disclose wealth under the searching eyes of prospectors. This year a number of parties have been scouring the upper heights of El Yunque, and rumors of finds are in the air. In the tributaries to the Rio Cibua, near Corozal, some fifteen miles southward of San Juan, gold

GEOLOGY

has been washed from the streams by the natives, and the San Juan merchants often purchase very small amounts of gold-dust in exchange for store goods. The method pursued by the natives in securing this gold, it is related, is primitive in the extreme, consisting of diving into the water, bringing the sand from the bottom in their clinched hands, and panning it out afterward on the banks of the stream.

Numbers of other minerals are named—none of them, so far as known, appearing in paying quantities. Copper, lead, garnet, and others of lesser importance are enumerated. Fine quartz crystals and agates have been picked up in many stream-beds, and small blocks of mica are said to occur in the streams of the southern watershed of El Yunque.

A geologic survey of the island would, in a year, settle most of the mooted questions as to the mineral resources of Puerto Rico, and would most likely save much useless expenditure of capital by individual seekers after wealth. The Spanish laws, which reserved all rights in mineral lands for the government, deterred individual investors; but the government, like the dog in the manger, has never taken advantage of the power vested in it to make either mineral or general geologic surveys.

While every possible avenue to wealth in Puerto Rico will be exploited within the next few years by Americans with money and without money, as a generalization based upon the evidence of small mineral finds in the past, and the known geologic formations, which promise little for mineral resources in the future, it may be suggested that there are many far more promising roads to fortune in industrial and agricultural pursuits than in the quest of a new El Dorado—that phantom which has lured the Spanish race, in centuries past, to its ultimate destruction.

CHAPTER V

THE MILITARY ROAD

THE finest road in the western hemisphere is to be found in the island of Puerto Rico; in fact it is a road equaling, for surface and as a feat of engineering skill, any in the world, with the exception of some of the marvelous roadways across the Swiss Alps.

It was built by the Spanish government at an approximate cost of four million dollars, for military purposes solely, and traverses the island from side to side diagonally across its very heart for one hundred and thirty-three kilometers (over eighty miles).

This magnificent highway was commenced in 1880, under General Sanz's military régime in Puerto Rico, and completed eight years afterwards by General Pulido Gomez. Thousands of workmen called " peons " toiled year after year with a daily wage of fifty centavos, together with gangs of civil and military prisoners who received ten centavos a day, under the direction of Spanish engineers, only kept from open mutiny by a strong guard of soldiers. While the construction of the thoroughfare contemplated no philanthropic purpose and was perhaps, financially, an expensive gift to the inhabitants, it will, in the future, be of incalculable commercial value, for it gives to the country the only road within the confines of the island which is really passable at all seasons of the year—except short stretches of a proposed road to encircle the island.

THE MILITARY ROAD NEAR JUANA DIAZ

THE MILITARY ROAD

It is macadamized from end to end with finely-broken calcareous rock, which cements itself into an almost solid floor. It has good bridges over the numerous fast-flowing streams, with the exception of four small rivers just north of Ponce, and the gradients are as low as it is possible to make them without extreme tortuousness of the highway. Every few kilometers are found substantial single-storied houses, with red roofs, called " camineros," in which the road-tenders lived, whose duty it was to keep the road up to the high standard originally set by its promoters.

There are other roads in Puerto Rico, all built for the needs of expeditious military maneuvers, but, for the greater portion of each year, they are vast rivers of mud and water. These dirt roads with no resisting surface almost encircle the island near the seacoast, and some few of them are branches of the main artery; but, whatever they may have been when originally built, they are now cut in deep ravines by the rushing waters, which find an easy channel through them, and are pitted with great mud-holes wheel-deep in places. It may be said, as a generalization, that no road can long be passable in this new possession of ours, unless it be rock-surfaced and drained with ample side ditches.

It is impossible to describe the beauties of scenery, the unsurpassed variety of emerald vegetation, and the charm of wonderful sunsets and more remarkable sunrises along this highway, without relating the personal experiences of a staging trip across the island from Ponce, the great commercial center, to San Juan, the capital—and, in the past, the political hotbed of Spanish diplomacy and intrigue—whither we were bound to witness the evacuation ceremonies. Owing to the difficulty of procuring horses, it was eleven o'clock at night when we began our wild ride from Playa.

Away we went at a dead run, the poor little rats of horses struggling in front of the heavy barouche, under the repeated lashings of the drivers. For the two miles leading into Ponce the road is lined with small suburban homes, and the old heavy-masonried buildings, with now and then a more modern white-balconied house nestled under the waving cocoanut-palms, made a very pleasing picture. Through the now silent city of Ponce we rushed, the drivers singing out a shrill cry of warning to a solitary sentry in blue, and then we swept out on the main road on our way to the mountains.

Just beyond the town we plunged into the rough and stony bed of the Rio Portugues, and shook and bumped across the bottom to the music of rushing water, hub-high. On our return trip we were held up by this stream, whose waters rose, during a torrential rain, some five feet above their normal level in less than half an hour, and would perhaps have run down as quickly had the rain not continued.

Four times in an hour were we yanked across these rough rivers, the startling sensation being heightened by the darkness.

At Juana Diaz we changed coaches, horses, and drivers. From here to Coamo, a distance of ten miles, the road becomes gradually steeper, with now and then a short drop, as it runs over the rolling foothills which become higher and bolder as the principal transverse mountain-range of the island is neared.

For the first forty miles this magnificent road, which is as smooth as a floor, follows a general direction toward the east-northeast, and then at Cayey, which lies in the foothills, it bends almost north, making for Caguas, and then for six miles to Aguas Buenas it turns west, and finally north for the rest of the distance to the city of San

PICTURESQUE BRIDGE ON MILITARY ROAD, NORTH OF CAGUAS

THE MILITARY ROAD

Juan. The intervening mountain-range is exceedingly steep and precipitous, and offers very few passes over which roads can be successfully constructed. The pass through which the military road threads its way before reaching Aybonito is the best one, but even here some wonderful feats of engineering were necessary to surmount this massive barrier to traffic.

Just at the faint dawn of day we pulled into Coamo, and pushed ahead for Aybonito. Only impressions of what we had passed through in the dark clung to us. Here was a great banana plantation whose giant leaves glinted in the starlight, as the softly-passing air waved them slowly to and fro; there stood the skeleton ruins of a fine villa, destroyed by the retreating Spanish soldiers. The windings of the road which carried us around starlit valleys and through the densely-verdured forests of the coffee plantations were very beautiful, but the panoramas which flashed upon us from bend after bend, in the morning light, were gorgeous beyond description.

A thousand feet below us the thousand little valleys cut by the mountain streams and walled by steep ridges, covered to their very crests with the green of growing things, lay partially veiled in darkness or lightly masked by the white, diaphanous clouds of vapor which seemed gently to caress each blade of green, as they slowly floated upward toward the now sunlit and tinted peaks above. It was a wondrous sight, such as could be found nowhere in our own country. Here was not the topography of the grandly-sublime ranges we find in the Rockies, nor the product of the awful powers of nature as displayed by the grim, barren, needle-pointed peaks and parched and barren valleys of our southwestern deserts. It was a landscape carved in surprising forms, with the elegance and symmetry of rounded hills and deep-set valleys, and everywhere covered with the magnificent foliage of a climate warmed by a torrid sun, and watered copiously, day after day, by a moisture-laden atmosphere.

We climbed the steep ascents of the backbone of the mountains just a few miles from Aybonito. The road doubled and twisted on itself in half a dozen places until it looked like a gigantic snake winding away in the distance. A great wall had been built at one point where the road scaled the steep side of a cone-topped mountain, and the advance carriage could be seen from below, laboring onward a hundred feet above us. In the wall, embrasures gaped empty where recently the Spanish guns swept the road below. It was this stretch that the Spanish soldiers commanded from an impregnable position on the mountains. It would have proved a fearful trap had our men marched into it, since, from the trenches which crowned the high hills, the artillery and small-arms could have annihilated an army of ten thousand men as easily as the three thousand men who were preparing to advance when the messenger arrived with the news of peace. On the side toward the enemy was a steep and precipitous mountain which fell into a narrow valley below; on the other, the rock rose bare and forbidding for fifty feet, and then, green-covered, at an angle of forty-five degrees for two hundred feet more. For over a mile extended this bare road, from which there would have been no escape except a retreat along its way, and the Spanish fire could have raked it with shrapnel and shell at perfectly-known ranges. Our military men who have seen this deadly and picturesque position agree that it would have involved great loss of life, if not utter rout, had the assault been ordered.

As the carriages passed over the highest point of the road, some seventeen hundred feet above sea-level, a

CLIMBING THE MOUNTAIN ON THE GREAT MILITARY ROAD, NORTH OF AYBONITO

double vista revealed itself, that already viewed in the rear and a new one to the front, even more impressive in its varied beauties of nature than the one behind us.

Down the mountain we rushed for three miles toward Aybonito, which came into view as a dream of fairyland, with castles floating in the clouds. Through the silver-white mists the square towers of the cathedral thrust their turreted tops, and below, through the semi-transparent clouds, a dim vision of a city revealed itself, topped with the ever-present red-tiled roofs of these southern climes. Unfortunately, all its beauty lay in the artistic touch of nature. In reality it was a dirty, squalid little town; one of the many where no evidence of progress is observable.

Between Aybonito and Cayey we began to notice the coffee-bushes, covered with berries turning red, and, in the early morning, troops of women and children trudged by us, swinging closely-woven baskets in which they gather the coffee-beans. The coffee plantations lie under the shade of forests, which are necessary to protect them from the fierce heat of the noonday sun, and the uninitiated would never dream that he was passing anything more than a jungle-thick virgin forest. On every mountain-side, clearings almost hanging in the air dotted the landscape and told a story of renewed vigor in the native breast, and the planting of his little crop of sweet potatoes, plantains, beans, and bananas. 'Way down in the valleys, lining the banks of the mountain streams, were the sugar-cane fields, and on the larger plantations the high chimneys of the sugar-boiling houses rose far above the plain. It was a scene of quiet, indolent life in which man works one hour and nature the rest of the day.

Cayey is the great tobacco center and the place of manufacture of the finest cigars on the island. It is also a hotbed of Spanish sympathizers, who make cigars for a living, and have worked under the patronage of the Spanish government.

Between Cayey and Caguas we saw stretches of waving sugar-cane, interspersed with small fields of corn. No great tobacco-fields were seen, and it is said that the best tobacco is raised on the mountain-sides toward the east and away from the main road. For miles along this section the road is lined with the beautiful tree-fern, whose delicately-traced fronds look like filigree-work, and here and there patches of high, slender bamboo wave their heads to and fro, thus heightening the artistic effect of the gorgeous scenery.

Orange-, lime-, banana-, alligator-pear-, nispero-, and gourd-trees fringe the road at every step, and their heavy burden of ripening fruit is a constant source of surprise and delight to the novice in tropical climes. It is a veritable Paradise, where one has only to ask and receive, and the tall, stately cocoanut- and royal palm-trees are scattered amid all this luxuriance, suggesting one's childish ideal of Biblical lands.

A second smaller mountain-range is passed over between Caguas and Rio Piedras, though the topography is less rough in character than that previously traversed, and the valleys have widened out into broad, level fields, covered with tasseling sugar-cane, which, in January, is taken to some of the dozens of tile-roofed sugar-houses now visible everywhere.

Rio Piedras is the suburban town of San Juan, and a narrow-gauge railroad connects it with the capital.

Little road-houses, typically southern, are found every few miles along the roadside from Caguas to San Juan, and add much to the picturesque effect, with their tiny gardens of brilliant-colored flowers, naked toddling chil-

THE TOWN OF AYBONITO, FROM THE SOUTH—THE HIGHEST POINT ON THE MILITARY ROAD

THE MILITARY ROAD

dren, bright-kerchiefed old hags, and the mantilla-covered heads of dusky, dark-eyed señoritas. Each one is a little store, with the counter opening on the road, and the drivers of the heavy-yoked and lumbering oxen stop often to drink a cup of *café negro* or nibble some dulce cake and pass rude jokes with the women of the house.

Around the doorways are mats covered with coffee-berries and chicory seed, rotting in the sun, and near by a robust girl, with the charm of nature's grace, steadily raises and lowers a heavy wooden pestle in a primitive mortar made from a log, grinding coffee for the family and the wayside customer. It is a happy picture, in spite of its poverty, for one knows that here no poverty can be so great that human beings cannot eat in plenty, and that no icy winds will ever blow to freeze the heart in bitterness of distress and woe.

The sun set in a mass of dark rain-clouds and colored them with heavy bands of golden hue; the topmost rolls of fleecy cloud were silver-lined and tinted with rosy light. Below and across the wide expanse of salt-water marshes the white buildings of San Juan reflected the failing light of day. Along the roadside fierce-looking walls guarded the way to the city's entrance. They were rows upon rows of ancient masonry, built for the protection of the Spanish soldiers, from which they have whipped invading armies in days gone by, and would have offered a serious resistance to our men. The great forts of San Cristobal and Morro, with their grim walls, showed their heads above the rest of the city, still held by Spanish soldiers who, on the morrow, would leave these historic walls forever. It was an impressive and never-to-be-forgotten sight.

Night came as we sped into the city, and the drivers yelled shrilly at loose-clad figures which thronged the roadway, and fled from side to side as the carriages dashed by.

The Spanish Guardia Civil saluted us as we passed opposite the flashing lights which filtered out of the store-doors; always courteous, even in defeat.

This ride should be taken by every American who visits the island. As a cycling trip it is unexcelled; as a coaching trip, with fine animals, it would be superb, and even with poor, badly-treated little ponies, driven by men with no feeling for animal suffering, it is a journey always to be remembered.

CHAPTER VI

OVER THE TRAILS

TRAIL-RIDING in Puerto Rico is both a terrible nightmare and a roseate-hued day-dream. In a single day's wild riding over the innermost rugged mountain country, one passes through blended feelings of terror and admiration, of sinking heart and buoyant ecstasy. It is a continual game of shuttlecock with one's senses, which are bounding one moment in the pure delight produced by wonderful panoramas, seen from clinging, bench-like pathways, and falling in the next with abject consternation before wild, headlong, rocky pitches on the trail, leading down to narrow troughs of waist-deep, sucking muds, where a single misstep would send you crashing down through the soft-fluttering banana-trees and creeping vines to the white limestones of the brawling mountain stream far below.

For mixed sensations it is ahead of the dizzy trail-skirting in our Rockies and Sierra Nevadas. Though those regions offer to the eye almost limitless horizons, and the barren, rocky steeps are aglow with marvelous tints of red and white and brown, while the trail is seemingly pasted shakily to the side of yawning abysses and bold canyons, comparison takes not one whit from the excitement and interest of the by-traveling in this tropical country.

One of the finest trail trips, where the greatest diversity

of topography and vegetation may be seen, is from Ponce to Mayaguez, by way of Adjuntas, Utuado, Lares, and Las Marias. It takes five days to make the trip, and good weather and a strong horse are required to accomplish the journey successfully. At the present time this region is designated as the " Heart of the Black Hand Country " by the military men, for it has been the seat of much marauding and incendiarism on the part of the lower-class Puertoriqueños, who are settling up old scores against the Spanish estate-holder.

It is only nineteen miles from Ponce to Adjuntas, but it takes fully five hours to traverse the distance. Though the first twelve of the thirty kilometers are over a good military highway, the rest of the distance is painfully traveled over an alleged road, which is in reality a " slough of despond " whose mires and bogs would try the patience of a patron saint.

On leaving town, the traveler rests a few minutes at the blacksmith-shop in the suburbs, where a cold shoe, without heels or calk, is carelessly tacked on the foot of his big American horse, while the admiring crowd of idle natives gathers round and remarks on the " Caballo grande del Americano."

On the great road a string of early market venders stride briskly toward the city, with swinging hips and stiffly-poised heads, on which are neatly balanced their sources of personal revenue. The patting of their strong, bare feet raises little clouds of white dust from the powdered limestones of the roadway, and envelops them in the distance in hazy mists. Through the pedestrian throng now and then passes a native, tiny, rocking-chair horse, whose gait cannot be described—nor felt, for that matter, for several hours, when, alas! it becomes much like that torture of water falling drop by drop upon an

TREE FERNS ON THE ROAD

unprotected head, so vividly described by ancient writers! On his back is the more prosperous citizen, the owner of a small plantation, astride a panniered saddle from the forward edges of which his legs hang unstirruped, swinging loosely from the knees.

The planter and the commercial man come townward, from their beautiful little summer homes and villas scattered among the foothills a few miles back, in island-made surreys, behind galloping, sweating ponies, whose drivers urge them on with cracking whip, uttering sharp cries of warning to the more slowly-moving foot-travelers. There is an energy and activity displayed, during the morning hours, in this erstwhile Spanish isle, not seen in other Spanish countries, and it augurs well for the future of the people under a new and more progressive rule, by another race whose talisman is the word " hustle."

The homes of the well-to-do near the great business centers are pleasing to look upon, with their white walls, big double-storied verandas, summer-houses, dove-cotes, and surrounding gardens of tropical flowers and fruits and beautiful foliage trees, and one always receives an open-handed welcome. After five or six miles out of Ponce, however, houses of the more pretentious kind are seldom seen, giving way to the more primitive road-house, where coffee, eggs, and dulces are ever ready to be served for a few cents to the hungry passer-by.

At twelve kilometers out, the revenues—or the good intentions of the Spanish government — became exhausted, and the beautiful macadamized road—at the turning of a rocky cliff—ends abruptly, so that, from here to Adjuntas, the horseman plunges through quagmire after quagmire. All that is lacking to convert the remainder of this road to Adjuntas into a fine highway is

PUERTO RICO

the macadamizing of its bed, for the survey and earth-cutting were completed many years ago. The natives will assure you that it is a " camino reale," but that it is " mucho malo " in rainy weather. Its frightful condition is much augmented during the coffee-packing season by the heavy ox-carts which are laboriously hauled through the axle-deep mud by many yokes of oxen. There are almost ten miles of uphill work from the oceanside before the high, sharp crest of the mountain-range, seventeen hundred feet above sea-level, which overlooks the valley of Adjuntas, is reached. There are many exquisite windings in this miry road: here it overlooks a gorge six hundred feet below, from which rises the hollow roaring of cataracts hidden away from sight by the rank and overarching vegetation; there it abruptly swings around into a deep re-entrant, across whose horseshoe form the meandering road may be seen half a mile away, and in whose deepest curve a beautiful cascade noisily dashes from rock to rock, embowered in the green of ferns and vines and lanias.

From the great crest at the top of the range, the ocean, a dozen miles away, seems to rise up on its outer edge like the curving of a huge saucer, and the few vessels far out on its waters are but tiny specks through the glasses. Toward Adjuntas range after range of mountains is seen to the northward, and it is seldom that so rough a landscape is found in such a small area. Not a foot of the country, so far as the eye can reach in this direction, seems to be level, and yet this valley and the one of Utuado beyond are among the foremost coffee regions of the island.

The road down the mountain to Adjuntas is formidable. Out on the ragged edge, overhanging the deep ravines, is a pathway good and firm; inside, for fifteen feet to the

HALF WAY TO UTUADO

edge of the heavy hanging wall of rock, it is knee-deep and even breast-high with mud, so tenacious, so well kneaded by floundering horses and cattle, that every withdrawn hoof gives off a report like drawing a cork from a bottle. It is a great temptation to trust one's horse to that better, narrower, outer path, but one experience in going downhill for fifty feet, through banana-tree tops and coffee-bushes, with a horse somewhere in the air behind you, is generally sufficient for the most daring man, and plodding, staggering, pulling through the glue-like mixture is far preferable to aërial flights through coffee plantations.

Adjuntas is a tiny town, with the ever-present church and brick-courted plaza. It is remarkable for nothing except its doorways decorated by the mystic " Black Hand," the insignia of Death placed upon them by brigands, bold, not in the face of an enemy, but behind his back. At the time this is written, the citizens of the town are filled with fear that the houses will be destroyed by the Black-Hand artist; but in truth there is little danger, as it is hinted by those on the inside that the signs are largely the work of a few townsmen themselves, worrying and working on the sympathies of American officers.

The town has a population of a little more than two thousand souls, a few negroes, much mixed blood, and at least a half Spanish and Puerto Rican whites. The Adjuntas province or jurisdiction has inhabitants to the number of eighteen thousand, and coffee-raising is almost the sole industry.

The next day's journey on the trail-riding up to Mayaguez is to Yauco, some twenty-two miles, though no one seems to know the exact distance. Spanish West Indians compute travel in hours, not distances, and it is very distressing to be told by a man on a clever, ground-covering pony, that it is " Dos horas, no mas!" when you are astride of a big, stumbling northern brute, that you know will require at least four hours to cover the same distance; you comfort yourself that this is not quite so bad as the Arkansas unit, " a jog," or the West Virginia one of a " right smart stretch up the road."

Formerly the travel-way between these two towns was nothing but a narrow foot-trail, but, when General Henry made his remarkable advance toward Arecibo, an attempt was made to construct a wagon-road over which artillery might be taken. For nearly two weeks, over a thousand men shoveled and picked and scraped into the precipitous mountainside, broadening the road quite uniformly to a width of fifteen feet, but the climatic obstacles were insurmountable, and, when the heavy rains fell, the new work became a sea of slimy mud. It was a great feat to attempt, but an army of a hundred thousand men could not construct a passable road in this mountainous country during the rainy season, without filling its way with crushed rock from end to end.

When I traversed it four months later, at many places landslides had taken place, and perilous footpaths, tottering on the edges of drops five hundred feet deep, wound round and over them.

I was given a detail of two army men, for fear the Black Hands might make way with me, and in fact I had some guard through the entire journey, but a milder, less warlike-looking being than the average alleged native villain could not be imagined, and there certainly is less danger of being held up on the road than in portions of our own country.

Practically the entire distance to Utuado is down a narrow mountain valley; not that the rider follows the river—far from it. At one point he crosses the stream after coming downhill for several miles, and then immediately — apparently — makes for the topmost rugged peaks, on an uphill journey of five miles, winding in and out around the steep faces of the mountain curves, until, on a cloudy day, all sense of direction is lost. If the beauty of the scenery and its constantly-changing forms did not hold the eye enthralled, it would thoroughly exasperate the hurrying tourist to see ahead of him a giant, almost-bare mountain-top, and then, after traveling for an hour without another glimpse, and with the growing feeling that he must have passed that mile-post, to find it looming up in front of him from a new direction, not appreciably nearer. There are no short cuts or straight lines in these tumbled ranges; only by great arcs—almost semi-circles—is forward progress made.

Every foot of the way is lovely; looking sideways through shaking banana-trees, one sees the trail a few hundred yards away, though he may have traveled a mile around, past the dashing brook in the course. On the precipitous hillsides are perched the palm-made huts of the peasants, braced up with shaky legs on their downward side, which promise some day to let them slide into the valley below. Ahead, the high-built road disappears at a sharp turning, as if its end was reached, and far beyond, five miles away—though it looks but the distance of a few minutes' walk—a great peak rises with an amazingly rocky and barren crest, for this land where nature's green finds foothold everywhere.

Off-shooting trails scour the hills in every direction, and one sees them creeping and winding up the steeps like tortuous snakes; only wide enough for the sure-footed little ponies, and leading to the homes of coffee-planters well on the top of the overhanging ridges.

Deep in the next winding two barefooted little girls

are filling their calabashes from the tiny rivulet, which finds its way to the great river below, with bounds and jumps, in crystal spray, refreshing the luxuriant, broad-leaved yautia lilies and the always-present banana. The little ones are timid and bashful in the presence of "Americanos," and, in reply to cordial salutations, one gets but a feeble "adios," though one hears their voices, merry with laughter, as they disappear, sliding down the side paths through the bushes to the house, hidden like a nest somewhere in the foliage below.

Another mile or two of swinging travel and the road is blocked by half a hundred men deep in the absorbing pastime of a cock-fight. The situation is a particularly odd one, on a narrow road, whose right side rises six hundred feet above, and whose left falls from the stilt-perched house skirting the edge five hundred feet below. The confines are small, but the fun is fast and furious. It is an orderly crowd of laughing, joking mestizos, who insist that we shall dismount and at least have coffee with them, if we cannot rest ourselves longer. The man who learns to appreciate the simple, open-hearted hospitality of the Puertoriqueños secures much that is pleasurable in life.

Nearer Utuado the valley broadens, and the trail finally comes down to the level of the stream. In the last few miles it has passed through magnificent coffee plantations, and wound under the moist shades of overhanging trees and vines, and from the invisible stream—now a rushing river—comes the music of a roaring cascade falling in the deep-carven limestone holes of its bed, and drowning the hoof-beats of our tired horses.

Utuado is a pretty little town with a population of some three thousand; a coffee town exclusively. Its streets are clean and the storekeepers prosperous. The

A BIT OF NARROW TRAIL OUT OF UTUADO

OVER THE TRAILS

town has an electric-light plant, coffee-mills, cathedral, jail, substantial residences for the better class, and an outlying village of thatched houses for the poor, called facetiously by the army, "Little Egypt." Its plaza is as handsome in horticultural designs as those of any of the larger cities, being brilliant in gay coloring of flowers and plants. On Sunday mornings the white-tented market scene presents itself like magic, on a brick-paved square which is bare and deserted during the week. The evident prosperity of Utuado, for an interior town, is largely due to its being connected, by fourteen miles of fair military highway, with the coast at Arecibo.

From Utuado to Lares is thirty miles, if it is a foot, though the map indicates but twenty; it feels more like sixty when you stiffly drop from your horse at sunset in front of the army headquarters, but there are compensations for sore muscles and tired backs.

The road out of Utuado towards Arecibo is a beautiful one, leading past the solemn, high-walled cemetery, over a handsome iron bridge crossing the Rio Grande de Arecibo, and down the river valley, banked high with mountains; but this is not the Utuado-Lares trail—this only leads to its obscure starting-point a mile away.

There is no rest for the weary—after one has ridden these mud-bound trails for two days on a strange horse, he feels like walking gently on his feet in place of lurching in rock-ribbed saddle. Up we go, toward the top of that near-by peak which experience has now convinced us is ten miles away, over a boggy, twisting footpath. This trail is unique; it follows one side of the ridge, fifty feet below the top, for a mile; then, without any apparent warrant, it sidles over to the other edge through a cut pass, and wanders aimlessly along for a mile or so before repeating the operation. On the off-side the sun falls blazing hot, and you swelter between the environing trees, but the trail is fine and hard, cut from the heavy, disintegrated rocks; while on the near-side it is shaded from the sun, and cold shivers run down your moist back, from the chilling air blowing fresh down the gorge, while your horse plumps staggeringly through stiff mud-holes two feet deep. It is a game of hide-and-seek, for ten miles, with sunstroke and pneumonia, with sunstroke *it* most of the time.

It is difficult to remember having seen a more beautiful panorama, even in the Sierra Nevadas, thán the one which greets the eye to the rearward, near the summit of the first climb. Utuado, clothed in dazzling white, lies cuddled in the cradle of a lovely valley filled with rank green grasses and waving sugar-cane, while, keeping guard over the little hamlet of men, rise mountains on mountains, fierce and jagged in giant outline, but softened by the mantling luxuriance of tropical verdure.

The trail hangs on the brink of deep gorges, that would turn the head with dizziness if one were not kept from fairly looking down the heights by the surrounding vegetation. At one point, fully a thousand feet above the valley, a maize-field is planted at such an inclination that even the earth which feeds its roots must find difficulty in staying at home. How it is cultivated is still a mystery, and the crop must be harvested from a balloon. I have been told by a veracious army officer that it is no uncommon thing for several men to brace their backs, from the downhill side, against an ox while plowing, but I have never witnessed the feat; it is either that or down-side stilts.

It is miles over the top of the mountain heights, through thick forests of guava-trees which protect the glistening leaves and reddening berries of the coffee-bushes. There are level stretches of mud where it seems absolutely im-

A SIDE TRAIL ON THE ADJUNTAS—UTUADO TRAIL

possible for a horse to pass through, and woe betide the man who is unfortunate enough to get his horse down; it is even chances whether he will get him up again, unless he secures a yoke of cattle and pulls his animal, by main strength, to firm land.

Over the range to the northward, the eye at last catches a new landscape; a strange, queer mountain-ridge—one which seemingly does not belong to Puerto Rico—looms up in castellated forms, almost like huge cathedrals, or like, perhaps, the wondrous middle-century fortifications the Spanish have been so fond of building. As far as the eye will carry you, twenty miles in either direction, these new mountains—the only ones in Puerto Rico like them —are in sight. When, after two hours more of downhill riding, you are under their curious walls, they appear to be sandstones, but are in reality old coral formations, which are crumbling and water-worn. The main trail follows the base of this configuration for ten miles into Lares, and clustered under the wrinkled cliffs are the homes of the peasants, pretty in themselves and their settings in spite of squalor.

As the day is dying, Lares bursts into view from the last hilltop, its white buildings gloried by the crimson sun. It is an exquisite scene; the little village with its high cathedral, its red-tiled roofs, and the smoke of evening fires burnished into gold by the setting sun. One long, steep hill into town, and the curious throngs in the streets watch us as we make a last gallant canter toward the barracks, and dismount gradually, but without assistance.

Lares is another coffee town, and it is said that one man alone ships annually a million and a half pounds of coffee, over the fearful wagon-road to Arecibo. It has been strongly Spanish in sentiment, and consequently there are many wealthy families in the city. The best houses are richly furnished from the Spanish standpoint, though American and Spanish ideas of æstheticism differ, ours seeming to run recently to tables covered with collections of fragile coffee-cups, and theirs to tables adorned with menageries of china images. The furniture, it must be admitted, is ample and comfortable, and there are no pipe-stem chairs needing the sign " Don't sit here! "

The fourth day's ride from Lares to Las Marias may be a fine one, but the writer got lost, and took, perforce, a most remarkable trip—through the stupidity of a Missouri recruit who accompanied him to guard his life, and who thought he knew the trail. It is said to be twelve miles, but, off the trail, I am convinced it is forty. The first few miles were good going, over a fair road toward the south; then the trail plunged abruptly to the left, down into a river-bed far below. The recruit—who was born and raised in St. Louis—struck the first trail leading upward and toward Aguadilla, and was hopelessly lost. Every mountain crest, every hut along the way, every river through which he waded, reminded him of the self-same thing that he had seen before, in his journey with the command to Lares. Poor fellow! there was a frightful sameness in the landscape, to a man without much travel-sense; in the green mountains covered with royal palms, in the vine-festooned brooks, and the palm-thatched huts with bits of cement floors for coffee-drying. They all looked alike in much the way that all coons do.

We were politely informed at the next shanty that the " camino reale " for Lares lay two leagues to our left, and that, by following the foot-trail which led to the rear of the house, we would come out on the highroad on the top of the next mountain. I could talk bad Spanish and he could n't, so I led. It was the wildest ride that one ever took on the back of a horse; the very first plunge was down a mountainside for two miles, over a path where the horses had to put all four feet in a straight line to walk at all, and the slightest misstep would have precipitated rider and horse into gulches twenty feet deep. I had given up my big army horse and taken to a small native animal the day before, and it was most interesting and satisfying to watch the way he actually let himself down long flights of steps cut in the steep face of the hill. All four feet together one moment, and then a hop with both front legs, and the next lower step was made. It was as clever a performance as a trick pony could give. A hundred feet down and alongside of a deep gully cut in the hillside, my guide's horse fell and landed with his rider in the deep ditch, the horse pinning his leg down. Fortunately it did not break, though it was so badly hurt that he could hardly stand alone, and his shaken nerves would not let him ride. Three hours were spent slipping, sliding, falling, over these by-trails in a search for the main road. It was like a tangled maze, with the right combination somewhere, but difficult to find. Now up, now down, through tangles of thicket and coffee-bushes, in the broiling sunlight of ridges, till we found a path that led clear to the stream-bed of the valley. On top of the next mountain the main road lay, but it had to be found by traveling over just such another network of paths as we had come down. Not a house had been seen for two hours, except burned ruin after ruin of the once homes of Spanish coffee-planters, whose property had become the spoil of the revengeful Puerto Rican laborers. On the main roads one cannot realize the immense amount of valuable property which was destroyed by the enraged natives, during the transition period from Spanish to American government. It was brought home very forcibly in such side trips as we were taking.

Two barefooted men were skulking through the underbrush, and stood hesitatingly at our call, then coming slowly forward. No doubt both were red-handed in the burning of the still-smouldering house near by, and their consciences troubled them. For twenty centavos, one of them agreed to guide us to the road, and, as his heart came back and his confidence became stronger, he waxed confidentially eloquent, assuring us, with grave face, that the Spaniards would have directed us to the wrong road, and that all Spaniards should have their throats cut.

At last, with steaming and strained horses, we crept to the top of the twelve-hundred-foot rise, and right on the topmost point of the crest, the long-sought-for main road ran, by the house of a lone coffee-planter who defended his eyrie home from incendiaries with loaded gun. The guide left us in the thicket; he and the planter evidently were not boon companions.

We were royally received, dined on curried chicken, served with delectable black coffee, and sent on our way with the well-wishes of our bowing host, who waved us a last farewell, as we disappeared over the well-beaten trail, from his balcony, hung with rifles like a veritable arsenal.

From here to Las Marias, the trail had originally been cut sufficiently wide for ox-carts, but the raging floods which had swept down its entrenching sides had long since destroyed its utility in this direction, by cutting huge gullies in the center, and forcing the bridle-paths out high along its sides. A long descent to a streambed again, and another climb to the top of the other side, and the American flag was seen waving fifty feet in the air, from a freshly-cut bamboo pole. It was the dirty, unkempt village of Las Marias. From the top of one mountain, over two mountain-ranges, and again to the top of the fourth—in addition to being lost—is enough

OVER THE TRAILS

riding for one day. The view from these immense ridges was extravagantly lovely. Off to the northwest, the placid sea near Aguadilla comes into sight, over and over again, while to the south the crumpled mountain-ranges lie in confused masses, with tiny clusters of planters' houses crowning the upmost points.

The region from Las Marias to Mayaguez—eighteen miles—is commonplace compared with the wilderness left behind, for the road is fairly good for nine miles to the great red half-way house, and excellent the rest of the way, over a macadamized bed lined with wealthy planters' houses, whose pretentious, arched, wooden gateways bear their names and the euphonious titles of the haciendas.

These five days of trail-riding should never be missed by visitors to the island, who have strong constitutions and are saddle-wise, for nowhere will you find the same combination of scenery—the serrated topography of Arizona, the flowering loveliness of the tropics, and the hanging homes of the Swiss in a new architecture.

CHAPTER VII

THE GREAT CAVES

IT is astonishing how little is known about the geology of the island of Puerto Rico, and the profound manifestations which Nature has there made of her power in earth-making.

At Ponce, San Juan, and Cayey, no one knew of caves in the land; the people had all heard rumors of mineral wealth, but could not definitely state the localities.

Even at Caguas, six miles away from a great cavern which may develop into as much of a wonder as our own Mammoth Cave, few people had ever heard of it, and no one had ever seen the interior of its expansive chambers.

At Aguas Buenas, which lies five miles to the westward from Caguas, the people of the little village were aware of great holes in the mountains toward the south, but only two negroes had ever explored them, and they only to a limited extent.

The owner of this unknown marvel of Puerto Rico is Señor Muñoz, a large coffee-planter. He told us that several years ago an Englishman, a member of some British scientific society, had paid a short visit to the cavern and was much interested, and it is quite likely that a report of its wonders has been published in the scientific journals of Great Britain.

The expedition over the surface of the earth to the cavern, known as the "Dark Cave," is filled with almost as many surprises to the explorer as the actual finish of

THE GREAT CAVES

the journey, when he finds himself environed in mineral walls of white and pendent stalactites, a mile beneath the earth's surface.

The trip proper begins from Aguas Buenas, after a five-mile ride over a bit of military road leading out of Caguas. This road is excellent—having a solid bed—though not as good as the main highway between San Juan and Ponce. It winds around the strongly-eroded mountain steeps, always climbing higher and higher, until one looks back into the fair valley of Caguas a thousand feet below, with its miles of rustling sugar-cane fields just tasseling into purple brushes, which foretell the coming of the cane-cutting season. Over the wide expanse are dotted the long, low buildings of the factories, relieved in their flatness by towering brick chimneys, from which curls a thin blue smoke produced by the test-heating of the pans. It is a fair scene, as are all landscape-vistas in Puerto Rico which recall, more and more strongly as they become familiar, the contours of Arizona and New Mexico in a new and strange dress; the rich reds and browns of the desert are clothed in one lovely gown of green, with settings of palms and bananas in place of the gaunt and wrinkled cacti.

Before us, around a turn in the road, perched high on the mountainside, lies the little village of Aguas Buenas, with its weather-worn and battered church prominently in sight; from the tower, the early morning hour is struck in cracked tones which reverberate among the houses of the scarcely-awakened town, and float still farther out to the clustering thatched huts of the poor, clinging to the hillsides in defiance of the laws of gravitation. The cool morning air, the sky filled with fleecy clouds through which the slanting sunlight streams in moving patches over the surface of the landscape, the women trudging with heavy loads of dirty linen on their heads to a near-by stream, the white-clothed, barefooted men astride of panniered, shambling ponies, the well-dressed planters, and shopkeepers yawningly opening their closely-barred windows, combine to make a new stage setting, part Eastern, part Spanish, part Mexican, and, last of all, part American, for over many houses floats our decorative flag.

Nine men with American uniforms—part of the First Kentucky Volunteers—protect the American interests of the town, under a lucky second lieutenant who lives at the Judge's house as his valued guest. We breakfast in the barracks for a second time on oatmeal, coffee, bread, and bacon. The two guides to the cave are found, and, with several more volunteers, we start for the cavern, which is said to be the distance away of that elusive Spanish measure, " an hour's ride."

In an air-line it is hardly a mile, but there is no telling how far it really is by trail, measured by any former training in covering space, as the way is narrow and tortuous. It goes up hills steeper than the roofs of shingled houses, it travels down declivities only short of actual precipices, and it winds into curves and S's and circles, until the body is racked with the slipping and sliding, and the points of the compass are obscured.

When the blasé man seeks new sensations, let him travel over the every-day trails of the interior portions of Puerto Rico. Rolling one's horse down the high bank of a dry-wash in Arizona, riding through the deep forests of the northern Sierras, and forcing one's way, foot by foot, through jungle mazes, are old and commonplace experiences, and without joy, as compared to the scaling, on horseback, of a knife-edged ridge on a narrow clayey path, always damp enough to make it an even wager whether

ON THE WAY TO THE CAVES

one's horse will slip down one side or stumble headlong off the other.

Here one strikes a fairly level stretch—a veritable corduroy road—filled in between the hard-earth ridges with soft, sticking mud, ten inches deep; the short-stepping native ponies walk in each other's tracks until deep holes are formed in mud between the earthen railroad-ties of drier soil. Our larger, clumsier American horses stumble and slip and snort with fear as they go through these new feats of stair-climbing.

Up one ridge we go—not wider, certainly, than four feet —for a two-hundred-foot rise, and every saddle has gone backward to the horses' rumps; one man even rides in front of his saddle, clinging vigorously to his panting horse's mane. On both sides, the coffee-bushes, filled with purpling berries growing under the shade of the guava-trees, brush against our horses' sides.

There a green but luscious orange strikes a traveler on the head, as he passes by; here a man ducks to miss the outspreading branches of the mocha-tree ; and there, again, another man has nearly been swept from the saddle by a huge bunch of bananas swung fairly over the trail.

Below us, on the right, lies the quite-modern frame house of the coffee-planter, with its tinned roof. Around his narrow yard—for his home is on a rounded knoll—are spread the coffee-cloths, deep-covered with drying coffee; while, not far away, four peons struggle with the handled fly-wheels of the crude berry-breaker, from whose shaking wire screens rolls a hail of green-hulled coffee.

From the summit of a sharp-pointed hill, after an hour's struggle of ups and downs, through stony creek-beds, along steep, grassy slopes, and under shady bowers of trees and pulpy plants, we have obtained our grandest view of the valley.

PUERTO RICO

Far to the east, over the valley of Caguas, lies the Loquillo mountain-range, and, through the banks of heavy cloud which screen its crest, El Yunque dimly looms, the highest point on the island. To the north, a second chain of mountains five miles away cuts off the view of the ocean and the city of San Juan. On the west, we look through long narrow valleys for miles away. On the south, right at hand, is the white, precipitous bluff of limestone, under which lie the caverns. Clinging to every tiny patch of earth are the vegetal growths of a tropical clime, and, at least a thousand feet below, in the narrow gorge, rushes a mountain stream, the sound of whose waters comes faintly to our ears, as it leaps over great boulders and down creamy-faced walls of stone.

A mile more of downhill in a wind-about fashion, and the horses are left at last, tied to calabash-trees laden with their huge green globes. A few yards to the right is a great opening in the wall of rock, but we are told that this passage is unknown, and that the main entrance is down the jungle-covered hill two hundred feet below.

The natural entrance to these caverns is very beautiful. It is down a narrow gorge, whose walls are the sides of great falls of rock. Over the uppermost end of this passage, which must be scaled with hands and feet, hang banana- and orange-trees. Between, and reaching out toward the cool, moist air which rushes upward, are the tropical ferns, with their leaves of filigree-work, five feet in length. On every side and from every cranny spring soft-leaved vines, and yet farther toward the bottom, pendent roots swing in great coils like inanimate snakes.

Forty feet down through this passage is the bottom—or rather the top—of the great rock-fall, and opening from it at each side are great yawning black holes, the mouths of the " Dark Cave."

THE GREAT CAVES

Our guides are carrying a big roll of native pitch lights, the ignitible material being a sweet, odoriferous gum which is poured into the hollowed end of a dried and rolled banana sheath, the whole being tied together with binding cord from a cocoanut palm. These lights burn fitfully, sputtering and red, sending up clouds of incense very pleasant to the nostrils in small quantities. A little, dark-faced native has scrambled down the rocky entrance, with a calabash shell, filled with water, balanced on his head, and, after we have all drank, we start into the left-hand cave.

The guide warns everyone against too near an approach to a great black spider which lives in this dark world, but we need no further cautioning after having seen him once. With a body as large as a silver quarter, and long, thin, wiry legs, stretched out four inches in length in a full-grown specimen, he may be as vicious and as poisonous as he is represented to be; we do not experiment.

The first passage of a hundred yards is not very high— not more than fifteen or twenty feet. The floor is muddy and slippery, and the condensed water from the moving air, which nearly extinguishes our primitive lights, drips steadily from the ceiling. We are all visibly disappointed in that the hanging stalactites are covered with dirt or vegetal fungi of dark brown, which makes the first gallery a dungeon, even with the flaring lights.

Now the chambers are opening out, and the sound of rushing water above our heads, among the thickening mass of lighter-colored stalactites, strikes our startled ears. We peer upward, and, as we strain our eyes, see a thousand, a million, fast-moving shadows. They are bats, with rushing, fanning wings, whose lightning flight gives out the sound of mountain torrents. They thicken as we move inward until the air is filled with them, a few feet above our heads; then one, then another, of us is struck by them in their panic-stricken flight. Their skin-like wings and soft-furred bodies produce an uncanny thrill, as they brush by our bare faces and necks, and it is quite impossible to repress a cry of alarm when the soft pulpy forms strike one fairly in the face. They are really harmless, but the incessant roar of their wings almost drowns our voices for the first five hundred yards.

These upper rooms—which we traversed for fully two miles, without seeing, probably, a tenth part of the surface-meanderings—are all the native guides are familiar with. Every deep hole which leads downward is an unknown world to them, and many were their expressions of horror when we crowded to the brink and cast stones into the depths, listening to the reverberations as they bounded from ledge to ledge, the returning sounds growing fainter as they sped downward.

Unfortunately, we did not carry any rope, and not a foot of it was to be had at Aguas Buenas or in the countryside, so we were stopped at this level; this detracted from our enjoyment of the great chambers, with their overhanging decoration of marble icicles and walls fluted into beautiful solid forms by the trickling, lime-impregnated waters.

The floor everywhere was covered with black, water-soaked earth, full of patches of mushy mud, over which crawled the loathsome, heavy-clawed land-crab of this region. Our guides seemed more interested in crab-hunting than in any other feature of the cave, and chased them through the slimy mud to a capture; when at last we saw daylight again, they dangled a great string of the unsightly creatures before our eyes with smiling faces, assuring us that they were "muchos buenos" to eat.

When we were at least two thousand yards from the

THE GREAT CAVES

entrance our guides became alarmed for fear our lights would not last, so we made our way hurriedly toward daylight again, passing ramifying hallways without examination.

It was a weird flight, in which the dark shadows of the manlike stalagmites fled backward as we passed out, and the great tessellated ceilings danced a red, flame-lit fandango to the music of the fanning wings of countless bats.

The entrance to the right was even more interesting, as the windings of the cave were more sinuous, breaking into great halls from passages through which we crawled on our hands and knees.

At one point we discovered a passage downward which our guides had never explored. It was very remarkable, as on one side was a highly-inclined mass of blue, shaly rock, almost black in color, while on the other was the creamy white of a finely-crystalline and metamorphosed limestone, which gleamed and scintillated in the flaring light.

Through this line of demarcation between two deposits, which had once been bedded on each other in a horizontal position and then lifted high by a great earth-flexure which probably raised the island of Puerto Rico from out of the depths of the ocean, we traveled for several hundred feet, letting ourselves down yard by yard until we could hear the babbling of a subterranean brook still many hundred feet below.

Two smooth, solid walls, four feet apart, with a drop of thirty feet to the next ledge, kept us from going lower. It was tantalizing to hear the hollow musical echoes which came back from falling stones, but without ropes we could go no farther.

From the second cave there are many exits; in fact our guides became lost through our enterprising explorations, and, after we had gone into many new chambers, and admired the spectral effects of sifting daylight from the high domes, mixed with the red tinge and smoke of our crude lamps, they were afraid to turn back to hunt for the original entrance, so we were, perforce, obliged to clamber out through a narrow opening on the opposite side of the mountain, and toil and scramble over the broken rocks toward the summit of the ridge, embowered in the wildest maze of tropical luxuriance that can possibly be imagined.

Many of the stalactites and the limestone rocks are stained with blue and green mineral salts, which would be very beautiful under the electric light, but which seem only darkened and dirty patches under the feeble light of torches. Their colors are exquisite when seen by the light of day.

At the entrance to the cave we were met by the chief functionaries of the town of Aguas Buenas, the Alcalde, the Judge, and a horde of servants, who invited us back to Señor Muñoz's hacienda to lunch. The lunch consisted of rice, eggs, and chicken cooked in the same vessel, coffee, red wine, and bread; and, after eight hours within the confines of the dark caverns, this simple repast seemed royal—its chief charm being the constant, thoughtful hospitality extended by the Puertoriqueños to the Americans.

When our new island becomes a great winter resort for people of leisure in the United States, these caves—situated as they are between fifteen hundred and two thousand feet above the sea, amid unsurpassed luxuriance of vegetation, with the ever-fresh vistas of this lovely country spread out before the traveler—will gain the renown which they merit and become a boon to the seeker after new sensations.

CHAPTER VIII

INDUSTRIAL POSSIBILITIES

PUERTO RICO is a veritable desert for the poor man today, unless he goes there with some definite commission to execute.

Just at present, there are few things which the American without a bank account can do in the island, sufficiently remunerative to furnish him with the staff of life; one of these is to enlist as a recruit in the army at $15 a month, and another is to drive a government mule-wagon at $40 a month and rations. There is nothing else in sight for him, unless he can speak Spanish, in which event he may become an interpreter for the army, or possibly, if he can mix drinks well, he may secure a position as bartender in one of the new saloons.

I should like to emphasize the statement that now, and for some time to come—until Congress adopts new laws for Puerto Rico, and American investors invade the island and create a demand for clever poor men—it is a good country for the impecunious to keep out of, however ambitious they may be.

At San Juan and at Ponce there are numbers of young Americans who rushed, hot-headed, into this supposed promised land, and who are slowly but surely wearing out their shoe-leather, with no immediate prospect of replacing it, in the search for openings which will build them a fortune.

PUERTO RICO

Everything is moderately high-priced, even with the exchange of silver in America's favor. The American army demands more and buys more than did the Spanish army, and, as a result, prices have risen, controlled to some extent, also, by the fact that the Puertoriqueños have discovered that Americans are more prodigal with their means, and are willing to pay higher prices.

At the Inglaterra Hotel in San Juan, and also at the Hôtel Français in Ponce—which are the leading hostelries of these two cities—the daily rate, including twelve-o'clock breakfast, six-o'clock dinner, and sleeping-room, is $3.75. Coffee, eggs, and bread in the café in the early morning are called an extra, which brings the bill up to $4.25 Spanish, or—at the prevailing rate of exchange—about $2.75 American, per diem. The service one receives in return for this would, in the United States, be considered high-priced at $1.50. It will be found difficult to live under $50 Spanish per month anywhere on the island, whether hotels, cafés, or private boarding-houses are patronized.

General outfitting goods are somewhat lower than in the United States. Thin clothes are very cheap; suits of good, serviceable linen and colored stuffs may be made up by the tailors at prices ranging from $5.50 to $10 Spanish money. Fine dress-goods command more than American prices. Shirts, underclothes, collars, and cuffs are as high as in the United States and not nearly so well made, though fabricated from quite as good materials. Good shoes—Puerto Rican hand-cobbled—may be obtained at prices ranging from $2 to $5 Spanish, and fine French goods are to be had at fifty per cent. more, in the same money, which gives one an advantage over America, so far as foot-gear is concerned.

Foods are both dearer and cheaper than in America,

INDUSTRIAL POSSIBILITIES

depending upon whether they are imported or home products. Butter is a luxury for which you pay 10c. a tiny pat; cooked eggs are five to ten cents apiece in the cities; milk can only be had in the morning, at 10c. a quart; ice, in the towns where there are ice-plants, is becoming the proper thing, but it comes higher, a few times, than an American combine can lift it; cold beer on ice is worth 30c. a bottle—a month ago every native café proprietor insisted that it would break the bottles to put them a-cooling, but he has been convinced of his error under our excellent tuition; coffee is a dream, at 10c. a cup, and chocolate a nectar indeed, at 20c.; pungent clarets, good withal, are cheap at 60c. a quart bottle, Hennessy three-star brandy at $1 a bottle, and rum—the devil's own—at two centavos a drink.

It is very difficult for the average American to hold his own against the combination of climate and native cooking, unless he has some Mexican blood in his veins or is a good campaigner. The continual warm weather is enervating, but the food-mixtures of olive oil, garlic, red peppers, stringy beefsteak which has not lost its animal heat, garbazos, frijoles, and half a dozen other kinds of beans, are too much entirely for a northern digestive apparatus, and one cannot live forever on coffee, bread, and soft-boiled eggs, which are the only elements of native diet not possessing distinctively southern flavors.

Garlic is going out of fashion in a few alleged American cafés, which is a relief to the nostrils and the sense of taste; a few months more will probably bring about Americanized meals.

Puerto Rican soups are always fine and palatable, though they usually suggest garlic.

Oranges can be bought two for a centavo, and are delicious. Bananas are as low as five for a cent, and this for the most approved style of " lady fingers " or little round fellows.

Where a man has capital to invest, there are many lines of business upon which he may embark with a fair assurance of the return of his money with interest.

Sugar-, coffee-, and tobacco-raising rank first, and will open the best avenues for investors of large capital. These three interests are treated in separate chapters.

Fruit-growing is as yet undeveloped, but the island offers many possibilities and a rich field for investors, in that every kind of tropical fruit may be cultivated to its highest perfection in the rich, well-watered soil.

Railroads and modern rapid-transit facilities are very much needed in the island. Don Ibo Bosch, in 1888, secured a franchise from the Spanish government to build and operate a railroad which was to encircle the island. The corporation was to be known as the Compañia de la Ferrocarriles de Puerto Rico. The road was to be finished in six years, and the government guaranteed eight per cent. to the corporation on the capital invested, not to exceed $10,000,000. This road was promptly begun at three points. At the end of four years, or in 1892, a single-track, narrow-gauge road had been laid northward and eastward from San Juan to Carolina, by way of Rio Piedras—sixteen miles in all—and the grading had been partially completed to Rio Grande, ten miles farther, while from San Juan westward it was completed for forty-eight miles to the town of Camuy. At Aguadilla, it ran southward through Añasco to Mayaguez, a distance of twenty-two miles. From Ponce, on the southern coast, it was built to Yauco—some twenty-four miles westward—making a total mileage of one hundred and ten of the two hundred and eighty-three contracted for.

DAILY TRAIN ON THE SAN JUAN-CAROLINA RAILROAD

INDUSTRIAL POSSIBILITIES

The equipment of these fragments of badly-laid road would disgrace a logging or mining region in our northwest, so mean and primitive are the cars, and so poorly kept are the engines. It is not essential to discuss the defective methods existing in railroading in Puerto Rico —beyond stating that the service consists of one mixed train of two cars each way, in twenty-four hours, and that the average speed is ten miles an hour—as it is rather intended to point out future needs. The corporation before referred to did not complete the road, and made no attempt to do so, within the stipulated time, so the Spanish government revoked the franchise. A renewal of the charter was requested and refused, and, at the beginning of the war, the matter was still under discussion, being held in abeyance at Madrid.

There are no other railroads on the island, except a tramway from San Juan to Rio Piedras, which parallels the other road that far; the equipment of this line is bad, but the service is comparatively good, as trains are run each way, on schedule time, an hour apart.

There should be a great future in the island for lighter tramway systems—such as trolley lines, with trains of two or three cars, capable of making twenty miles an hour. It is not believed by the writer that, in this small area, there is, or ever will be, sufficient commercial inducement to warrant the construction of heavy road-beds, equipped with large engines and standard rolling-stock. The distributing points for both imports and exports will lie around the periphery of the island, at the best waterfronts, and the railroad handling will always consist of very short hauls. Passenger traffic will be mainly of the same nature, from small inland towns to the port-towns and vice versa.

The offsetting advantages of electric as against steam

roads lie in the possibility of more rapid and cheaper construction, over heavy grades, to the interior towns, which are large exporters of coffee and consumers of merchandise, and in being able to furnish light, heat, and power to many small towns along the routes. Apropos of this subject, it may be said that the scarcity of fuel is everywhere felt, and, for this reason largely, charcoal—which is an economical and intense-heating medium—is used almost universally for cooking purposes. Instead of depending upon this fuel, the cook-stove of the future might be some form of electric heater. Also, it must not be forgotten that every coffee-planter is desirous of introducing his own machinery, but is confined to the use of animal- and hand-driven mills, mainly, for the reason that steam-boilers requiring fuel are an unprofitable investment unless the operations are carried forward on an extensive scale.

Owners of sugar-mills, which run day and night during the grinding season, would gladly welcome cheap electric light. For fuel, however, they depend largely on the cane-begasse which is burned under the boilers; and the feasibility of furnishing such mills with electric power, to replace their present batteries of boilers and engines, remains a matter for future determination.

It is generally conceded today that electric transportation is not profitable where the traffic is small, as the plant must be kept in nearly maximum operation. If, upon examination of the railroad problem, however, it is found that the maintenance of electrically-driven cars will not give a satisfactory return, for lack of continuous traffic, or sufficient current cannot be sold to make it profitable, then compressed air—which has long since passed the experimental stage—may be substituted, with a view to economically centralizing the generation of power.

INDUSTRIAL POSSIBILITIES

San Juan and Ponce have gas-plants, against the product of which the average American citizen would cry aloud. Gas, as an illuminant, is an antique in the present age, and it is doubtful whether it can be made to compete with electricity in a country where every pound of heavy piping must be imported from abroad, and where, for some time to come, there will be small objection made to overhead wiring. Heating-gas would subserve an excellent purpose, at present, in every town on the island, in place of the ancient charcoal kitchen-furnaces, which give off noxious and deadly vapors; but, as before suggested, some type of electric stove may be preferred to either.

Railroad construction on the island offers many difficult engineering problems, excepting, perhaps, in the case of roads which will skirt the littoral levels along the coast-line. The interior country is so broken with heavy and steep mountain-ranges, so devoid of extensive level valleys—where they do occur, they are flooded from time to time by freshets—that perforce it will be necessary to carry the contemplated roads around the multitudinous windings of the mountainsides. This being true, it means that almost every yard of road-bed must be blasted from the close, underlying limestone rock, and that, at every transverse rivulet which cuts a deep V-shape basin, it will be necessary to heavily grade and bridge.

The east-and-west extension of the rugged mountain-ranges will strongly militate against trans-island roads, but the present location of interior commercial towns does not seem to demand more than two such roads; one following the military highway from San Juan through Rio Piedras, Caguas, Cayey, Aybonito, Coamo, and Juana Diaz to Ponce (I understand that a charter has already been granted for such a road), and the other possibly from Ponce, or some harbor farther west—say Guanica—to Adjuntas, Utuado, and finally to the northern coast at Arecibo. Both routes would be through the very heart of the largest agricultural sections of the island.

Ice-plants offer another inducement for the business man; a few such plants, with limited facilities, are now in operation at San Juan, Ponce, Mayaguez, and Guayama, but the interior towns are sadly lacking in refrigerants. In connection with such enterprises, there should be introduced cold-storage rooms for cooling and preserving the beef, which is now killed in the morning and eaten before night. The household refrigerator is an almost unknown article, and, as a side line and persuader to the use of ice, it is very desirable.

Cattle-raising has a bright future in this country, where the tall, succulent bunch-grass grows as high as one's head, and the cropping of hay is never required, since the rich, green food grows perennially. In 1895, only a little over 4,000 head of live cattle were exported from the island, which brought an average of $38 apiece. There are no statistics as to the home consumption of beef, and it is impossible to even approximate that consumption, when dealing with a people who are large meat-eaters among the well-to-do, and use little or none at all among the vast army of poverty-stricken peasants. Assuming that the annual exportation of hides, which amounts to about $11,000, represents one-fourth of the cattle slaughtered, the yearly consumption would be in the neighborhood of 50,000 head.

The accredited great cattle region of the island, whose reputation is borne out by personal observation and the fallible testimony of the eye, is in the northeast section, a great district around Carolina and Rio Grande. The

BEEF CATTLE OF PUERTO RICO

INDUSTRIAL POSSIBILITIES

rolling, low-lying hills, adjacent to the immense flat and fertile cane-bearing bottoms, are covered with grazing cattle. These animals are much like the famous long-horned cattle of Texas, but are far finer in appearance, and heavier, a condition brought about by the ease of grazing in fields where every step gives an abundance of nutritious food. The island of Vieques has been a large producer of beef-cattle for the main island, and each year many thousands are shipped to San Juan and other seaport towns, Santo Domingo and Haiti being also purchasers from this point.

Raising cattle for market in Puerto Rico has no drawbacks like those known to our people in the United States—such as carrying them through the hard winters of the northern and eastern sections, and feeding them with hay and grain, or, as in the great southwest, suffering from a shortage of pasture caused by biting blizzards, or the withering heats of summer when the grass becomes crisp and brown. It is a paradise for cattle; plenty of food the year round, flowing water in every hollow, and never a need for housing. With the United States as a market, and free entry for cattle, there will be great inducement for money-makers in a land where hundreds of thousands of fine animals may be raised with a minimum amount of expense. The use of cold-storage plants in the island—already contemplated by some of our great beef-packers, with a view to introducing American fresh meats—might, and probably will, be reversed, in a very few years, to handling an island product for the benefit of consumers in the United States. The high price of land may be cited as an argument against cattle-raising, but, within given areas on the island, many times more cattle may be grazed than in any portion of our own country, and, if Pennsylvania and New York farmers can raise cattle with profit on lands valued, on an average, at $200 an acre, their only advantage being near-by markets, certainly, in a region averaging $100 an acre and rejoicing in a superabundance of rich food, much profit must accrue to the investor.

Dairy-farming is another opening which has a future, notwithstanding the attendant drawbacks of a hot climate, no cold springs for cooling the milk, and ice at a premium. If entered into on a sufficiently large scale to warrant the installation of an ice-plant, the returns would leave a large margin of profit. As things are today, the cattle are milked but once in twenty-four hours—before daylight each morning. The warm milk must reach the consumer in a very few hours, or be lost by souring. The selling-price ranges from eight to twelve cents a quart. Cream is unknown, not because, as one of the army officers put it, "This damn Puerto Rican milk is so poor that never a particle of cream can rise," but because it is never sufficiently cool for cream to rise. Canned butter sells for from 60 cents to $1 a pound, in two-, three-, and five-pound tins. This article, which delicate people should never have analyzed, was imported in 1895 to the extent of 365,000 pounds.

Cheese—another of the by-products of the milk farm—is annually imported to the amount of a million and a quarter pounds. Also there is made on the island good, palatable, hand-pressed cheese, too white, too dry, and too tasteless for the average foreigner, but largely consumed by the natives.

Dairies supplied with proper refrigerating facilities, near any of the larger towns, will be able to more than compete with the methods in vogue. Cream, fresh butter, and cheese would find a ready market at prices—for the present, at least—much higher than those of America.

INDUSTRIAL POSSIBILITIES

Poultry culture, as it exists today, seems to consist mainly of breeding game fighting-cocks. Miserable little chickens of a pound and a half bring 50 cents each. Eggs are to be had in limited quantities, at sliding-scale prices ranging from 30 cents to 50 cents a dozen, determined largely by the age of the hen-fruit, which becomes painfully overripe in forty-eight hours.

Fresh mutton is always in demand in the market, and it is an easy matter to keep sheep fat and in good condition. Wool-growing would not be a success, unless haircloth becomes fashionable, as the imported lamb soon turns into a goat, judging by his bristling coat.

Pork, to the amount of nearly 10,000,000 pounds, is annually imported by Puerto Rico, and is almost wholly purchased from the United States. The raising of hogs in large numbers would, however, be a doubtful experiment, owing to the high price of corn, though there is much mast in the mountain regions upon which they are said to grow fat; the indigenous animal is an extremely poor specimen of the razor-back species.

Corn is scarce and high-priced, and cannot be raised with much success on the northern half of the island, on account of the quantity of rain. The lands of the drier southern portions of the island are capable of producing very excellent corn, though, during exceptionally wet seasons, it is apt to mature badly and be injured by canker and must. The failure of corn-crops in certain years is made apparent by the variable importation of this grain, which sometimes rises as high as 20,000 bushels, and falls, in other years, to one-fourth this amount. This year (1898), the island crop is very promising, and, in the Yauco and Mayaguez districts, several thousand acres of this cereal wave ten feet high, usually bearing two large ears to the stalk. While the local price of corn is high,

PUERTO RICO

ranging from 80 cents to 95 cents a bushel, it is not at all probable that, in the future with open markets, island corn can compete with the American product. The benefits, therefore, will accrue to American exporters of maize.

It is said that cotton can be grown successfully on the island, and, in the past, the crop has been referred to in consular reports. The raw product, however, has not been able to compete with foreign-grown cottons, and the raising has fallen into desuetude. In view of the oversupply of this commodity in our own country and the prevailing low prices, there is no remunerative future promise from the growing of cotton in Puerto Rico.

A mountain rice is grown quite extensively by the peons, and, at some points, by the larger landholders and planters, but it is usually considered inferior to the foreign, lowland-grown rice. In 1895, over 74,000,000 pounds, averaging a little more than three cents a pound, were brought into Puerto Rico. These figures indicate to what a large extent this cereal is consumed by the native population—being a little over eighty pounds per capita annually, not including the home product, which is consumed mainly by the poor people, and which would readily bring the consumption up to and over one hundred pounds. This remarkable quantity of rice is purchased principally from Great Britain, Germany, and Spain; the United States never having furnished more than 10,000 pounds in any one year during the last ten.

It may be impossible, even with the cheap labor of this island, to compete with the cheaper Indian and Chinese rice, but one wonders, nevertheless, why sugar-cane planters, who have been running behind financially year by year on account of primitive machinery and the disastrously low price of sugar, do not attempt the cultiva-

INDUSTRIAL POSSIBILITIES

tion of rice in lieu of sugar-cane. Many of the estates are admirably adapted to such a purpose, with irrigation ready at hand and sufficient in quantity. It would, at least, pay a considerable margin over the cost of cultivation, and would be far preferable to the present custom of making muscovado sugar at a loss.

Bay rum and the essential oil of the bay-tree, which grows luxuriantly on the island, bring an annual income of no mean proportions into the coffers of a number of men. Up to the present time, however, no systematic culture of this tree, which furnishes us with the delicious bath and tonsorial perfume, has been attempted. While this is now an industry of minor importance, there is no reason why it should not readily be expanded into a commercial enterprise of magnitude. The destructive distillation of the leaves in rum, and the extraction of the essential oil from the leaves, are both extremely simple and require no extensive plant.

Market-gardening for the cities is not apt to prove very remunerative in a region where every negro or mestizo, by stirring up the earth with a stick and planting seed, secures a tenfold return for his labor, and further where the primitive gardener is in the habit of trudging miles, on his own bare feet, with a few centavos' worth of produce, which he sells in the market-place. Americanizing the island will mean a greater demand for a larger variety of fresh vegetables, and supplying the new population may offer inducements to a few men. Rich returns will accrue, however, only through the raising of agricultural products which may be exported. The rearing of fruits and vegetables, with the attendant industrial possibilities, will be treated in another chapter.

Lumbering has no future in the island, as it has long since been on the wane. There are no extensive sections covered with virgin forests; here and there, on the rugged mountainsides in the eastern-central and western-central portions, a few hundred acres may be found clothed in heavy timber, but beyond these regions and scattered patches from which the best woods have been culled, no timber remains. The vast wildernesses of trees, which often mislead the unknowing into believing that forests abound, are usually the spindling guava- and mocha-tree coverings for rich coffee plantations beneath.

There have been, and yet remain, many small areas of rare and fine woods, but, in the commercial sense of lumbering, there are no business openings of any magnitude. The small, rare growths will be cut out, as the clearing of land for agricultural purposes proceeds, and will be sold abroad as the years go by, the larger, common timber being used, as in the past, for the framing of local buildings.

The balance of trade in lumber—excepting the types of rare woods—will be largely in favor of the United States, though, up to 1896, only an average of a million dollars' worth of wood and its manufactured products was shipped to Puerto Rico. At Lares, in the heart of the mountain region, lumber is worth $50 a thousand, and the cost of erecting frame houses and buildings, at this high price for building material, may readily be imagined. There should be a great demand for cheap American lumber.

Wood for fuel is becoming scarcer each year, and commands, delivered at the big sugar-mills in small ox-cart loads of about a third of a cord, the exorbitant price of a peso to a peso and a half, and this, too, for the roughest kind of firewood—crooked, with knots and knobs and much small stuff among it.

Among the woods still found on the island may be

INDUSTRIAL POSSIBILITIES

enumerated the "asoubo," which grows very large, is very hard, reddish in color, a little like mahogany, and is used for house-framing, principally; the "capa blanca," which grows large, is hard, fine-grained, white in color, and used for framing and furniture manufacture; "capa prieta" is a beautiful wood, fine-grained, with black and white streaks, grows large and straight, rather rare now, and is desirable for export trade; "capa de sabana" is a soft wood, with a white ground having yellowish veins; looks— by optical illusion—semi-transparent, when polished; rare now, and used by the natives for the manufacture of beautiful canes; "aceitillo" is another fine hard wood, of yellowish color, which makes good plow stuff, carriages, and framing; "cedro" (cedar) is found rather plentifully, and is used to a limited extent for cigar-boxes; it is not, however, the fragrant species so common in Cuba, and is therefore less desirable, commanding a much lower price; mahogany is found in small trees, but is not profitable, commercially; it is used for making fine canes; lignum-vitæ occurs in some districts, in limited quantities, but the major portion of the best wood has long since been exported; "tachuelo" is interesting for a hardness so extreme that a nail will not penetrate it, and for a weight which causes it to sink in water; the "ciera" or silk-cotton tree is one of the most imposing of tropical growths, rising to great heights, with far-outspreading branches, and with immense encircling ribs, which stand out like braces at its base.

There are hundreds of other woods, many of them very beautiful with variegated colors, but not growing in sufficient quantity to make the handling of them profitable.

There are a number of small manufacturing projects which may be carried into effect by quick-witted men, and, through them, a few men with small capital will undoubtedly make a beginning in this new territory. Straw-hat making and straw-plaiting offer opportunities, where rice-straw and a score of grasses and barks are abundant and adaptable to this end; rope-making from vegetable fiber is another; tortoise-shell cutting still another; fan-making, cane manufacture, basket-weaving, and many others, dependent on the natural resources, will be found profitable in a small way.

Manufacturing of any kind in Puerto Rico, for home consumption, will probably be profitable only when the raw material is found or grown on the island, as the want of mineral fuel—unless it is discovered later—will be a serious drawback.

The United States, by reason of the abundant supply of cheap fuel, will be able to furnish Puerto Rico with all commodities, manufactured from raw materials not found on the island, at less cost than she can fabricate them herself, and it may even be discovered that many of the raw products of the island—where they are not perishable—may be more economically enhanced in value in America.

Whether Puerto Rico manufactures on a large scale or not in the future depends greatly upon what action Congress may take in determining the form of government for the island. With free-trade relations between the United States and her new possession, manufactories will be slow to develop; on the other hand, high tariff will force her to increase the value of crude materials at home.

Brick-, flagging-, and tile-making should prove good openings for capital. While every town of any importance has its brick-kiln, and some of the largest several, their fittings are crude and the machinery and methods in vogue very primitive. The pug-mill consists of a circu-

INDUSTRIAL POSSIBILITIES

lar trench dug in the ground, some two and a half feet wide by two in depth. Around this excavation an ordinary wheel travels—one from a cart usually serves the purpose—through which is thrust a long wooden pole, attached to a swivel-head in the center of the circle, which answers for both axle and draft-bar. A yoke of oxen on the outer periphery furnishes the motive power. Clay and water are thrown into the trench, and the wobbling, revolving wheel does the pugging. The pugged clay is all molded into brick by hand, and often a form is not used, but the plastic clay is paddled into brick shape. Drying takes a long time, as the clay is worked very moist, and the atmosphere is usually damp. Burning is done with wood, in fairly good kilns of small dimensions. Good brick of this character brings $15 a thousand.

From this meager outline of the process, it will be readily understood by brick-makers that, through the introduction of modern brick-making machinery—the dry-clay variety being preferable—far finer brick could be produced, and the present price could be almost halved, and yet leave a handsome profit to the investor.

Roof-tiles are also made by hand, the proper curves being given over a wooden mold. The same brick-machine, with an additional die, is easily adapted to the manufacture of simple, curved roofing-tiles.

The clays of the island are exceedingly fine for all purposes to which burnt clay is applied. There are many clays with only a small percentage of iron, which will burn light, but the majority of them are the iron-bearing kinds, which burn into bright reds. The texture and homogeneity of most of the clays cannot be surpassed, where a hard, firm, clear, ringing brick is desired. It is claimed that kaolin of fine quality appears in the western portions of the island, but, in view of the fact that there are several earths identical in appearance with kaolin, though totally different in chemical composition, this point must first be determined before being finally announced; there are, however, other clays well adapted to the manufacture of the heavier and coarser pottery-wares.

Every small town in the island has its alleged hotel, and the larger cities have several, among them some very good abiding-places for the traveling public. Cafés are found by scores and hundreds, in the cities, towns, and villages, as well as scattered along the highways and trails; in fact, any house or hut bearing on a highway may be approached with perfect confidence that at least coffee, bread, and dulces are served for the benefit of the passer-by.

From an American standpoint, however, there are no good hotels on the island of Puerto Rico. The rooms are meanly furnished, the beds are without mattresses, the victim sleeping on a blanket spread over wire springs so short that the head must be skilfully perched on the infantile pillow to keep it off the wooden cross-piece, while the heels rest on the bottom of the wooden frame in such a position as to cause one to feel as if he were sleeping with his feet on top of the mantelpiece. It requires months of practice to slumber easily, and not get up with a broken back. The partitions between the rooms are usually made of a single planking, and the next-door neighbor's midnight idiosyncrasies may be a source of entertainment, more painful than pleasant, to the insomniac. American hotels, run by Americans, will be hailed with delight by the army officers, and, in the large towns, the fear of lack of patronage need never be felt, as the English-speaking population is large and will rapidly increase.

THE HOT SPRINGS AT COAMO

INDUSTRIAL POSSIBILITIES

The cafés are fair; that is, in all the big centers, there are establishments where one can be reasonably well fed. They are so numerous, moreover, that few Americans will be able to sandwich in among them with much chance of a brilliant business success.

For a winter resort, the climate of the island is everything that the æsthete, the tourist, or the invalid could desire. The balmy days and cool nights of January and February, the exquisite flowers and tropical verdure, the rolling mountains and the rushing brooks, all blend to charm the eye and the senses, and should, in a few years, make Puerto Rico a much-sought-after winter home for those who roam the earth in search of more genial temperature. Winter-resort hotels will, in every probability, be one of the successful financial ventures. There are many spots in the lovely mountain regions which offer sites of natural beauty, encompassed by natural wonders. One might suggest the great caves of Aguas Buenas, or those near San German, as desirable points, though there are many other places in this great limestone country where unexplored caves may turn out to be caverns rivaling, in extent, those of America.

Thermal, mineral, and medicinal springs occur in numbers all over the island, the one of chief present importance being two miles from Coamo, where the heated mineral water rushes out of the earth in great quantities. This has been a favorite resort of the island population for many years, and a fairly comfortable establishment exists. There are also mineral springs at Ponce and Caguas, which have been, to some extent, developed commercially, and there are a number of others scattered through the land, to whose curative properties enthusiastic praise is given.

The most serious hindrance to the immediate development of winter resorts is the lack of roads. The great traveling public, excepting the brawny, danger-loving tourist, is not willing to be carried over wild mountain-trails, even to witness the most profound natural phenomena. The military road across the island is the only travel-route now feasible for the mass, and along this line certainly not over three fashionable resorts would prove profitable; however, not many years will elapse without bringing to this land of sunshine and flowers its needed highways, and, with them, crowds of seekers after pleasure, comfort, and health.

General merchandizing is held well in hand by Spanish and Puerto Rican storekeepers, and Americans will err if they assume that, as business men, they are more capable than their newly-acquired, dark-haired brethren; for the Spanish tradesman is thoroughly clever and competent, usually well educated, polite to a fault, and eager to meet the wants of the incoming American population. Most of these men are well-to-do capitalists, and they have often carried on the same business in the family for generations. It will be no easy task for shopkeeping Americans to compete with an element of this character, which controls all the native trade, and is capable of meeting all the exigencies of the new.

CHAPTER IX

COFFEE CULTURE

COFFEE-RAISING ranks first as an industry in Puerto Rico, bringing wages into the pockets of thousands of earners, and substantial profits to the coffers of the plantation-owner and exporter.

Beside the assured income from a well-planted coffee plantation, the life of the planter and owner has many desirable features which recommend it as an occupation to be followed by the American investor: First, coffee must needs be raised in the higher altitudes of the picturesque rolling hills, and on the faces of the steep, mountainous inclines which finish upward in sharp, zigzagging, narrow ridges, thus giving him a healthful, cool place of residence, away from the hot lowlands and fever country of the coast. Second, in the hills and mountains, living springs for uncontaminated water-supply are found, and, at the worst, he has always at hand the cooler, frothing, dashing torrents of the rock-bound mountain streams, from which to draw crystalline water. Third, and perhaps most important, no great technical training is required to raise coffee successfully, as is the case in raising sugar or tobacco. Fourth, the life is an easier one for the proprietor—which is no small factor in a torrid zone, where excessive activity is sure to bring on fever in the case of the unacclimated—in that he travels in the shade of the forest which shelters his coffee-trees from the hot sun, as he makes his overseeing tours, and works under cover, where the pulpy berry is changed into the finished and polished bean of commerce.

Good coffee-land ranges in price from twenty to five hundred dollars an acre, depending upon location and the topography of the site, and again whether it be virgin soil, or in crop of varying age, the highest price being asked for five-year-old, full-bearing trees, near the great military highways, within easy-hauling distance of coast shipping-centers.

It may be said that five hundred dollars is a fictitious value for any coffee plantation, and that the owner naming such a price is usually a Spaniard, filled with a desire to return to Spain, but inwardly fearing, even in his dislike of the American, that the new rule may mean unparalleled progress in the island. Two hundred dollars an acre for well-grown trees, with adequate shade above them, has hitherto been considered a good round sum for a plantation, though as much as three hundred has been paid under Spanish domination.

There is no favored section in the mountain districts where coffee grows to greater perfection, or with better flavor, on account of more fertile ground, and this assertion is made in the face of a prevailing opinion that the Yauco region, in the southwestern part of the island, grows the best coffee. "Yauco" has become a trade name in France, so it is almost a universal practice to mark the higher-grade coffees with the word "Yauco," whether they come from the east, west, north, or south.

The western end possesses some topographic and shipping advantages over other portions of the island, for, in a section running in a great arc around this district, the mountain country has more rounded foothills, and less angular and precipitous contours, thus making the work

HAULING THE CROP OVER A HEAVY TRAIL

PACK-TRAIN CARRYING COFFEE TO MARKET

COFFEE CULTURE

of planting and cropping easier, and also permitting expeditious gathering of the berry. The shipping advantages lie in that a fair military road connects all the coast towns, and that good harbors are not far away. Ponce is reached by rail from Yauco, and the deep-water and picturesque harbor of Guanica is not over six miles away. Ponce also has a military road leading up into the Adjuntas country, which is almost solely devoted to coffee culture. There are the ports of Guayanilla to the eastward of Guanica, Cabarajo on the lower western end of the island, Bramadero several miles to the north, and the large city and harbor of Mayaguez in the center of the western side. After Ponce, Mayaguez is the great coffee-shipping city of the island, and a large area of country to the eastward is tributary to this city. North of Mayaguez is Aguadilla, which exports a fair proportion of coffee; and Arecibo, on the northern coast towards the west, receives nearly all the coffee grown in the Utuado district, as a good military road connects the two towns.

The coffee country on the great military road across the island from San Juan to Ponce is just as rich, and on it are raised as prolific crops as in the western end of the island, but the region is rougher and the hauling is a large item of expense, reaching eight cents a pound where it is necessary to bring the product in by pack-mules over frightful trails to the military road, and then laboriously haul it in ox-carts to San Juan or Ponce. Electric railways will relieve this burden of excessive tolls, which is now, in some places, so destructive to profits.

The development of coffee-raising in the eastern half of the island has no doubt been retarded by lack of roads, less water, greater area of rough, rocky country, and no convenient harbors; though there are many fine coffee plantations scattered through the mountains.

PUERTO RICO

The clearing of virgin soil in Puerto Rico for coffee-raising, or for any other purpose, represents much labor, but it is a far easier undertaking than in Cuba, where virgin land presents the densest of tropical jungles. In Puerto Rico there are few areas which have not been cultivated over and over again, during its three centuries of occupation, and the overlying vegetation consists, except in rare cases, of small trees and heavy undergrowth only, which, at a wage of fifty cents a day per laborer, may be economically cleared away and burned. The man who essays in this way, however, to create a coffee plantation *de nuevo* must be prepared financially to tide himself over four years of waiting for a remunerative crop of coffee, and to meet attendant expenses of cleaning, weeding, and the final introduction of coffee machinery.

Here is a fair estimate of the cost to a man contemplating the purchase of 100 acres of coffee-land and converting it into a paying investment:

One hundred acres of land, with trail leading from it, not over twenty miles from coast harbor, at $40 an acre	$4,000
Clearing of land, preparing the soil, planting coffee-bean, platano, and guava-trees, at $30 an acre	3,000
Weeding for four years, cutting out the platano, at $20 an acre	2,000
Introduction of machinery	8,000
Buildings, plain residence	2,500
Coffee-houses	2,500
Trail-building and repairs and ditches for water	500
Incidentals	1,000
Total	*$23,500

This represents an establishment with modern machinery, but plain buildings, boiler and engine, pulping machine, steam-drying drum, huller for second shell, polishing machine, classifier, blowers, bins for handling

* Puerto Rican pesos.

and final sacking. The machinery, except the pulping machine, may be dispensed with, and the coffee-bean, in its last casing, dried in the sun on cement floors, or in flat, shallow boxes supported on rails to be run under cover; but the saving would not exceed five thousand dollars, and the expense of handling the coffee would be increased, while the marketable price would be greatly reduced, as it is necessarily sold to the coast merchant, who finally prepares it for market in his own mills.

The returns for this outlay would, approximately, be as follows:

Second year, coffee (5,000 lbs.) at an average of 15 cents a pound,	$750
Third year, coffee (10,000 lbs.) at same price...............	1,500
Fourth year, coffee (20,000 lbs.) at same price..............	3,000
	$5,250

Cost of picking, at 1½ cents a pound.....................	$525	
Cost of hulling and washing, at 2 cents........	700	
Cost of easy transportation, at 2½ cents...................	875	
		2,100
Net returns at end of four years....................		$3,150

At five years of age the plantation should be in full bearing, and by careful attention 500 to 1,000 pounds of coffee per acre can be raised in the following years, the decline in yield not being apparent until after the trees are twenty years old. Assuming that the average crop is 500 pounds to the acre, the annual output would be 50,000 pounds, and, gauged by the present standard price, controlled by the French, Spanish, and German markets, of 15 cents a pound—though in the last few years it has been as high as 25 cents—the returns—after deducting the cost of handling, which in itself may be reduced by the introduction of greater transportation facilities—would yield a net income of $4,500 a year.

It must be understood that 15 cents a pound represents

an average price to the grower of coffee for his entire crop, paid by the local exporters of coffee at the coast towns, and does not refer to the selling figures for the special classes of coffee supplied to the foreign market. This subject will be developed in the course of the relation of the growing, handling, and exportation of coffee.

Coffee, as it is raised today on the island, is planted with very little system. The bean is poked into the prepared land, and platano or banana slips are set up in the ground at intervals. The platano, making a full growth in each year, affords the first year's shade, which is absolutely necessary for the well-being of the young coffee-plants. Melango, known in England as tannia, a big lily with an edible root, is often used for this primary shading, particularly where the clearing of the ground is undertaken by a native laborer, who is granted the privilege, by the plantation-owner, of living on a plot of ground for two years and raising his subsistence, provided he prepares the ground for coffee.

With the planting of the platano, it is customary to plant small guava- and mocha-trees; the former are preferred, as they are speedy growers, and give the essential shade for years to follow in the life of the plantation. Both are slender, high shade-trees, branching out toward their tops into a fairly-dense covering of fluttering leaves, and they bear little fruit and lose few leaves during the year.

As time passes, loose berries drop from the coffee-trees and sprout to form new plants. These are transplanted when they interfere with the parent plant, and from them it is possible, in a few years, to secure a solid mass of coffee-trees, and to advance new areas each year, by transplanting under the shade of growing banana trees, which in themselves furnish a marketable food.

COFFEE AND TOBACCO LANDS, NEAR CAYEY

COFFEE CULTURE

The flowering coffee-tree is a thing of beauty, with its myriads of white flowers clinging close to the slender, waving, nearly-vertical branches of the bush. The flowers give way to green berries, and the tree looks much like a nature's rosary, so closely do the green beads crowd one another. In the month of October the berries begin to ripen and get their rich red and glazed coloring, which foretells the coming of the picker.

The commercial man perhaps does not care that the ragged, tattered pickers, large and small, father, mother, and a brood of partially-clothed children, make one of the most picturesque sights in this island of loveliness. In the early morning they trudge out from their little thatch-roofed huts, with home-made baskets slung on bands from their shoulders or balanced carelessly on their heads; straggling along the trails and roads, the little elfin children chasing each other in glee as they go to work. The bright-eyed, comely girl wishes you " Buenas dias" with half-timid, half-flirtatious smile, and the father and mother salute you with the deference born of generations of training. Later, from the depths of every thicket, comes the chant of singing voices, and the chorus is feminine, the woman of poverty, somehow, knowing how to be happier than the man.

The little children gather all the low berries which may be reached by their tiny hands, while the grown-ups bend down the tall bushes and rapidly strip the fruit into their baskets. At dusk, from every side burdened figures struggle up the steep hillsides, to the winding trails, or ease themselves down, step by step, from the heights above. The men and women are carrying the berries now, sometimes laden down with a large basket on the head and smaller picking baskets swung around the body, while the sleepy, tired tots stumble along, with all the brightness of life gone out, for that day, from their worn-out little souls. It is no uncommon sight to see a mother carrying a sleeping child, beside all her other load.

Down at the plantation, the coffee-berries are weighed up or measured up and paid for, usually with mild protest from the lips of the picker, for it is the common practice to underweigh and underpay. A centavo more or less to these poor people means much.

For a hundred pounds of berries $1.50 is an average price. A man can gather, in a heavily-fruited coffee plantation, an average of fifty pounds a day, and, with the addition of the earnings of the whole family, he becomes quite opulent for the first few weeks, but as the berries grow thinner—for they must not be picked green, and they ripen at different times—the work grows more arduous and the daily wage less.

All told, the native coffee-picker gets on an average not more than four months' paid work in the year, and this estimate includes his work of weeding and transplanting. Assuming his family to number five pickers—two grown people and three children—they perhaps pick an average of 100 pounds a day for eight weeks, and not more than 50 pounds a day for the remaining four or five weeks. His annual income for his entire family, at this rate, could not possibly amount to more than $125 Spanish, including one month's labor in caring for the field. It is little wonder, then, that he and his family, on an average wage of $10 a month Spanish, have few clothes and live in plain thatched huts, anæmic and fever-stricken from fruit diet and no medicines.

In consequence of this low wage, much stealing of coffee prevails, the spoils being exchanged or sold at the little stores along the roadsides. One sees everywhere, bordering the military highways, small mats with drying

COFFEE CULTURE

coffee upon them, and while some of it is the legitimate raising of the present owners, most of it has been pilfered by the laborers. All this side-issue coffee is handled by hand; the berry is bereft of its pulp in crude wooden mortars with hand-pestles, and dried in the sun, the outer shell being removed by a similar beating process in the same vessel. It is said that this system of peculation prevails in all the large exporting coffee-houses, and, in consequence, every poor family whose members work in the big mills and houses is always prepared to serve the most delectable beverage which the highest-grade coffee can produce.

When the berries arrive at the plantation house, they are stored away in sacks or bins, and, as speedily as possible, are put through the pulping machine, which removes the outer juicy meat from the two coffee-beans, which rest—with their flat sides together—within. This machine is extremely simple and is generally of local manufacture. A heavy wooden roll, eight or ten inches in diameter and two or three feet long, studded with round-headed nails, much like the bottom of a hobnail boot, is the principal element in the machine. Into a hopper above, the berries are poured, and come down through a narrow slit upon this moving roll, which is guarded by a steel-edge, adjustable rule, just separated far enough from the hobnails to macerate the berry and release the beans. This product, pulp and beans, falls onto an inclined, shaking wire net, through which the beans pass by oscillation, while the pulp travels over its surface to a refuse pile.

This finishes the handling of the coffee by machinery in most of the sun-drying establishments, though in the larger ones the entire work is done by mechanical means. Where the coffee is sun-dried, large, square cement floors are laid down on the open ground, with a slight dip for drainage, or, elsewhere, shallow boxes on small flanged wheels are used, which travel on tram railways from exposed positions in the sun to cover, under the house or shed, at night and in time of rain. The cement-floor system represents much work, for the berries must be housed at night and in damp weather, and it is a common occurrence to see men frantically raking the coffee into bags and onto squares of burlap, in haste to get the valuable product under cover from a coming shower.

At Lares, the entire public square is rented to one coffee-seller on week-days, that he may spread his coffee for drying, and every morning a hundred men file out with huge loads of coffee, tied in burlap sheets, on their heads, and begin the work of laying them open to nature's heat-rays. In this instance, it is all kept on the cloths, so that it may be quickly gotten under cover. It is an interesting operation to watch the deftly-trained men laying these cloths so that they overlap into one solid carpet of cloth, and following this maneuver up by spreading the coffee into a vast field an inch in depth. It takes from two weeks to thirty days to dry coffee well by this means, depending largely, of course, upon the weather.

The greater percentage of raisers ship the coffee thus dried, and yet enveloped in a thin brittle shell, to the steam-mills on the coast. A few of them, however, have hulling-mills which remove this last coat and afterwards polish the bean. These mills are primitive in character, consisting of two great wedge-shaped wheels five feet in diameter and covered with tin, which chase each other round and round from opposite ends of a great axle, in a circular-walled and tinned trough two feet deep. The motive power is a yoke of oxen. The heavy wheels ride over the coffee and crush off the outer hull. It is then

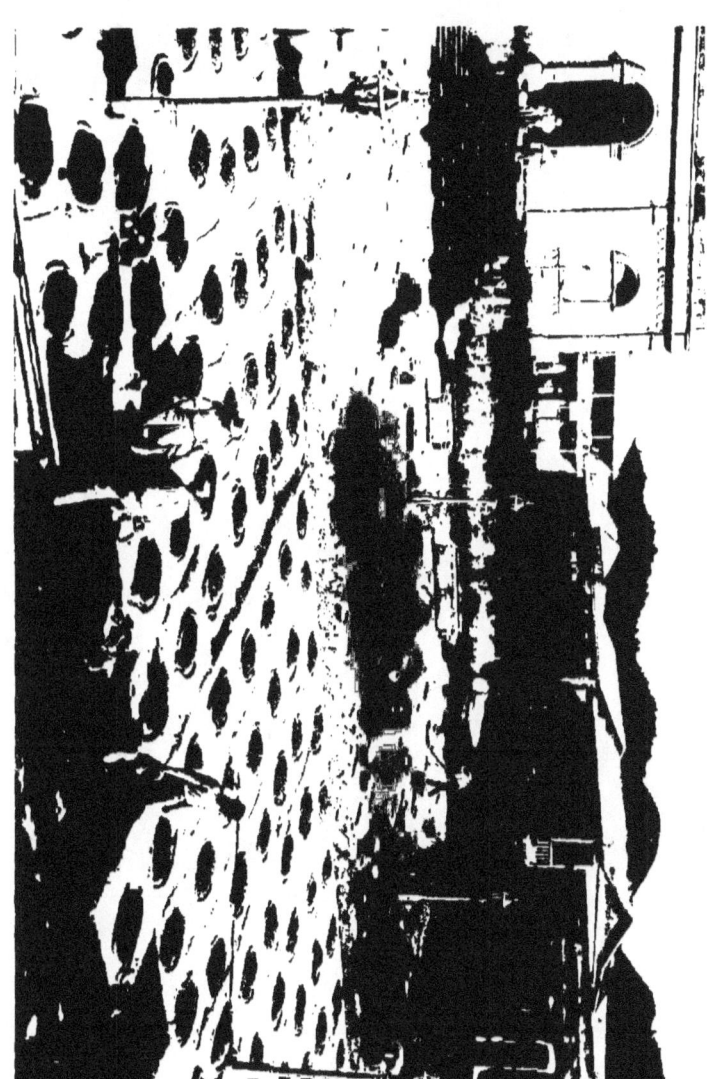

PUBLIC SQUARE OF LARES
Rented Six Days in the Week for Use in Sun-drying Coffee

COFFEE CULTURE

placed in an ordinary fanning-mill, such as we use for cleaning wheat or other cereals, and the dust and light hulls are blown out. It is passed back to the big rolls, and a small quantity of blued water—a quart to a hundred pounds—is poured into the runway, the wheels going round and round until every individual berry is polished till it shines and possesses the blue tint so prized in French markets. One coffee-burnisher of this character, at Cayey, run by steam, polishes and blues 16,000 pounds of coffee each day.

When the mountain coffee-growers have their crop of berries ready for the market, pack-trains of the sturdy little mules (not burros) pour in from the pasture-lands along the coast, under the charge of expert packers. Everywhere over the tortuous, precipitous, muddy mountain-trails, one finds, in November and December, long, snaky lines of these muscular little animals crawling carefully along narrow, rocky paths, or floundering through mud-holes belly-deep, laden with such huge packs as would put our government mules to shame. From the tolls of this pack-animal business many men make a comfortable or even comparatively sumptuous living.

On the alleged passable highways two-wheeled ox-carts are used, and it is a common sight to see four and five yoke of these lumbering animals, lurching and straining in the plastic muds, in an almost vain attempt to start five hundredweight of coffee on its impeded journey.

Where the work is done entirely by machinery, the wet beans may be run directly into the steam drier, though it is the usual custom to spread the mass out under cover for a few days until it loses its first water. The driers are of two types; a huge rotating cylinder filled with iron pipes through which hot steam circulates, or the more usual kind containing hot air sucked from the fire under the boilers and blown into the turning cylinder, where it escapes through close-meshed wire doors. From the drier the coffee is dropped into bins, carried to the top of the building by travelers, and deposited in bins. It then passes into the huller, which is of American make—outside of the pulper and the polisher, most of the coffee machinery comes from the United States,—where the hulls fly off, after slight crushing by fast-moving teeth. It is then polished and blued as described, and finally passes to the classifier, a cylindrical framework six feet long, wound with piano cord, in four sections, each set of wires being more open than the preceding. Inside this wire-work, a fixed-screw shovel moves the coffee along, and, according to size, it falls through into different compartments beneath.

No machine-method has been invented by which defective and marked beans may be separated from their better brethren, so hand labor has still to be expended on this part of the work. The hand-picking of coffee is again one of the picturesque phases of the coffee industry, as it is carried on by women and girls. In the poorer establishments they sit on the floor with a lapful of coffee, and, one by one, throw out the bad beans, shoving the lapful of good coffee finally into a bag at their feet. In the big marts on the seacoast, picking-tables are supplied, from whose compartmented boxes dangle bags connected to the table by open spouts. The girls work rapidly and deftly. Some woman in the corner starts a church chant, which is taken up by one after another, until the whole room is singing; then this is changed to a wild native love-song, and, through the stronger voices of the grown ones, sounds the weak treble of little children, that one wishes might be out in God's air, instead of stooped day after day, thin and white, over their

A COFFEE-PLANTER'S HOME, LARES, LOS MARIAS TRAIL.

COFFEE CULTURE

tables, their baby fingers flashing back and forth as they seize the discolored beans, piping amorous songs while their unmatured bodies grow round-shouldered, and their eyes lustrous only in fever. Bagging, labeling, and shipping follow.

Four grades of coffee are handled; as has been said before, geographical position is not an index to quality or flavor. The prime coffee is the male bean, which grows alone in a berry-pod. The shape is ovoid, instead of having one flat side, like the double bean. There is but five per cent. of this coffee, and it has brought a price at the wharves, in years gone by, ranging from twenty to thirty-five cents, the average being above twenty-five cents silver. The second coffee is the largest of the flat-sided beans, and is a very fine coffee. Its price has ranged between fifteen and twenty-five cents. The third coffee is a good bean, but smaller than number two, with a price of thirteen to eighteen cents. The fourth coffee is usually the irregular-shaped, small bean, with more or less discolored coffee intermixed. Its price ranges between six and twelve cents silver, depending upon how many bad beans have been thrown in. This coffee is very fair, measured by American cheap-coffee standards, and it is hoped by Puertoriqueños that it will compete with the grades of Rio so extensively consumed in our country.

55,000,000 lbs. a year seems to be a conservative estimate of the amount of coffee exported from the island in 1897, though the amount may fall somewhat this year (1898). Of this amount, Ponce ships from her seaboard nearly 25,000,000 lbs., Mayaguez between 10,000,000 and 15,000,000 lbs., and the rest goes from the ports of Arecibo, Aguadilla, San Juan, Guayama, and Guanica.

PUERTO RICO

Yauco district raises		8,000,000 lbs.
Lares "		5,000,000 "
Adjuntas "		6,000,000 "
Utuado "		6,000,000 "
Las Marias "		5,000,000 "
Mayaguez "		4,000,000 "
Cayey "		500,000 "
Aybonito "		500,000 "
Total		35,000,000 "

The other 20,000,000 lbs. is scattered over the island. It is not to be understood that these figures represent accurate statistics; they are merely an average of estimates given by various coffee-planters and shippers.

It may confidently be stated that the coffee industry is in its infancy in Puerto Rico, as compared to its possibilities under the progressive management of American capitalists. Not more than 100,000 acres are under cultivation, and the methods in vogue for handling the crop are very primitive. With American energy, proper machinery, and accessible electric transportation, there can be no doubt that Puerto Rico holds out the promise of becoming one of the leading coffee-producers of high-grade coffee in the world; the topography, soil, physical conditions, and climate favor an immense production of this one of the world's needs.

The quality of Puerto Rican coffee is held in high esteem in France, Germany, Italy, Austria, and Spain. France has always been the heaviest purchaser of high-grade coffee, Spain the largest buyer of the poor grades. Cuba, in some years, has been a heavier purchaser even than the foreign countries. In the United States, hitherto, this coffee has not been sold, except in small quantities, as our coffee-buyers will not handle the commodity at the high prices asked and received abroad. In flavor, it is as fine as our best mixtures of old government Java

COFFEE CULTURE

and Mocha; it has less of the pungent acridity of the Mocha, and is stronger than the Java. The half-way point reached between these two coffees makes a cup of Puerto Rican coffee a beverage of fine aroma and most delicate flavor. It should, as fads go, become the coffee of the future in America.

The progressive growth of the coffee industry during a century in Puerto Rico may be illustrated by the following table, though it should not be assumed that these figures are more than approximate statistics, for Spain and Spanish provinces have always been, in a marked degree, weak in accurate statistical reports:

Date.	Lbs.	Value.	Rate.
1783	1,126,225		
1803	294,784		
1832	2,800,000	$33,600	12c.
1834	11,596,500		
1851	12,111,900		
1887	25,102,000	3,415,666	13.6c.
1893	44,612,000	11,297,723	25c.
1896	58,780,000	13,379,000	22.7c.

The 1783 estimate is undoubtedly a guess made by De la Torre, author of "Cuba and Porto Rico," 1861, as there were no tabulated statistics of imports and exports of the island until the year 1803, and his figures for 1834 and 1851 are hardly to be credited, in that the careful writer Flinter ("State of Puerto Rico," 1834) gives but one-fifth the amount of the other author, for a coffee-crop two years earlier (1832). Flinter states, however, as his belief, that the official returns represent but one-half the actual quantity raised. The figures for 1887 and 1893 are taken from the English consular reports of the island, and are reliable. The returns of the 1896 crop are from

99

the exhaustive report of the Department of Agriculture, by Frank H. Hitchcock.

The discrepancy or apparent increase of the later over the earlier selling-price, ranging from an average of 12c. per lb. in 1832 to 25c. in 1893 and a little less in 1896, is probably to be accounted for by the constantly-augmenting depreciation of the silver currency of the island, which difference the consular agents have failed to consider. The Spanish official returns of the exports of Puerto Rico are reckoned in the island currency and not upon a gold basis. A material increase in the selling-price of coffee per pound would naturally follow, however, for, by the introduction from year to year of coffee-handling machinery, the quality of the marketable bean has been much enhanced, and the old methods of selling the bean for foreign exportation in its second hull and in an unclassified condition have wholly given way to modern methods, which place a carefully-classified, highly-polished, and blued coffee in foreign marts, where money is paid for fine appearance as well as flavor.

CHAPTER X

SUGAR CULTURE

A GENERAL impression seems to prevail that sugarcane raising and the manufacturing of the products from cane—sugar, molasses, and rum—form the chief industry of Puerto Rico. This is an erroneous idea, for, while the products, measured by avoirdupois, do greatly exceed those of all other industries, if gauged by money valuation, they rank second in importance; coffee being first, with a crop worth over three times the sugar output.

The growth of the sugar industry, from the beginning of the century, is told in the following table, though it should be remarked that twenty years earlier—or in 1783 —the annual amount of sugar grown was quite as large; there was a profound stagnation in island industries, however, between the years 1776 and 1811.

1803	Sugar	263,200 lbs. at 6 c.,	$15,792	exported.
1810	Sugar	3,796,900 " 6 c.,	$227,814	exported.
"	"	4,000,000 "		home consumption.
		7,796,900 lbs. total raised.		
1828	Sugar	19,788,600 lbs. at 4 c.,	$791,544	exported.
"	"	7,000,000 " 6 c.,	420,000	home consumption.
"	Molasses	2,245,044 " 2 c.,	44,900	exported.
		29,033,644 lbs.	$1,256,444	

PUERTO RICO

1838	Sugar	69,138,500 lbs. at	4 c.,	$2,765,540	exported.
"	"	8,000,000 "	6 c.,	480,000	home consumption.
"	Molasses	19,619,458 "	2 c.,	392,389	exported.
		96,757,958 lbs		$3,637,929	
1847	Sugar	104,178,200 lbs. at	4 c.,	$4,167,128	exported.
"	Molasses	26,922,126 "	2 c.,	538,442	exported.
		131,100,326 lbs.		$4,705,570	
1853	Sugar	115,666,200 lbs. at	3½ c.,	$4,038,317	exported.
"	"	11,000,000 "	6 c.,	660,000	home consumption.
"	Molasses	28,510,872 "	2 c.,	570,217	exported.
		155,177,072 lbs.		$5,268,534	
1887	Sugar	180,974,080 lbs. at	2.8 c.,	$5,041,444	exported.
"	"	16,000,000 "	5 c.,	900,000	home consumption.
"	Molasses	55,210,880 "	1½ c.,	978,163	
		252,184,960 lbs.		$6,919,607	
1896	Sugar	122,946,335 lbs. at	2.9 c.,	$3,603,852	exported.
"	"	16,000,000 "	6 c.,	960,000	home consumption.
"	Molasses	32,221,619 "	1½ c.,	493,638	
		171,167,954 lbs.		$5,057,490	

It will be noted that, from 1803 to 1887, there was a constant increase in the weight of sugar exported, and it may be said that during the next ten years, or up to the present time, a marked decline took place in the sugar industry, the crop of 1896 being about two-thirds that of a decade earlier.

The money value of the crop, however, has not, for fifty years, kept pace in ratio with the constantly-increasing acreage and output of marketable sugar. In 1847 the export sugars, at the then-prevailing high price of the commodity, sold for a sum within a million dollars of the high-water crop of 1887, though 77,000,000 more pounds of sugar were exported, or an increase of 77 % in the total crop over the year 1847, with a gain of but 20 % in money value. There are so many confusing factors to

SUGAR CULTURE

be taken into consideration, in an attempt to compare the past with the present condition of the sugar industry, and so few statistics in which confidence may be placed, that it is an almost hopeless task to attempt to prepare a critical analysis. The principal elements to be taken into consideration are:

1. Fertility of soil, which returned, sixty years ago, nearly double the crop of today.

2. Methods of cultivation, cutting, and transporting cane from fields, all of which have made giant strides, in some sections, over the primitive ways of the past.

3. Difference in machinery; modern machinery returning over thirty per cent. more sugar than in 1847.

4. Manufacture of by-products, rum and alcohol, which are produced very cheaply today, and with considerable profit.

5. Scale of wages; free labor in the forties received twenty-five cents a day and board, while today sixty-two cents Puerto Rican silver, or about forty cents gold, and no board is paid. Slave labor, of which there was never over fifteen per cent., cost as much as free labor, in housing, clothing, etc.

6. Cost of transportation to seaports, which has been materially reduced in sections with contiguous military roads.

7. Cost of fuel, which has more than doubled in price in forty years, but has decreased in quantity required by over one-half, through the introduction of better methods of firing, use of begasse for fuel, and use of vacuum pans and tubular boilers.

In 1847 it was possible to raise from 3,500 pounds of sugar per acre on the poorest lands, to as much as 8,000 to 9,000 pounds on the best; this was accomplished with little resting of the soil, and, further, the ratoons sprang up from the cropped cane for six or seven years in succession. Today little land on the island proper ever gives more than 4,000 pounds of sugar, and the average is near the ton mark; the cane grows from the ratoons but four or five years, and then lands must be rested for several years before replanting. The island of Vieques may be noted as an exception to this rule, and its productive lands yet return immense yields of cane, the fields not requiring replanting under six or seven years; but excessive and prolonged drouths occur now and then.

The modern methods of cultivation are greatly advanced over the earlier ones, through the almost total disappearance of the primitive single-stick plow and one yoke of oxen, which have given place to modern, heavy breaking plows (not gang-plows) with three to four yoke of oxen to each. The fields are carefully prepared for planting, though fertilizing is not indulged in, as it is said —with mistaken ideas of economy—that it would not be profitable.

The cane is still cut by hand, as no machine can do it, but the picturesque ox-cart, which sinks deep into the soft earth of the fields, has given way to steel tramways and cars, on the great estates, as a means of transporting cane to the mill, while, on one estate at least, whole trains are drawn by small steam-engines. This has much reduced the cost of labor, and insures expeditious movement of the cut cane to the crushers.

The machinery used before the forties consisted principally of wooden single- and double-roll crushers, driven by bullock power, open kettles for boiling, wooden vats for crystallizing out the second sugar, and dripping-rooms in which hogsheads of crude sugar, set on huge beams, were drained of their surplus molasses. Steam-engines for motive power and iron crushing-rolls were introduced

SUGAR-CANE FIELDS AT VIEQUES, OR CRAB, ISLAND
One and Two Years' Growth

in the forties, but the open-kettle and -pan boiling gave way very slowly to the modern process of vacuum pans, "triple effects," and centrifugals, and even to this day the industry is seriously handicapped by the continued use of antiquated machinery. Most mills boast of a vacuum pan and centrifugals, but, in the majority, the juice-boiling is still done in the open air, which necessitates a wasteful use of fuel and a finished sugar little above the old muscovado in quality.

There are but two central factories in all Puerto Rico which have really modern machinery, consisting of tubular boilers heated with begasse, fed automatically from carriers, double crushers with triple rolls, clarifiers and eliminators, triple effects, vacuum pans, mixers, centrifugals, sugar-carriers, bagging bins, and all the auxiliary vats and transferrers for making third and fourth sugars from the molasses. It may be said that most mills are a heterogeneous combination of old and new machinery in a most incongruous fashion, and that, in consequence, the mechanical equilibrium of the process is so easily upset that often one portion of the mill must close down, to wait upon some slow, weak link. The result of these unscientific methods has been to close down, permanently, mill after mill in the last ten years, since the price of sugar has been low, as it cannot be manufactured with profit without the most skilled handling.

The by-products, rum and alcohol, are manufactured at every big central factory, and furnish no inconsiderable return in the sugar-making business. It is almost impossible to estimate the annual production of rum on the island, for, as there are no internal-revenue taxes on the quantity manufactured, it is never returned as a portion of governmental statistics. The consumption of this fiery liquor is almost entirely confined to the native population, though some thousands of gallons are exported each year to Spain. Newly-made rum sells as low as twenty-five cents a gallon. The profitable side of molasses distillation will be found to lie in the manufacture of alcohol.

In regard to wages, the writer feels it may safely be said that labor is cheaper today in Puerto Rico than fifty years ago, when free men received twenty-five cents a day and board; for, with the depreciated value of the island silver, the best laborers do not get over thirty to forty cents a day gold, and must board themselves, while the sugar-planter receives an equivalent in gold, at the seaboard, for his crop. A fact which prospective investors in Puerto Rican sugar-estates must not lose sight of, is that financial legislation by our government for the island will place the silver used in the future on a gold basis, but it is not at all likely that the wage of the laborer will be any less, as measured in cents per day, this wage being now fifty to sixty-two cents of the present depreciated silver. If this is true—and all history of national financial fluctuations bears out the assertion—the wages for labor will be materially appreciated, as computed by the employer and charged against his profits. This promises to be one of the most serious obstacles in the way of profitable sugar culture in Puerto Rico, if not in all of our new possessions, unless the price of sugar shall advance.

All contracts for sugar from foreign buyers contemplate a delivery at the water-front of one of the great seaport towns, in bags or hogsheads, and the transportation of the sugar from the factory to the wharf is no small item of expense, amounting, in one instance known to the writer—from Carolina to San Juan, sixteen miles by oxcarts—to twenty-five cents Puerto Rican silver per bag

PRIMITIVE METHOD OF REMOVING THE "BAGASSE"

OLD SINGLE-STICK PLOUGH

SUGAR CULTURE

of two hundred and fifty pounds. Where railroads may be used, the transportation charges are materially reduced, but the tariff is exceedingly high, compared with American freight rates, and the carrier binds himself in no way to the safe delivery of the freight. The factor of transportation is one to be carefully considered by capitalists intending to invest in agricultural enterprises.

The scarcity of fuel has become a bugbear of monstrous proportions to sugar-makers, as the island has been almost denuded of wood; no mineral fuel has yet been discovered, and foreign coal is very costly. A small ox-cart load of very poor fuel wood, certainly not half a cord, costs, in most sections, a dollar and fifty cents a load. Begasse (the refuse cane) is used everywhere as a part of the fuel, but, where muscovado sugar-making still prevails, the proportion of wood consumed is at least seventy per cent. of the total amount of fuel, and it is only in the most modern establishments, where begasse is employed under forced draught for heating tubular boilers, that the ruinous wood bill is materially reduced.

Sugar-making on a gigantic scale is one of the deeply interesting industries of the world, and in Puerto Rico it is particularly fascinating to the observer, in that he can, while traveling over the island, follow the evolution of the industry objectively. The old wooden crusher, with its two upright, creaking rolls—driven round and round by slowly-plodding oxen, who snatch, now and again, a mouthful of the sweet cane—may be seen in operation in some of the out-of-the-way places. The juice is boiled, perhaps, in a single kettle, frailly housed from the weather by palm thatch, and the bubbling liquid seems almost to dance to the rhythmic strumming of the primitive guitar, in the hands of the native watcher. The little nude, round-bellied piccaninnies sit in circles and stare with

PUERTO RICO

wide-eyed approbation and contentment at the operation, while they munch huge mouthfuls of cane, and lather their faces with the sweet juice, or cement more firmly the kinky hair to their pates. Sugar for home consumption only is made at these extremely primitive mills, and it is doubtful whether the return is at all commensurate with the labor involved.

The next visible stepping-stone in the industry is shown in the scores of small mills, built fifty, sixty, and seventy years ago, which dot the valleys of the sugar districts. Many of them have been abandoned, and the majority are slowly passing away in dry rot, as the poverty-stricken owners cannot afford to operate them, and have either let their fields grow up in a wild luxuriance of weeds—as in portions of the Mayaguez district—or are cultivators of cane alone, for which they are paid, in a certain proportion of sugar, by the great central factories with their better machinery.

A few of the little mills are still operated, and turn out the lowest grades of muscovado sugar. The crushers are double rolls, driven by ancient condensing-engines of marine type, or by undershot water-wheels. The juice is boiled in batteries of circular, round-bottomed, cast-iron kettles, cemented and bricked in over a fireplace, in a single row. The juice is slowly heated in the first one farthest from the heat, and crystallized into sugar in the last directly over the hottest fire, where the thickening syrup rages like a tempest-tost sea, in foaming, sputtering ebullition. The molasses is drained from the semi-crystalline mass in wooden bins, and the remaining sugar, of very poor quality, packed in hogsheads or burlap bags.

At a conservative estimate, not more than seven per cent. of the lowest quality of sugar is returned from the

SUGAR CULTURE

canes, even when the first molasses is painstakingly converted into a second sugar. It is today utterly impossible to operate such a plant without constant loss to its owners, and one wonders at the almost asinine persistence with which some of the Spanish estate-holders continue the practice of making crude sugars by cruder methods, which each year involves them deeper in debt. The only explanation ever offered the writer was that the government had put an almost prohibitory tariff on modern machinery; it is true that American machinery was discriminated against in such a way that its introduction into Puerto Rico, by an unfortunate estate-owner, meant the doubling or tripling of its original price, by a subtle system of shuffling classification, which would lead the owner to believe that, unawares, he had imported a gold mine instead of simply a gold brick. Incidentally let me say that most of these unfortunate agriculturists hail with delight a bonding of the island's interests with those of the United States, in the firm belief that it means for them financial salvation.

During the last thirty years, what is known as the "central factory" system has arisen, the buildings being owned by capitalists, who may or may not own the canelands. The outlying landowners send their cane to these mills to be converted into sugar, and receive for it four and five per cent. of the weight of the cane in sugar. It is not usual for them, however, to receive the actual sugar, but rather the value of such proportion, at the ruling market price. The writer will later give fairly accurate figures of the cost of raising cane per acre, and placing it at the mill. It has been difficult, even under this system which places the burden of expense upon the mill-owners, for the agriculturist to even up, and it has been a common practice for mill-men to advance money to the farmer for the necessary cultivating machinery and expense of cropping, charging him 12 % interest, and taking, as security, a mortgage on his property. The result is most likely the same the world over—the mill-men each year add to their landed domain, and then sublet such properties on shares, perhaps to the scion of a once-powerful family.

Up to within ten years, or before the pressure and competition of beet-sugar were severely felt, it was possible for central factories, making as low as eight per cent. of sugar, to secure a fair rate of interest on the capital invested, but since that time, with sugar falling several times as low as $2.20 per hundredweight, only factories which possess the facilities and machinery for producing ten or eleven per cent. of sugar, and which have contributory cane-lands to furnish them with at least fifty million pounds of cane annually, can be run profitably.

One of the best-equipped central factories in Puerto Rico, which produced, in 1897, 6,500,000 pounds of first, second, and third sugars, made a net profit for the year of $19,500 on a capital investment of $800,000, or a little less than three per cent. This factory is capable of making 13,000,000 pounds of sugar a year, but has contributory to it but 2,000 acres of cane-lands, which can supply only about half the required amount, and hence it is forced to shut down, from time to time, during the grinding season. It costs the mill almost an even $18 per ton, or nine mills a pound, to make the sugar which sold, on an average, at a little below two and four-tenths cents a pound in 1897. The cane-raiser's five per cent. commission gives him half the sugar made, leaving, as a profit to the mill-man, three mills per pound. If this mill could be run up to its full capacity, the expense of operating

TYPICAL SUGAR-MILL NEAR PONCE—ANTIQUATED AND MODERN MACHINERY COMBINED

SUGAR CULTURE

would be so lessened as to easily afford four mills' profit per pound of sugar, and an easy return of seven per cent. on the total capitalization.

This particular illustration has been drawn with a view to pointing out that, while the sugar industry of the whole island is in an apparently precarious condition, in point of fact a thoroughly equipped establishment with sufficient cane territory, and the whole properly managed, will give, to the investor of large capital, an adequate return. But the factors which are today ruining the sugar-mill owners, of Puerto Rico at least, are antiquated mills and insufficient cane to keep them in operation. The promise of a successful future lies in more profound centralization of the industry, and there are now a number of sections on the island where single valleys of twenty to thirty thousand acres might easily be made contributory to a single factory; sections which, if necessary, might readily be irrigated from the constant and fast-flowing waters which course the center of the valleys.

Approximate cost of cultivating an acre of cane-land:

Plowing, first	$2 50	
Plowing, second	2 00	
Plowing, third	1 50	
		$6 00
Planting cane-tops	8 00	
Draining and ditching	4 00	
		$18 00
Weeding, first	$6 00	
Weeding, second	4 00	
Weeding, third	2 50	
Weeding, fourth	1 50	
		14 00
Thieving (pulling leaves from cane and laying in the rows to keep grass from springing up)		2 00
Cutting cane and loading on cars		6 00
Total cost per acre		$40 00

These figures are only approximate, based on wages of sixty-two and seventy-five cents per diem, and on contract jobs let to field bosses.

The expenses of the succeeding years, when the ratoons are springing up from the roots, are much less, not usually exceeding $20, but it should be remembered that the annual crop is becoming lighter, until a time arrives—after three or four years on poor lands, and four to six on rich bottoms—when the land must be rested or reset.

In years following the first one it is usual to "line up" the "trash" or leaves, in the drainage ditches, and "break bank" by plowing; that is, to plow down the ridge between the rows, which covers the trash with earth and creates a new drain, or reverses the topography of the field.

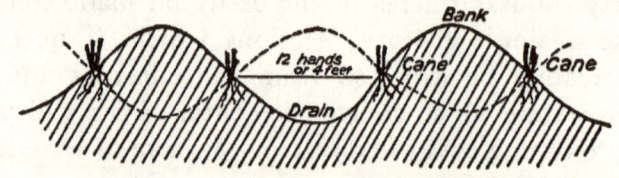

CROSS-SECTION OF BANKS AND DRAINS.
Dotted lines indicate method of breaking bank.

The diagram will give an understanding of the operation. Only one plowing is required, and the weeding does not exceed $10 in cost.

The plowing, weeding, and cane-cutting may be let out by contract to native Puertoriqueños who make a business of handling cane for estate-owners. The price per acre for plowing, weeding, etc., has been given, but it may be said that the cutting and loading are usually paid for at the rate of two cents a hundred pounds of cane, so the amount is variable, depending upon the size of the crop.

SUGAR CULTURE

The expense—to the cane-grower—of moving his crop to the sugar-mill falls heavy or light upon him, depending upon long or short hauls; whether it is necessary for him to transport the crop in ox-carts to the mills, or only a short distance to steel tramways owned by the central factory. It is an expense of sufficient importance in short years to materially reduce his revenue.

There are still many small valleys in Puerto Rico, where the rivers annually overflow, leaving behind, at the recession of the waters, a rich fertilizing silt where forty thousand pounds of cane may be raised per acre, and there are handsome stories of nearly double that amount in places. Good rich land will average thirty thousand pounds of cane or three thousand pounds of sugar per acre. Assuming this to be a big average, and the cane-raiser to receive one-half the value of this amount as his share, at the ruling price of 2.4 cents his gross receipts would be $36 per acre, as against liabilities of $40 an acre in planting his crop, a loss of $4 per acre. During the next four years his ratoon crops would run down from 3,000 to 2,000 pounds per acre, making his crop average 2,500 pounds to the acre, or his share in cost $30 per acre. Losing $4 an acre the first year, and netting $10 per acre the succeeding four years, leaves him an average annual profit of a little over $7 per acre.

Cane-lands range from $50 to $100 an acre in price, the latter figure representing rich lands.

This summing up appears, on its face, to be a fairly-pleasing exposition of how the landowner may net seven per cent. or more on his investment, but it is very doubtful if the figure for crops herein given will, year after year, reach the estimate. One estate raising over five million pounds of sugar is said to have averaged 3,600 pounds per acre, but many of the cane-lands of the island

PUERTO RICO

have been utterly worn out by generations of contract cultivators, and, in the writer's opinion, 2,000 pounds of sugar per acre would represent a nearer figure to the truth than a larger one.

It should be pointed out very forcibly, however, to sugar-cane growers in the United States, that even today, after decades of cane-growing in Puerto Rico, on lands which have never known the taste of fertilizers, and whose readily-accessible streams have never been diverted to irrigate a soil which blossoms under a drop of water, they do average, per acre, double the crop of the United States, and further that the cane throws up its ratoons for at least four years, instead of being planted annually.

There must be a remunerative future in Puerto Rico for just such men as have struggled for a hundred years, in Louisiana, to rear sugar-cane in an artificial environment. The climate is no more difficult to live in, and, with northern methods of cultivation pursued in the island, with Puerto Rico recognized as a portion of our country, and with duties removed, the prospects of making fortunes are exceedingly flattering.

It has been suggested that Puerto Rico's chances as a factor in the sugar market would be small if she competed with Cuba and the Philippines. The only argument which can be legitimately advanced to confirm this statement is the one of difference in price of labor, for, under similar methods of cultivation, the islands differ little in average crop.

CHAPTER XI

TOBACCO CULTURE

MORE tobacco was exported from Puerto Rico in 1828, by nearly two hundred thousand pounds, than in 1896, and in 1846 there were shipped abroad 6,693,900 pounds, or over three times the amount exported in 1896. For seventy years the amount of tobacco exported has been surprisingly uniform, usually between the two- and three-million-pound mark, with now and then a year like 1846, which blossomed into promise of a future for tobacco, when the crop has doubled or trebled that of preceding years. These increases have been sporadic and far apart, being accounted for usually by shortage of Cuban crops.

It is exceedingly difficult to find a solution for the non-progressiveness of this commodity, which is grown so well and so easily on the island; the explanation lies possibly in several directions: First, the rapid increase of tobacco culture in Cuba, and the world-wide attention called to a particularly fine leaf—grown only in a very restricted area, however—which soon made Havana tobacco famous. It was not until the forties that Cuba rapidly strode ahead of Puerto Rico in her annual exportations, and since then the latter has been completely eclipsed, if not almost forgotten, in tobacco-raising. Second, in the early days, as well as today, the peasant almost exclusively raised the entire crop on the island, in meager patches of from a quarter of an acre to several acres, mortgaging his crop beforehand to the shopkeepers and petty dealers. The landed proprietors and capitalists, with curious conservatism, chose to risk their all in sugar and coffee, preferably buying their manufactured tobacco from the expert cigar-makers of Cuba and the Peninsula, rather than fostering and promoting the poor home industry. Hence in all time—excepting possibly the last few years—the manufactured products of tobacco in Puerto Rico have been execrable, the work unskilled and slovenly, while the leaf itself has been raised by careless hands, eaten by insects, badly cured, and improperly packed.

The increasing demand for Havana tobacco has excluded Puerto Rico from the foreign tobacco marts, and the premium set on Cuban-grown tobacco has been so great that not only have her entire crops sold at high figures, but, to meet the growing commercial preferment, she has for decades imported the bulk of the Puerto Rican raising, branding it with that magic word, "Havana." Spain has been the second great buyer, the heaviest in quantity but not in quality; in fact between them they absorbed the tobacco-crop, leaving a few hundred thousand pounds in some years for Germany, and a few thousands for Italy and France.

The United States smokes its Puerto Rican tobacco through Havana; it is more expensive, but the label increases the flavor some fifty per cent. Only in exceptional years, during Cuba's struggle for liberty, and the concomitant restriction and destruction of her tobacco, have we imported any from Puerto Rico, and then only to the amount of a few thousand pounds. We have returned to the island, in manufactured tobacco, many times the value of her exports to us.

Cuban tobacco-growers would probably insist that the

GIRLS STRIPPING THE LEAF-TOBACCO

TOBACCO CULTURE

suggestions advanced are not vital in retarding the tobacco industry, and that the real explanation lies in the poorer quality of the tobacco grown in Puerto Rico. However, with a leaf as fine today as Havana's, Puerto Rico could not compete, until her reputation had been much advanced, and solidly built up.

They do not grow as good tobacco on the little island as on the greater. That they *can* grow it, there can be no doubt. The soil and the climate both favor this assertion, but until such time as careful methods of cultivation, handling, curing, and manufacturing shall prevail, and the growing be done on large estates, in a scientific manner, the quality of the tobacco will be lower, and the surplus product necessarily be controlled and sold at a low price set by the consumers.

The change of island ownership will, perforce, cause the current of the crop—both raw and manufactured—to set towards America's shores, and, if our government legislates for open markets, a sharp impetus will be given to the manufacture of cigars, cigarettes, and smoking tobacco on the island, which will redound to the financial benefit of its people. As an argument in favor of such a course, it may be said that it is generally conceded that finer cigars may be manufactured in the humid atmosphere of the tropics than in more northern, drier regions, where much of the pristine flavor and aroma is lost.

Spain has, in the aggregate, been much the heaviest purchaser of Puerto Rican tobacco, but, in years that the Cuban crop has been small, Cuba has purchased everything in sight, and the Spanish sales have fallen off, as illustrated in the second part of the table on next page.

The apparent rise and fall in the size of the island tobacco-crop, as illustrated in the following table, does not, in the writer's estimation, indicate any great excess

PUERTO RICO

or decrease in the acreage planted; neither does it point to a failure, in certain years, of the crop, as the average exportation for many consecutive years is rather uniformly low. The answer is found in the fact that, in years where there is exceptional demand for the tobacco, almost the entire crop is sold abroad, and in the years of small demand the surplus is largely consumed at home.

The following table may be of interest, showing the exportation of tobacco from 1828 to 1896, giving some maximum and minimum years:

	Amount.	Total Value.	Price per Pound.
	Pounds.		
1828	2,396,500		
1842	6,693,900		
1847	2,270,600		
1852	5,807,000		
1853	2,099,500		
1887	6,924,000	$1,125,770	15.7c.
1894	3,369,616	619,474	18c.
1896	2,219,907	408,110	18c.

EXPORTED TO FOREIGN COUNTRIES

	1894.		1895.	
	Pounds.	Value.	Pounds.	Value.
Spain	2,378,573	$437,280	1,375,751	$252,920
Cuba	580,256	106,675	2,160,347	397,161
Other countries	410,787	75,519	128,953	23,706
Total	3,369,616	$619,474	3,665,051	$673,787

There are no statistics by which one may arrive at any conclusion as to the annual quantity of tobacco raised, but island tobacco-dealers estimate the crop at from eight to twelve million pounds, and a few somewhat higher. As the use of tobacco is almost universal, the local con-

TOBACCO CULTURE

sumption of the five to eight million pounds' gross weight, which would remain after deducting the average export, by a population of a million, is not excessively high.

On the crowning, round-knobbed crests of the lesser hills, and surrounded by the guava-trees or bananas which screen them from the wind, little patches of close-growing tobacco, sprouted from the seed, may be seen almost anywhere on the island, during the months from July to November. It is here, in these primitive hotbeds which catch the first and last rays of a summer sun, that the life of the coming tobacco-plant germinates.

Early in November the great green hills which reach far up toward the sky, overrun by creeping vines and the general luxuriance of plant life run wild, slowly bare themselves to somber brown under the laborious attacks of groups of ragged, white-clad peasants, armed with broad-edged hoes. It is a pretty sight for the traveler who may pass across the land, over the great military highway—this agricultural panorama, stretched out perhaps so far from him that the landscape becomes a map, with manikins in white, mere specks moving on the earth. 'Way over there across a rare, deep valley is a charging army in a thin and straggling line; behind them down the steep slope is clean, bare soil, sprinkled with little rubbish bonfires, whose white smoke curls upward in the lazy air, while in front of them is the barricade of green, eaten away foot after foot by the heavy hoe and gleaming machete. The sharp-edged height is their objective point.

On the opposite side of the hill another army of workers creeps up to the same objective, and, when they meet on the mañana, possibly there will be a war of cigarettes, for the clearing of the field is done, and it is ready for the planting of the baby tobacco.

PUERTO RICO

The great tobacco-field is of rare occurrence, and found nowhere except in the Cayey district, on the military road, which holds the prestige for high-grade leaf, of fine color, softness, fragrance, and combustibility. The greater part of the tobacco is still grown by the peasants in little patches. At Cayey, however, in the last few years, a number of energetic men have gone in for tobacco culture on a large scale, and the prompt return in richer tobacco, handled yet too primitively, pays a tribute to the possibilities of the soil, and promises an immense future for the backers.

The land, before planting, is made soft and mellow, and drawn into high ridges with gutters or drains between. Each young plant is set two feet away from its neighbor, and the youngsters which die under the galling sun are replaced by vigorous ones, until the entire field is alive with growing plants.

The best lands are considered by some to be those of the low-lying foothills, near the narrow valley levels, and beneath, and protected by, the more rugged mountain-ranges, but there is a very limited amount of such land, made by the disintegration of the massive limestones and fertilized by the decaying vegetable matter of the upper slopes; consequently the higher ridges are resorted to and cultivated to their very tops. Where the growing tobacco is fairly protected from constant winds and secures plenty of warm sunshine, the matured plant returns a beautiful leaf, and the differences which exist between the top and bottom of ridges are marked in the varying quality of the tobacco; that at the top being a rougher, darker leaf, while that at the base is thin and good for wrapper.

By March, or the middle of that month, the tobacco is ready for its first cutting. Before this time arrives there

TOBACCO CULTURE

has been much work done on a tobacco-field. Weeds must never be allowed to spring up; the leaves of the growing plants must be examined for the eggs of cutworms, and the pests themselves, which must be killed promptly; the budding flower-stalks must be cut off so that the leaves will grow larger, and the small, defective leaves are often taken away for the benefit of the plant. It is for lack of this constant care that so much black, spotted, thick-leaved tobacco appears in the markets of Puerto Rico. The lower leaves of the ripening plant are first taken when they begin to get their yellow color; following this are two other pickings, and sometimes a third, until the plant is stripped bare. The first leaves are usually the finest, thinnest, and of the best color, being used for cigar wrappers principally, while the last are small, thick, and rough, and serve only for filler or cigarettes.

The weakest side of tobacco culture on the island manifests itself in the methods pursued in drying. Long, low, open sheds, on the hillsides and in the fields themselves, serve for this purpose, being built lengthwise downhill, in many instances, that the air may draw through them like a chimney. These buildings are a very inadequate shelter from the weather, and much tobacco—which might otherwise be good—is allowed to deteriorate by a drying process through prolonged periods of time, dependent upon the sequences of dry periods in a climate of prevailing moisture. Artificial heat will probably be found in the future to be the only safe and perfect method by which fine leaf may be dried in this constantly-humid atmosphere.

Forty days is considered the proper length of time to cure the tobacco, and, as many planters follow this rule without regard to what the weather may have been during the interim, there is a marked difference from year to year in the quality of the tobacco grown by the same man. At the end of this time it is placed in huge piles and allowed to " sweat," which process gives the leaf its final color and makes it soft and pliant.

The growers of tobacco all carelessly bale their product in burlaps, and one never sees the careful handling of fine tobacco so prevalent in the western province of Cuba.

The price of good tobacco-land ranges from fifty to one hundred dollars Spanish, though the contemplative purchaser, unless he be exceedingly diplomatic, will be asked a much higher price at the first conference.

Field laborers can be had in numbers for fifty centavos a day. Some of the large growers are in the habit of giving their field hands, during the clearing and planting season, besides this amount of money, two very frugal meals a day.

There are representative tobacco-buyers and -exporters in all the large coast towns, the more prominent being in San Juan, Ponce, and Mayaguez, in the order named.

Only a small percentage of the tobacco exported is manufactured, as pointed out; Havana and Spain, in the past, have been the principal purchasers, and in both these countries the leaf is made into cigars and cigarettes at home; the Cuban importation finding its way ultimately to the United States as Havana cigars, which are sold at a lower price than locally-grown Havana leaf; while in Spain it is known as Puerto Rican tobacco, and used as such, though even there the prejudice in favor of Havana tobacco causes many manufacturers to disguise it with the mystic name.

Rich Puertoriqueños in the past largely imported their fine cigars and cigarettes from Cuba, but within recent years, since the introduction of more skilful cigar-makers

TOBACCO CULTURE

and cigarette-machines, this practice has been almost discontinued, and today the native tobacco connoisseur is not only satisfied with his home product, but will assure you that quite as fine tobacco can be raised and just as perfect cigars made on the island as in Cuba.

This will not voice the sentiment of the casual visitor to the island, for the vast bulk of the cigars which are sold to and consumed by the native population are vile in the extreme; however, they are correspondingly low in price; the cheapest—green, badly hand-rolled, and wrapped with heavy, coarse black tobacco—sell as low as fifty cents American a hundred, and range from this upward to the ordinary cigar used by the average clerk and shopkeeper, which brings a dollar and a half to two and a half a hundred. Really good cigars—though too green and strong for the American taste—sell for three to five dollars a hundred, American money. These last-named cigars, when given time to age and dry, would sell readily in the United States for two for a quarter and five for a dollar. They are well made, burn perfectly with a clear white ash, and are pleasing in color and fragrance.

There is a very limited output of yet finer cigars, selling as high as twelve dollars a hundred at the manufactory. These are made with the utmost care from the rare, fine leaf and wrapped singly in tinfoil. It is doubtful if any Havana-grown tobacco can greatly exceed this particular brand.

The centralization of employees in tobacco factories is practically unknown. There are, perhaps, all told, half a dozen houses which might be dignified by the title of tobacco factories, but the major portion of the manufacturing is done in the homes of the laborers, who carry the leaf to their shanties, do the work, and return the finished product to the owner. This system is open to serious condemnation, as the homes of the laborers are usually in an extremely unsanitary condition. It is no uncommon sight to see a man seated at a bench in a house of a single room, rolling cigars from a stock which lies on the dirty floor beside him, while his houseful of children tumble over each other in youthful abandon, or idly stir the green scum of stagnant pools before the door, and then, in all innocence, trample a few million bacteria into the tobacco with their pattering bare feet.

Another universal habit which tends to make a man swear off is the final licking given to the drawing-end of the cigar, between the moist lips of the workman. It is a detestable—nay, an almost vicious—operation, when one stops to consider that among these people lurks a loathsome hereditary disease, which may be readily transmitted to the smoker by the use of this infected cigar. This practice should be stopped by stringent legislation, as it was in some of our own states years ago.

At Cayey, where the best cigars are made, are clustered a number of establishments, but none of them employ more than a dozen men, and the largest output from a single place is about three thousand cigars a day. Every cigar is hand-made, the mold being unknown in the island. Each man selects his filler and binder, cuts his wrapper, and makes a complete cigar. There are very few really skilful cigar-makers, though in one factory in Cayey a few clever men make a great variety of shapes, and those of the most approved form.

The classifying and assorting of cigars by color is very defective, and a source of irritation to the buyer, as a box marked " claro " may have all shades packed within it from the lightest to the " oscuro "; it has also militated against securing a permanent and high-priced market. During the past few years more attention has been paid

CIGAR-MAKING IN THE LARGEST FACTORY, CAYEY

TOBACCO CULTURE

to this side of the business, and a few men are turning out a fairly uniform cigar.

Wages are very low; the "head selecters" and shop bosses receive from $1.25 to $1.75 per day; good cigar-makers, $1.00; strippers—who are usually girls—about $1.00 per hundredweight; and learners receive their clothes and board, and poor board at that.

San Juan has a cigarette factory which turns out a hundred and twenty-five thousand cigarettes a day, eighty thousand being the output from the most approved of American machinery, and the remainder from old-fashioned machines which roll from single papers and crimp in the ends, instead of the modern method of a continuous paper-band feed and chopper. They make three varieties of cigarettes, two of white paper—one ready for smoking and the other requiring to be rerolled—and the third with a licorice-stained paper covering, which is very sweet and pleasant. The tobaccos used are usually the cheapest, smallest leaf called "boliche," which is also used in the first class of filler. There are some higher grades of cigarettes which contain a better leaf mixed with the poor grade.

It may be said in favor of Puerto Rican cigarettes that an unflavored, pure tobacco is used, which, while it does not satisfy the average American cigarette-user, pleases a cigar-smoker. Their worst faults lie in the use of too heavy a paper, which imparts its fumes in burning, and in loose rolling. With a thin paper and less draft, cigarettes made from these tropical tobaccos would find a ready sale and win reputation in the United States.

Home-made, molasses-soaked plug tobacco, in ropes a hundred feet long, is one of the primitive wonders of the island. On any market day one may see the tobacco man with his little table piled up with bad cigars—black as

PUERTO RICO

your hat, so green that you may wring water from them, and so cheap that a silver dollar will buy out his stock in trade,—but the objects which catch the eye are the cylinders, eighteen inches high by six in breadth, made up— you would swear—from bights of hawsers soaked in tar, but in reality chewing tobacco. Try it once and quit. A tobacco-chewing Jacky from Georgia, with a day ashore at Ponce, volunteered the information: " Yes, suh, that 's the most pow'ful stuff I ever stowed in my wisdom teeth. Yes, suh, that 's right." I agreed with him.

Smoking is almost universal in Puerto Rico, the cigar and the cigarette being alternated by most natives without any apparent preference. The better classes of the women seem never to use tobacco in any form, and to one accustomed to seeing the dainty fingers of Mexican señoritas hold lighted cigarettes, after the black coffee is served, something seems to be lacking in the familiar ensemble of tropical home-life.

The peasant woman dearly loves her black cigar, and a sight which arouses risibility is the common one of a huge, black aunty rolling down the center of a street, burdened with head-balanced load heavy enough for a horse, placidly smoking an inky cigar of able proportions, whose clouds of smoke enshroud her head, and waft into her contented, half-closed eyes. Envy her; she has only half enough to eat, but is rich in the soothing of nectar nicotine.

It may interest the tobacco man to know that the island tobacco is graded at present into the following classes (valuations are in Puerto Rican silver):

1st class, wrapper superior, worth $100 per 100 pounds.
2d   "   wrapper inferior, $80 to $95.
3d   "   wrapper and filler superior (this distinction is made because one-half the leaf is good for wrapper, while the other half is used for filler), $70 to $80.

TOBACCO CULTURE

4th class, wrapper and filler inferior, $50 to $70.
5th " filler superior, $40 to $50.
6th " filler inferior, $20 to $40.
7th " filler, $12 to $20.
8th " boliche (worst filler), $5 to $12 (and used largely for cigarettes).

This careful grading is never done by the grower, however, who simply gets a lump sum for his crop, but by the exporter, and it may be said further that this is not done as skilfully as in Cuba. The high-grade wrappers are beautiful in color, soft in texture, and thin as paper, and they are, in the opinion of the island experts, quite as fine as any raised in the far-famed Vuelta-Abajo district of Cuba.

There is, apparently, a very bright future in Puerto Rico for tobacco-raising and -manufacturing, but it will be restricted by the impossibility of great expansion in any direction on an island already so densely populated, and by the possibility that only certain sections will prove suitable for tobacco culture.

CHAPTER XII

FRUIT-RAISING, MARKET-GARDENING, AND FLORICULTURE

IT is when the writer comes to descriptions of the fertile possibilities of fruits, which bud and blossom and ripen to sweet maturity, and market produce which returns a hundredfold the work of man, in one, two, and sometimes even four crops a year, and of the vast flora of beautiful shrubs, of gorgeous foliage and flowering plants, which dazzle the eye by mazes of odd rich forms and colors, and overpower the senses with subtle perfumes, that he is inclined to rhapsodize over beautiful, tropical Puerto Rico and call it, truly, a promised land.

It is in the early springtime of March, April, and May that the little island becomes one glorious flowering mass; such a wilderness of gay blossoms that even the wonderful green settings of new and bursting leaves are smothered beneath the glorious tints of flowers, which dance with delight in the pink of early sunrise, bedecked with scintillating, dewy jewels, or go to sleep at the close of day, under a fiery, cloud-flecked sky and overarched with wondrous misty rainbows which seem to have caught their color from the very earth itself. It is a region of languorous dreamland, where the oppressions of life and the struggle for existence fade away as some past nightmare, and, if it were not for the high shrill voice somewhere outside the sacred garden wall, monotonously

FRUIT-RAISING

crying "Pescado! vendo pescado!" as its owner trudges through dirty streets, one might feel that at last he had reached the land of the eternal Fountain of Youth.

It is small wonder that the early Spanish explorers, who were, beyond their inbred cunning, craftiness, and martial desires, imbued with a profound sentimentality and love for nature, should have indugcd in wild rodomontades regarding this new world. With a heart warmed by tropical sun, and under the deft spell thrown around the senses by aromatic odors and exquisite blending of color, even the stolid Briton might have been unbalanced in his cold mental poise, and made to believe that just before him, somewhere in this ideal land, were the waters of everlasting life, or if not that, at least it must hold out the promise of gold which glitters—the material panacea for human misery.

While the spring months rollick in the greatest wantonness and profusion of bloom, to the tourist there seems to be no period of the year when the landscape is not an immense flower garden, for most of the wild plants blossom and go through the stages of fruitage several times a year, and the cultivated fruits, vegetables, and flowers are planted in successive intervals of time, so that matured products may be had the whole year through.

The Floridian orange- and lemon-grower, who has struggled against the perversities of his sandy soil, where his carefully-prepared fertilizers straightway proceed to enjoy the society of subterranean fossils rather than to give renewed life to his tenderly-husbanded trees, and where the climate is all gentle zephyrs one day and a black frost the next, would do well to move to this country of vegetal luxuriance, where fine sweet oranges will grow well in the dense thickets, in spite of choking and entwining vines and overarching shade-trees.

PUERTO RICO

The same advice applies to the fruit-grower of arid southern California, who, by constant irrigation and by the sweat of his brow, raises his crops from the sandy soil, creating, upon the desert, spots of green loveliness, and securing in return, it is true, an exuberance of fine fruit.

The same amount of capital and energy, however, expended in Puerto Rico, would insure twice the crop of the Floridian and fully as great if not a greater one than the Californian can raise on his artificially-prepared ground.

With Puerto Rico as an integral part of the United States—and there is every promise that it will come into close relationship with us long before those hotbeds of revolution, Cuba and the Philippines—there is no doubt that it will literally become the fruit and vegetable garden of this country. Almost every known tropical and semi-tropical fruit can be grown to its highest perfection there, and many of the growths of temperate climes find the soil congenial. A northern man fails to comprehend the meaning of the word " fruit " until such time as he has lived on this lovely island and tasted, each day for a year, some new edible creation of nature. The descriptions of flowers and odors fail me, as there are no adequate comparative terms or sensations in which they can be expressed. They are sour or sweet, savory or insipid, pungent or mawkish, fragrant or malodorous, and all degrees between, but, above all, with an individuality in each and every fruit which should debar one from remarking that it is, in taste, a near approach to others.

It is quite the habit of the native population to speak of the western province of the island as the fruit-raising region. From a commercial standpoint—that is, in the sense of supplying large markets with fruit—there exists

FRUIT-RAISING

but a meager industry in Puerto Rico. At Mayaguez, which is looked upon as the export center for small fruits and vegetables, there were shipped in 1898, principally to the United States, some six or eight million oranges, which brought an average of $4.50 a thousand; a million and a half cocoanuts at $25 a thousand; and fifty thousand pineapples at $2 a dozen (money in Puerto Rican silver). These figures sum up, practically, the foreign fruit-trade done by an island which, area for area, is capable of producing much larger crops than any portion of the United States.

It seems astounding that bananas, plantains, yams, sweet potatoes, and half a hundred more fruits and vegetables which would find favor in our country, have never been exported, to any extent.

Plantains and bananas form the principal food-products of the island, and exceed many times, in quantity and weight, all other food-stuffs combined. There are no statistics bearing on this point which are more than mere conjecture, but it may be safely said that the diet of the peasants, who number ninety per cent. of the population, is mainly these two nourishing fruits.

To the eyes of the novice, the banana and plantain are alike in fruit, though there is a difference in the veining of the leaves and the shape of the fruit. The plantain is almost tasteless and mawkish when green, and is not fit for food until baked over a hot fire.

There are no less than eight varieties of banana which are indigenous and grow wild. They are known under colloquial names relating to their form and color, and range in size from the giant triangular-shaped yellow banana, some eight or ten inches long, down to a tiny variety with cylindrical barrel and rounded ends, known as "lady-fingers." There are two varieties of the red banana, which are not considered by the natives to be particularly good, but which command high prices in our country. The large yellow varieties have a fine flavor and penetrating fragrance, but the little ones, with a slight, delicate aroma, are considered the most palatable.

Flinter, in his book on Puerto Rico ("State of Puerto Rico," page 197), entertainingly shows the product of one man's labor for a year (1832) in raising plantains. He can cultivate eighteen acres, growing 11,875 plants, which will bear annually, allowing twenty-five plantains to a shoot, and three shoots to a tree, 890,625 plantains, or enough food for 244 men for one year, allowing them each ten plantains a day, or they will bring in money, selling them at the then lowest market price—192 for a dollar—$4,639. He further calculates that this amount will pay for the land at $100 an acre, buy oxen and horses for cultivating, and two slaves at $400 each, and still leave a net profit of $1,479 on the capital invested. The changes necessary in his figures to meet the conditions of today are rather in the grower's favor. Land may be had for $50 to $75 an acre, and free labor at about $200 a year; the product, on the whole, will sell for more, if the larger varieties are cultivated, as they bring about fifty cents for bunches six to eight hands high, in the market at Mayaguez, and, allowing a single full bunch to a tree in place of the possible three, the grower would receive about $6,000. The factor of transportation, which Flinter does not calculate, must be allowed for, and will materially reduce the profit.

There are two varieties of oranges which are indigenous to the soil and grow wild in the dense thickets, yielding, under unfavorable conditions, heavy crops of fruit. The only orange grove actually cultivated as such, of which the writer has knowledge, consists of fifteen acres of

FRUIT-RAISING

trees, and is near Mayaguez. It is customary to let all young plants live where they spring up, in the shade of the coffee plantations, in the fence-rows, and on the roadsides, no particular attention being paid them beyond the harvesting, perhaps, of what remains of the crop after the wandering poor have enjoyed many a luscious globe stoned from the branches.

There grows another variety of orange in the island which is bitter-sweet when green, known by the natives as " naranja " (the Spanish name of orange), in contradistinction to the sweet green orange called " chino." The trees differ slightly, in that the " naranja " has a supplementary tip or heart-shaped pendant on the end of each leaf. The " naranja " is seldom used, though when it goldens it is very pleasant and sweet.

What a veritable paradise this land will be for the American orange-grower who carries with him his often bitter experience, and careful methods of cultivation, gained in the sandy wastes of Florida!

The thin-skinned lemon is not indigenous to Puerto Rico; there is, however, a small citron which looks like an immense lemon, with a rind nearly half an inch thick, which cracks open as the fruit yellows. It is rather dry and not very sour, and the juice is used with sugar and water as a beverage. The rind is highly aromatic and has an economic value. There are no drawbacks to future lemon culture, the soil and the climate of the mountain uplands being very suitable. Sweet lemons, with a bitter-sweet taste, grow very profusely in several sections, though they are seldom gathered unless it be to make from them a sort of conserve, or to use them medicinally, since they are considered of some therapeutic value in malarial fevers. Shaddock grow to fine proportions, and are eaten to a limited extent.

Limes, which are used most universally on the island, are very abundant, and, during the flowering season, perfume the air for yards around with the delicate odor of their blossoms. The fruit reaches a size and perfection seldom seen elsewhere, and the large, paper-skinned varieties almost cause one to mistake them for lemons. They are never raised with intent, and never exported, but they may always be found fresh in the market-places. The extraction and bottling of lime-juice has been found very remunerative elsewhere, and is offered as a business suggestion.

Puerto Rican pineapples are famous for their delicious flavor and wonderful bouquet; in fact it is even admitted in Cuba that the pineapple *par excellence* is grown on the sister island. It has only been within the last decade that any attempt at systematic culture has been made, and the industry is yet carried on in the most primitive manner. The Mayaguez district is the one in which they are grown mainly for export, and in other portions of the island, where never above a hundred or so are grown in a single patch, they are used for home consumption, the inferior ones alone finding their way to the local markets.

The raising of the above-named fruits—bananas, plantains, oranges, limes, lemons, and pineapples—offers industrial openings of much merit for men of small capital, who cannot or dare not indulge in the high-priced luxuries of sugar-growing, coffee, or tobacco plantations. It is a sure way to modest wealth, and it is believed that no investor, for the next ten years, can go amiss by putting his money and his wits into this form of toil. What is sorely needed today, however, to assure complete success, is direct lines of fruiters running from the island ports to the great marts of our Atlantic seaboard. It is possibly on account of the lack of such transportation

FRUIT-RAISING

facilities that the more perishable fruits have never found their way to the United States from this bit of fertile land and sunny sky.

Cocoanuts grow everywhere along the sandy coast-lines, and old coral rocks, which have been covered over with rich silts and sands, afford a perfect soil for their prolific growing. It is said that cocoanut-raising is very profitable ; that is, it gives large returns for the money invested, but there is much more labor connected with the industry than the casual observer would imagine. The sandy margins of the coast-line, where sugar-estate holders are willing to part with them, are sold for very low figures. The trees rapidly spring to maturity and, after a very few years, bear immense annual crops of nuts. The heavy expenses lie in the laborious methods of gathering the nuts by climbing the trees and hacking the branches from the lofty heights, and again in the difficulties which are met with in releasing the nuts from the heavy fibrous husks. Cultivation of the sandy loams in which the trees grow is unnecessary, and hence there are no expenses in this direction. A very profitable business is the extraction of oil from the nuts, as half a dozen large ones will furnish a quart of oil. The writer hesitates to make too much of a point regarding this industry in Puerto Rico, as the suitable areas are not numerous, and there are so many far more desirable localities along the coast of Cuba, where thousands of acres are available in single stretches; it is, however, one of the economic possibilities, even here, which should by no means be overlooked.

The cocoa-tree (cacao) grows well, and the product has a ready sale on the island, as cocoa and chocolate are made at both San Juan and Mayaguez, the best chocolate bringing as much as a dollar a pound. It takes seven or eight years for a grove to reach full bearing, but the industry is sure to expand rapidly.

Among the many other valuable fruits which might be shipped to northern markets, if rapid steam facilities were at hand, is the "aguacate" (alligator or avocado pear, *Lauraceæ*), which grows on a tree with laurel-like leaves, from thirty to seventy feet high. The fruit is like a huge pear, with smooth, green skin, turning brown if allowed to hang too long; it has a soft, buttery meat, half an inch thick, which melts in the mouth and is eaten as a salad in combination with lime-juice or vinegar and salt and pepper. While it is almost tasteless without condiments, it is so agreeable with them that the "aguacate" habit becomes a fixed one after a few months' sojourn on the island. In the center of the pear is a large, hard kernel, an inch or more in diameter, which is not edible, but from which may be extracted a reddish-brown, indelible dye, needing no mordant to fix its color. This salad fruit is sometimes seen in New York, in small quantities, where it sells for from 25 to 50 cents, though it may be purchased on the island for a copper piece. There is no reason why it should not be shipped to the United States in quantity, but it requires careful packing, and should be picked from the trees while firm and green. The trees require from five to ten years to mature.

The "nispero" is another delectable fruit with an indescribable nectar flavor. It grows on a rather small, bushy tree, and looks much like a round, rough-skinned, baked potato. It has a number of large, shiny, black seeds set in the meat, which make it difficult to eat successfully. This fruit would be extremely hard to ship, unless packed with great care. Its delicate aroma, however, would cause it to find instant favor with our people. The tree does not bear fruit until the fourth or fifth year.

A DATE-PALM

FRUIT-RAISING

There are two varieties of fruit, much like plums in shape, and known as Indian plums or "jobos de la India." The larger kind is an exotic which grows well and bears a fruit as large as a lemon. It is fine-flavored, slightly acid, and, when ripe, is of a golden-yellow color. The native variety is smaller, but very pleasing to the taste. It contains much tannic acid, and is often eaten for its medicinal properties alone. The tree exudes, when tapped, a gum which is made into a powerful mucilage.

There are two kinds of guava-tree (Spanish "guayaba," *Psidium*) in Puerto Rico, known as the red and white guava; they grow luxuriantly from the lowlands to the mountain-tops, and when their white flowers are in blossom they send off a delightful fragrance. No attempt is made at systematic culture of this tree, whose fruit is so universally used to produce the fine guava jelly of commerce. Its culture in orchards will be found very remunerative, especially if, in connection, an establishment for jelly-making is considered. It is possible to make delicious jellies and pastes from the fruit, but the average product from the hands of ignorant natives is dark-colored, sometimes burned, and doubtful as to its cleanliness. An American embarking in business, in the line of preserve- and jelly-making, will find half a dozen other fruits which are available for this purpose, such as the tamarind, pomegranate, "grosella," Indian plum, orange, etc.

Pomegranates grow to a very perfect maturity, and the fruit is finer in the mountain regions of the island than in any portion of the sub-tropical mainland. It is not raised extensively, and there is little demand for it in the local markets. It offers, however, a factor in fruit-raising for foreign markets, as it can readily be transported.

The "grosella" is a small, irregular-shaped, yellow fruit,

PUERTO RICO

about as large as a cherry, sub-acid in taste, and it makes a beautiful, transparent jelly. It is never seen except in private gardens, where it is raised without difficulty.

The date-palm, while not indigenous to the West Indies, grows to magnificent proportions, and is a prolific bearer of fruit. Its culture has never been attempted for commercial ends in Puerto Rico, and one sees only now and then some magnificent specimen in the yards or picturesque gardens of the great sugar-planters.

Figs grow readily and well, but, for some inexplicable reason, they are not raised on the island in sufficient quantities ever to appear in the markets. The few trees which the writer has seen were literally loaded down with the juicy, pear-shaped pendants.

The tamarind is little grown, but reaches a high degree of perfection, with little care. The jellies and conserves which can readily be made from its fruit will cause it to impress favorably future fruit-growers.

An odd growth in Puerto Rico is the pawpaw tree (*Papaya* or "lacheza"), which grows all over the West Indies. Under the low crown of its large leaves, which are often a yard in length, clings the green fruit like squashes, in bunches, packed closely around the trunk of the tree. These are filled with small, black, pungent seeds, and the inner rind, which is eaten either raw or cooked, tastes much like a muskmelon of fine flavor, though the meat itself is rather gummy. The fruit is used medicinally for indigestion and gastric troubles, and possesses marked pre-digestive powers; the seeds are also used for the expulsion of tapeworms.

The sugar-apples or "carrosones" are interesting, as they look like small inverted Swiss cheeses hanging from the trees. They are white and sweet inside, and very palatable.

THE PAWPAW-TREE, WITH EDIBLE FRUIT

FRUIT-RAISING

The "mayama" or "mamie" is a tree which looks much like a small magnolia, with the same leathery leaves having a wax-like polish, and bears a bright yellow fruit about as large as an apple. A taste for it must be acquired, as it has a suggestion of acridity not generally pleasing.

The fruit of the granadilla, a species of passion-flower, is often eaten, and has a very delightful flavor and aroma.

There are many other fruit-trees which grow almost spontaneously, and whose products are relished by the natives, but industrially they hardly come within the category of fruits for foreign export, and the writer has omitted them, feeling that this work has, for its purpose, the pointing out of possible business opportunities for Americans.

Among the edible products called fruits are the breadfruit and breadnuts, which are used in large quantities by the natives. The first-named had its original home in the islands of the Pacific, and is known as "fruta del pan" (*Artocarpus incisa*). The trees grow very large, with wide-spreading branches and trunks bare sometimes fifty feet from the ground. The leaves are huge, with rough outlines, and the fruit, which hangs on the outer limbs, looks much like a giant Osage orange, as large as one's head. The ovoid fruit is picked green, and the outer skin and rind are pared away from the white, cellular center, which is baked in a hot oven or smothered in the ashes of the fireplace. When done, it looks somewhat like a browned loaf of bread, and, while extremely wholesome and palatable, it has not a wheaten flavor, but rather one similar to that of baked plantain.

The breadnut is indigenous, and, to the untrained eye, is identical in outside appearance with the breadfruit; its interior construction, however, differs, in that it contains a great mass of closely-packed nuts, like large chestnuts, which are not edible raw, but are very fine when boiled or baked for half an hour. They would catch the fancy of the American public, and would find as ready a sale on the streets as roasted chestnuts.

Vegetables, Edible Roots, and Seeds

The list of vegetables, if enumerated separately, would probably exceed that of the fruits, and market-gardening on the island will doubtless be profitable locally to the skilled gardener, as well as offering possibilities for supplying the northern marts.

Sweet potatoes and yams reach a remarkable degree of perfection, with but the smallest amount of care in cultivation, and, next to the platano or plantain, form the chief diet of the natives, who grow small patches for family consumption everywhere on the sides of the steep mountains, and in other places where the lands are not considered available for money-making crops. There are many varieties, but no more than four are commonly used; two sweet and orange in color, and two white when cooked, and near to the Irish potato in taste. The great poisonous yams, with tubers thirty pounds in weight, which require careful cooking to dissipate the acrid juices, are seldom raised. The Irish potato is raised, but it is said that it does not do well on account of the excessive moisture. Still the Irish potato which finds its way to the town markets, and which is grown on the high hillsides where the drainage is perfect, is as fine a specimen as we grow in the United States. In view of the immense yield of the sweet tubers which may be obtained within a given area, these crops should be money-makers, provided cheap transportation may be had.

Among other roots used for food are manioc, yucca, or cassava and the "yautia," "tannia," or "melango." The

MARKET-GARDENING

former is well known to most readers as the bread of primitive tropical tribes. There are two kinds, sweet and sour, one being palatable even when raw, and the other filled with the deadly hydrocyanic acid, which is removed by pressure and heat before it may be eaten. The cassava is not used to any extent in Puerto Rico; the other root, however, known commonly as "yautia," is much cultivated by the peasantry and held in high esteem, being always on sale in the markets. The plant is like a big lily, with large spreading leaves, not raised much above the ground, and the tuber-like roots, which weigh from three to ten pounds, are particularly fine when carefully baked. The "yautia" and cassava both yield starch and starchy foods. From the "yautia" roots considerable starch is made in the town of Rio Grande, in the northern part of the island, and is sold principally for laundry purposes; the cassava yields the tapioca so generally imported from tropical countries, and in this direction alone cassava-raising would yield a fair revenue to the cultivator.

"Gedianda,"* a small bushy weed bearing a narrow pod some four inches long, filled with little disk-shaped beans, is a curious plant, in that these seeds are largely used by the peasant population in this coffee-growing country in making a substitute for this beverage. The bean is said to have great medicinal virtue, and allays inflammation of the membranes of the stomach; the writer can testify that it produces a very potable beverage. If there must be a substitute for coffee, a decoction from this little bean is much to be preferred to chicory, and would perhaps, in a commercial way, meet with greater favor than the frightful stuff sold in small tin cans in some of our backwoods regions as "coffee-essence."

It may be safely said that any vegetable not requiring

* Spelled "Hedionda" in Appendix.

an extremely dry soil and cold climate may be well and successfully grown on the island. The foothills of the southeastern portion of the island, where rain sometimes does not fall for weeks, are remarkably well adapted for the raising of vegetables of temperate climes, and, under the strong suns and in the rich soils, the yields will far exceed those of the United States.

The vegetables which are grown everywhere now, as common articles of diet, may be partially summed up as follows—yams, sweet potatoes, Irish potatoes, " yautias," cassava, celery, carrots, turnips, egg-plants, beets, radishes, okra, beans of many varieties, pease, tomatoes, cabbage, ginger, sweet and pungent peppers, pumpkins, cantaloupes, watermelons, and squashes.

Spice-raising can be carried on with great success on the island, though, so far, but little attention has been paid to it beyond the growing of a limited amount of " pimiénto." Black pepper, nutmegs, mace, cinnamon, ginger, and cloves may all find a fruitful home, and their careful culture is an enterprise well worthy of consideration. It is said that the vanilla bean would find the soil congenial, but this is doubtful.

There is an immense range of medicinal trees, shrubs, and herbs which now grow wild in the forests, and are gathered by the women and children, sometimes sold to the pharmacists, but oftener hung upon the walls of the native huts, to be administered by the old women versed in plant-lore to their own sick ones. The average observing native has usually accumulated, by experience, a large fund of information concerning the plant-life of his hillsides, where he is constantly searching for some possible utilitarian value in every living thing.

As a generalization, it may be said that, in this tropical climate which varies considerably from the low seacoast

FLORICULTURE

to the mountain-heights, and in the rich and fertile limestone soils, almost every form of plant-life, which does not demand cold weather or an arid earth, will spring to luxuriant maturity and fructify in a way to gladden the heart of every agriculturist. Americans who have struggled early and late upon their little farms, against adversities of cold and leaden skies in spring, dry and blistering heats in summer, freezing blizzards in winter, and, worst of all, glutted markets, will find Puerto Rico a land flowing with milk and honey, where, even if they do not amass a fortune, they may be sure that financial ends will meet, and that they cannot starve.

There are many dyewoods and plants on the island, the chief among them being—the brazil-wood (*Cæsalpinia echinata*), in limited quantities; fustic (Spanish "fustoc," *Maclura tinctoria*), of the nettle family, which furnishes a yellow dye from its wood; divi-divi (*Cæsalpinia coriaria*), a small tree from whose bark and long curved pods is extracted a reddish-brown dye; mora (Indian mulberry, *Morinda cetrifolia*), which belongs to the madder family; and indigo, a shrub of the family *Indigofera*, whose leaves and berries furnish the well-known bluing. It should be remarked that indigo is easily raised, and that considerable profit accrues from its culture, but in Puerto Rico it has hardly risen to the point where it may be dignified by the term "industry." There also grows on the island a bastard indigo, which can be made to produce a small quantity of dye. Annotto (Spanish "achote," *Bixa orellana*) grows wild over the entire island, and the symmetrical plants, crowned by the gorgeous fuzzy red and yellow pods, like chinkapins, may be seen by the hundred in every fence-row. It is from these soft burrs, filled with tiny seeds, that the fugitive yellow dye, known as annotto and used for butter- and cheese-coloring, is extracted. On the island it is used to a limited extent for coloring foods fried in oil, and a few people have gathered the seeds for export. The gathering of this crop would add many dollars to the pockets of small farmers, and, if a mordant might be found to fix the beautiful yellow in fabrics, it would at once become a really valuable article.

Many of the dye-plants are easily cultivated, and the business might be profitable if entered upon systematically, but so far little enterprise has been shown by the native population in this direction.

A number of gums and resins are exuded from indigenous trees and plants, and small quantities are gathered by the peasants and sold to the pharmacists. The more prominent are—guaiac gum from the lignum-vitæ tree; gum from the seeds and leaves of the Indian (Spanish "copey") tree, and balsam of copaiba from the plants of the genus *Copaifera;* there are also the algarroba, which exudes a gum, known as catechu, used for dyeing and tanning, and the cashew (Spanish "pajuil"), from whose acrid fruit is obtained a gum which may be used as varnish.

It is impossible to devote much space to setting forth the innumerable flowering plants, the bedazzling foliage-plants, which are such freaks of nature that one almost pronounces them artificial, and the sweet shrubs and trees which exhale from their leaves and bark penetrating perfumes. Puerto Rico is a land of orchids, of flower-forms which make one silent with wonder, of painted leaves which vie with the daring colors of the flowers themselves, and of an atmosphere where one breathes, not the dew of morning off new-mown hay, but redolent, languorous ether distilled by the mystic alchemy of nature.

CHAPTER XIII

HOME-LIFE

IT is a hospitality highly seasoned with garlic and sweet oil which the true-born Puertoriqueño proffers to Americans, but it is no less beautiful in sentiment for all its odoriferousness.

Perhaps never before in history have a foreign people, who talk an alien language, and who have been trained under a monarchical system for centuries, so gladly and with open hands extended welcome to a nation who differed from them in physique, customs, habits of thinking, and religion, as have the Spanish-speaking Puertoriqueños received the Americans. That some of this evident display of friendship is due to politic motives on the part of individuals is no less true, but it would be a mean and small spirit which would attribute to mercenary motives alone the constant extension of the right hand of fellowship which has met the army on all sides since its advent on the island.

There are many circumstances which have combined to bring about a felicitous relationship with America. For centuries Puerto Rico has lain in the grasp of the military; a small and much-favored number of men controlled the political and financial reins of the island, to their own personal betterment and self-aggrandizement. They kept down in poverty those who could be of little use to them by the basest and most open discrimination. They built up those who were willing to share their daily profits of hard labor with the gold- and lace-bedecked, and yet even those who were successful through their fawning upon the governmental representatives were not at all sure that their tenure of favor would be continuous. In a sentence, it has always been possible for the politico-military body, in whose hands rested the fate of the island population, to make a man powerful and rich, and to beggar him as easily.

The process has brought about a social and financial condition in Puerto Rico not possible in the United States, and quite incomprehensible to our people, who instead of remaining silent under abuse, kick lustily for their rights as free-born citizens. It has meant abject poverty to the great mass of the inhabitants. It has meant almost as low a rate of wage for the laboring classes as in China. It has meant that the poor man can never be a landholder. It has meant that the landowner, unless in high favor, must grind the vitals out of his peons, with scant profit to himself after government excises and official tips have been paid. It has meant that a few, a very few, might become rich and prosperous, and it has meant, most of all, that no one, except the handful of men in despotic power, has had the slightest voice in molding the laws governing a million people.

It is little wonder, then, that this same people stretch out their weak hands in joy, with the manacles riven at last, toward a government whose very spirit is supposed to breathe the perfume of individual freedom. May we meet the expectations of these people in full, and may the greed of American legislators and American financiers do no overt act which will lower the standard of our government, as the Puertoriqueños fancy it.

COUNTRY HOUSE OF A WELL-TO-DO PUERTORIQUEÑO

GUAVA TREE—FROM THE FRUIT OF WHICH GUAVA JELLY IS MADE

HOME-LIFE

There is a handful of Spanish malcontents in Puerto Rico—men who hate American institutions, men who have been favored under the old régime, and who bitterly dislike the change; but how large this element really is will probably never be known, as it is masked under the Spanish smile of approbation, always ready to stab in the back.

The home-life of well-to-do natives is extremely simple, due largely to the fact that excessive duties, lack of transportation facilities, and abominable roads—except the military roads—have militated against the introduction, into their homes, of the comforts which we consider so essential to life.

Even the finest haciendas are meager and barren in their interior fittings. The floors are always bare. The walls have few pictures, though now and then one is surprised to see a clever painting by one of the masters of the modern French school. The usual wall decoration affected is a pair of Spanish bas-reliefs in colored plaster or papier-maché. Chromos and vilely-executed woodcuts often make an appearance, and seem frightfully out of touch with the oftentimes beautiful architectural finish of the drawing-rooms, whose wide, doorless archways are framed in carved woods and relieved of severity by scroll latticework.

Marble-topped mahogany tables with carved legs occupy the centers of the rooms. On them are flowering-plants, vases of artificial flowers, and the photograph album, and above the table is a hanging lamp or chandelier, usually of cut glass, with a profusion of swinging prisms, sometimes gaudily decorated with bright-colored ribbons, or festooned with artificial vines and flowers.

Cane-seated furniture is used exclusively. The great

rolling rocking-chairs constitute the principal furniture, with a sprinkling of straight-backed chairs and cane settees. Many of these chairs would set the lover of novel forms and finely-carved furniture wild, for numbers of them are rare antiques, handed down for generations. The woods of the carved furniture are heavy and highly polished, while the more modern is lighter, without carving, depending upon the twisted and bent frames for beauty, and it is invariably painted a rich black.

Incongruous decoration is seen in every home, in the way of cheap porcelain vases, covered dishes with molded figures upon them, antimacassars and tidies on the chairs, while in the doorways hang the cheapest of cheap lace curtains, held back by brass chains, with perhaps nearby some piece of wonderful hand-made native lace or drawn-work.

The mathematical precision with which all the furniture is placed in a well-regulated household always creates a thrill of horror in the æsthetic breast. Around the centertable, equally spaced, are the great rocking-chairs; against one wall, like guarding sentries, are the straight-backed chairs, while flat against the other wall is placed a cane couch or two. Even in the Governor's summer palace, this primness in furniture arrangement was found. Out on the broad balconies encased in closed white shutters, the beautiful chairs were also ranged down the side walls, with the tables in the center, for all the world like a dairy lunch-room.

The beds, of brass and metal, are dreams in design, covered with canopies of lace, having auxiliary mosquito netting gathered up on the top during the day and let down at night. Wardrobes and not closets are used for clothes. Heavy carved dressing-tables, bureaus, and washstands are often seen, but to the majority these have

HOME-LIFE

been too great luxuries. Now and then one sees mirrors framed in heavy antique frames, which are delightful in their symmetry.

Bad soap is found everywhere, and a single comb and brush seem to meet the needs of the family. One seldom sees manicure sets, though the powder-puff and rouge are in evidence in every well-conducted house. The lack of toilet articles, dressing-stands, chiffoniers, and pier-glasses is painful to those who are familiar with the profusion of implements of dainty toilet.

The dining-room is always quite bare, with the exception of the table and chairs, and perhaps a side-table which holds the multitude of dishes for an ordinary dinner.

The kitchen has much of interest and novelty, and much dirt and many squalid children, so it is better not to see it near mealtime. Modern ranges are seldom a portion of the culinary furniture, and when they do make an appearance, they subserve the end of a quick-baking apparatus, in lieu of the slowly-heated brick ovens of an older period. Every house has its charcoal cooking-pit built out of brick, waist-high, the top of the bench being covered with a series of small, square, grated holes, over which pots and kettles and frying-pans are placed. Charcoal, in a country where coal is expensive and gas unknown, is an ideal fuel for cooking food. It makes a quick, hot fire with a minimum amount of fuel, and the many small holes permit a large number of dishes to be cooked and kept hot at the same time.

The opinion of most of the volunteer privates who have seen duty in Puerto Rico is that the population consists of a lot of dagos, linked together to see how much they can raise the price of every commodity and to steal everything they can lay their hands upon. A striking exception, among enlisted men, to this state of feeling were the Fourth Ohio boys, who went home gladly, but with regret at leaving a people who did everything they could for their comfort. Their good fortune was the result of a kindly spirit which imbued the entire regiment, and was exhibited toward the native population, and reciprocated in full measure. There is no intention to criticise other organizations, for the men lived hard lives in a hot climate, and were homesick and discontented, but there has been shown over and over again a wilful malice, by a certain type of volunteers, resulting in ordering and cuffing the natives about, as if they considered them conquered animals instead of human allies and friends. This conduct, in a few towns, has thrown the volunteers out of touch with a people who, from habit, at least, if not from better feeling, are inclined to show courtesy and graciousness to the military.

Those whose actions have been tinged with good intentions toward the native population have received a cheerful welcome, which has made many a lonely heart feel that service in Puerto Rico was not all hardship.

The officers have always been received in the best houses, where they have shown themselves appreciative of hospitality extended in a manner not known even in the United States. Everything in the Puerto Rican houses has been theirs, from the host's horses to his underwear and collar-buttons. Their entertainers struggle to cook American dishes, and swell with pride when they procure American fruits, cheese, and crackers for their tables.

A swell dinner in a Puerto Rican home is a trying gastronomic ceremony. The menu is made up of astonishing viands, and the dishes seem to follow no conventional sequence in their procession to the table. Soup is as apt to be the second or third dish as the first. Roast-

THE DRAWING-ROOM OF A PUERTO RICO HOME

HOME-LIFE

beef and beefsteak are served at most unheard-of moments. The disastrous effect of a meat diet in tropical climes has been dwelt upon by medical experts, yet at one dinner no less than eight meat dishes were served—combinations of bacon, of ham, of kidney, of beef, and of chicken.

The following is the menu of a dinner given to two Americans by a rich sugar-planter:

Fried eggs and two fried corn-cakes. Vegetable soup filled with garlic. "Gondinga" (a hash made of chopped kidneys and liver, seasoned with garlic and split olives). Larded beef—cooked juiceless and hard—flavored with garlic and oil. Beefsteak, onions, and garlic, fried in oil and served in overdone fragments. Potatoes, sweet and Irish. Rice and scrambled eggs. Guava jelly, in rectangular blocks. Cocoanut and brown sugar. American apples and cream cheese. Coffee and cigars. Champagne.

Claret was served through the entire dinner, and the coffee was either black or served with hot milk. Broken bread was kept always at hand.

There are many queer dishes—for example, vermicelli soup with whole pork chops, sausages, and tomatoes incorporated made its appearance on one table; on another was a boned goose stuffed with sweet red peppers, olives, and garlic; on still another, roast chicken stuffed with sausages and the usual olives and garlic.

Sweet peppers bathed in olive oil are a common relish.

"Garbonzas"—a succulent pea not unlike a cooked chestnut in flavor—form a national Spanish dish. "Frijoles"—the Spanish red bean—come on as a separate course. A number of dulces or sweetmeats are used, the oddest one being peanut taffy with chopped garlic.

Deviled land-crabs are a novel dish and would be pleasant-tasting minus the olive oil.

PUERTO RICO

The "aguacate" or alligator pear, a salad plant, is often eaten in one of the earlier courses with salt, pepper, and olive oil or wine vinegar.

Oranges and small bananas form another dinner course. Dry native goat cheese, hand-made, is used very commonly and widely. Sweet-potato soup is good and nourishing. The bread is generally better than ours, and is a close approximate to French bread.

Dinner is served, one article of food at a time, and the plates, knives, and forks are changed with each. At least a dozen such changes take place during a single meal.

Smoking goes on at the table with the ladies present, and unfinished cigars are carried into the drawing-room.

The table decoration consists of a huge bouquet of native flowers, which are magnificent in their profusion and variety.

Napkins, where used, are generally as large as towels, but in many of the interior towns table-linen is at a premium, and it is slightly shocking to catch a pretty, black-eyed señorita slyly wiping her rosebud mouth on the edge of the table-cloth.

Rum, white wines, and cognac are brought out before and after dinner, and at any time the host may think the American taste craves stimulation, though, in his daily life, the average Puertoriqueño is remarkably abstemious, drinking perhaps before dinner a brandy-and-water and before breakfast a little white wine.

The native early-morning meal is a cup of coffee with milk—addiction to the black-coffee habit does not exist on the island—and a piece of bread. Breakfast is served at eleven or twelve o'clock and is seldom elaborate, unless guests are in the house. Boiled eggs, bread, and coffee satisfy the ordinary man, but the hungry man eats his garlicky beefsteak in addition.

HOME-LIFE

Dinner is *the* meal of the day, and is eaten between six and seven o'clock. This is the native's only full, heavy meal, and this fact may account for his ability to eat a quantity of food which leaves the average American a victim to indigestion and remorse.

The positions of honor at a dinner-table are, among the older and non-traveled residents, in the following order: the head of the table to the most distinguished guest; the rest, in the order of their rank and importance, ranged around to the right, the host occupying the last seat after his guests. The women sit at the left of the table, all together. Among the more cultured classes, the host occupies the head, the hostess the foot, the places of honor being the seats to the right and left of the host.

The evenings in the home, for instance, of an alcalde —the mayor of a town—are spent around the marble-topped center-table, lazily rocking to and fro in the big chairs. The men smoke their cigarettes—the women never smoke—and a flow of small talk, filled with simple jokes and sallies, constitutes the entire evening's amusement. Where they have pianos, the daughters exhibit their limited skill on instruments which are jangled and out of tune. One never sees a book or a magazine in these houses, though in two or three of the larger cities there are many literary men. Reading is not a strong point of the island population. The women are pictures of self-complacent indolence in the evenings, though it must be understood that Puerto Rican women are far more assiduous in their interest in household economy than are the women of the other Spanish-speaking territories of North America.

Every little comfort which these people can provide for the stranger within their gates is offered with a whole-

PUERTO RICO

souled cordiality that appeals to the heart by its true and unaffected ring, and, as Americans coming among them, we should remember that, by meeting this spirit measure for measure, we shall follow one pathway to a sincere and lasting mutuality of interests.

CHAPTER XIV

LIFE AMONG THE PEASANTRY

THE life of the peasant, the peon, of Puerto Rico is not a dream of ease and luxury; neither has he ever passed through the nightmare of wretched hunger and biting cold which adds so vitally to the hardships of the poverty-stricken in northern climes.

In squalor and filth, in crudity and ignorance, the larger number of the inhabitants go through their comparatively short lives, for one does not see many aged people among them. They die off from fevers, contagious diseases, and troubles handed down from sickened forefathers, at a comparatively early age.

At no period of the poor man's existence can he suffer the tortures of starvation because his job of work has given out, for, while during whole months of the year he may not earn a single centavo, he still has his little plot of vegetables on the hill; then, if worst comes to worst or the landowner turns him out, he may live on the profusion of fruits and roots of the forest, or, as is a common practice of the country, upon the fruits filched from his more opulent neighbor.

In the dry season he complains of the cold of early morning, yet he needs but the merest rags to cover his nakedness, for on no day in the year is it colder than our mildest autumnal weather. Shoes are a useless burden to his bare and sole-leather-lined feet, which have trodden the rocky, briary trails in their nakedness from infancy; and a hat, if he must have it, he makes in his own house from the grass grown around the doorway.

The house in which he is domiciled he builds in a few short days from poles and thatch and bark-rolls of the royal palm, and a good house it is, in spite of its primitive appearance, for it screens him from the colder winds of night, and sheds the water of the driving rains like a duck's back.

As a story-book life of primitive simplicity, in which the human needs are few and readily met with a minimum amount of labor, it is idealistic, but as an existence for civilized man it is a horrible fantasy.

The average wage of the laboring man is less than fifty cents Spanish a day, and the work for which he is paid does not cover a period of more than four or five months in the year. It is not customary for the employer to hire his laborer by the month or the year, but to secure his assistance only at cropping times. Sugar-plantation workers in the field are usually paid sixty-two cents Spanish a day, though the skilled labor of a few men in the mills brings from one to one and a half pesos. The tobacco-field laborer gets about fifty cents, depending upon the locality and controlled by the supply of laborers. The coffee-pickers are almost equally divided as to sex among grown people, with a large sprinkling of children who receive so much per measure, a hundredweight of coffee-beans delivered at the hacienda of the planter bringing about a peso. This makes the wage very variable, as quick and skilful pickers, when the crop is heavy, can make one peso a day, while in less prolific fields they secure only starvation wages. The little children add materially to the sum-total of the family's revenue, but it is not over a few centavos a day. At the coffee-mills

LIFE AMONG THE PEASANTRY

and drying platforms, where the work of handling the coffee is constant and heavy, the wage is often a peso a day, but the numbers engaged at these places are small. Girls do most of the assorting of the coffee—though a few owners do this work with machinery—and seldom get above forty centavos per diem.

It may be said, then, that the wage of the Puertoriqueño is exceedingly small, and the time he is employed short. His earnings hardly amount to enough to supply him with clothing and trinkets for his family. In idle times of the year he must support himself from his garden patch, high on the steep hillsides.

The employers in Puerto Rico all maintain that the returns in work done by the laborers of this tropic zone are much less per day than what is accomplished by laborers in the United States, and that their purchasing power for necessities is greater.

House-rent is an almost unknown factor in the country, though in the towns many people huddle into one house and live, amid dirt and disease, at an expense to each family of a few pesos a month. It is customary for landed proprietors to grant to their peons small patches, on the steep hillsides, which are of little value for tillage. This meets the end of assuring their services to the plantation-owner upon demand, with no expense to himself, and secures him the éclat of being apparently a philanthropist.

One enterprising Spanish coffee-raiser gives garden spots to his laborers rent free, with the understanding that they may raise garden stuff, provided they plant guava-trees, the shade for the coffee-plant. By this means he gets virgin soil under cultivation, and grows the tree so necessary to successful coffee culture, while he becomes a benefactor with a string tied to it, for his laborers move every two years to new land, and the coffee-plant springs up in a rich and fertile soil.

These little garden patches of the peons, divided by green, untrained hedges hanging high against the hills and over the steepest ridges, with their thatched houses boldly clinging to some sharp spur or bench, all clustered together under close-growing banana-plants, or, in lonely singleness, watched over by a naked baby or two playing in the dirt, add greatly to the general picturesqueness of the entire region.

In the gardens they raise principally "batatas," or sweet potatoes, which seem to be the staple article of food. They have three varieties of this potato, one as sweet as ours and two with a taste much like our Irish tuber. Rice is often grown, and it is a curiosity to northern people to see, in place of lowland, carefully-irrigated areas, luxuriant, heavily-laden rice-fields on the highest mountain-peaks. Beans of various kinds, squash of odd forms, muskmelons which look like pumpkins, peppers—big and little,—a substitute for coffee called "gedianda," gourds and calabashes of great size, "achote"—a bean-like pod filled with edible seeds,—bananas and plantains, and "yautia" or "tannia"—the tuber-lily—make up the list of vegetables grown by cultivation upon these baby-farms of the poor.

One sees, now and then, a lean, razor-backed pig or two, held in tow by a hobbled leg, nosing around the doorway of a hut, and the fighting-chicken is always present; beyond these and the cur-dog there are no domestic animals.

Children are an ever-present and abundant factor in the domestic economy of the peasant's life. Domestic economy is a fitting term, since it costs nothing to supply the air of day for the lungs of these little waifs, and it costs nothing for their clothes, for they run about in the sun-

NATIVE TYPES—A MOTHER AND CHILDREN IN STREET COSTUME

LIFE AMONG THE PEASANTRY

shine and the rain just as God made them, and sleep in odd corners without cover, for the first half-dozen years of their baby lives, while, when older, a single discarded, tattered garment adds to their natural grace the shield of decency. So they live, without expense and with little tenderness bestowed on them in the shape of material comforts, though the mother's kiss is often given, and the father pats the little head. They soon toddle, at the command of the mother, to do small errands, to help weed the garden, to bring in a handful of wood for the fire, to dig the tubers for a meager meal, and lastly to hold up their tiny hands and, with pleading eyes, gain a copper from the passer-by on the roadside. They are a good investment in the family; the majority of them die at an early age, and it costs but a few strained hours to the mother's heart, a bit of cloth for a shroud, and the energy needed to carry the tiny form to the potter's field. Offsetting this is the usefulness of those who, by the laws of survival of the fittest, pull through with sturdy forms, to pick berries, work in the cane- and tobacco-fields, and add to the common fund, until, at a varying age, they rebel against the paternal banker, and live for themselves, in poverty and in bondage to the landed kings, just as the generations who came before them.

Among these people, the houses and house-building of the poor are always interesting. The methods, the material, and the interior fittings are quite as primitive as among any of our aboriginal tribes of North America. In fact there are less skill and less art shown in their construction than those exhibited in the highly ornate tipis of the Sioux, or the cleverly-built adobe houses of the Zuñis. The type and shape of house vary little. A framework of lashed poles is thrown up, with a ridge-pole lashed above the rectangle box, and to the side walls are tied the broad bark-curls unwound from the upper green trunk of the royal palm, the walls sometimes being doubled by lining the interior. The bark overlaps and is drawn taut by thongs in such a way as to make a perfectly solid wall. One opening suffices for a doorway, and window-openings are unknown. The interior is often divided into two rooms, with the door-opening of the second compartment in the hallway, but as the dimensions of the entire house seldom exceed ten feet square, the quarters become rather crowded. At night, four or five people sleep on the floor or swing in small hammocks, and, blocking the outer room or passage perhaps, lies the man of the house in a low-swung hammock. The house is a shelter from the wet weather of day and the damp of night, and at other times the inhabitants live outside, the women squatting on their heels, when domestic labors are not pressing, chattering at each other like a flock of parrots. In the ditch-water paddle a dozen naked babies, with protruding stomachs due to fruit and vegetable diet, good-natured and aimless in their play.

The roofs are all thatched, preferably with the great leaves of the cocoanut or royal palm, or with the heavy, long, rank grass of the fields. One never sees ornaments in the houses. Now and then some of the very few religiously-inclined will possess a rag-baby saint, covered with dangling bits of silver blessed by the local padre. The children have trinkets and playthings of the crudest character, and a naked baby boy is a happy youngster when riding a piece of stick for a horse, while his nude sister sits and fans herself, with haughty mien swaying a bit of palm-leaf. The walls are hung, not with decorations, but with various eating-utensils, made commonly from the calabash, though the richer element sometimes proudly dangle a tin cup against the wall. Cooking is done on the

LIFE AMONG THE PEASANTRY

outside of the house in dry weather, on a sheet of iron or in a small, badly-battered iron kettle, and the foods are served in gourd dishes, and eaten with gourd spoons. The powdered rice, corn-meal, and seed-coffee are ground in wooden mortars or broken between stones. In continuous bad weather the life of the peasant is hard, as he is perforce obliged to cook within the confines of his house, which soon fills with a damp, clinging smoke that finds egress only through the openings under the eaves.

Marriage is almost unknown among the very poor classes, and the distinction of having the written word and the blessing of the priest carries with it no special meed of honor; it is suggestive only of another poor man gone wrong and a grasping padre a few pesos richer. It is a much easier matter for a man to select his companionable partner, and set up housekeeping in a new wickiup under the banana-trees, without more ado.

A legal marriage by license has less in it which meets approval, in the native mind, than that performed by a church functionary, for the padre might always save them from hell, while the nation's sanction is an absolutely barefaced robbery. General Grant recently gave hearing to a much-agitated man who stated that the priest would not marry him to the woman he loved without excessive fees, and he prayed that his excellency would order the erring father to marry him at a rate commensurate with the size of his pocketbook. The General sorrowfully told him that he could not pretend to interfere with the church's rulings, even though his sympathies were aroused, and suggested that he be content with the legal form, which meets all the lawful needs of our own country, and pay the small fee to the civil authorities. The man glared at him and disappeared; it being beyond his power to express in words the manifest cupidity of American officials.

It is to be remarked that there is little quarreling among these people, paired by nature's approval, and that their relations, while not the acme of conventional modesty and virtue, are on the whole constant. A belief has arisen in the American mind that virtue, as known to us, has no existence among the poorer classes of Puerto Rico. It should be remembered that wretchedness, poverty, and oppressive rulers beget, as an offspring, abject humanity with no great sense of moral honor. After admitting that this is true, it may still be said that fidelity and devotion between the couples so paired are universally found among these black-eyed, soft-voiced peons of our new island, and it is not to be believed that an excessive amount of immorality exists.

Chronic diseases are common, engendered by bad diet, total lack of sanitary measures, and an almost equal shortage in personal cleanliness. Among the distressing evils is elephantiasis, said by some to be a pseudo-leprosy. It begins by an enlargement of one or both ankle-joints, then of the toes, until finally the entire lower extremities are involved, and the toes and feet slough off. Fortunately most of these sufferers die before the frightfully-acute stages are reached. It is a common thing to see men and women limping, slowly and feebly, on limbs twelve inches in diameter. It is said that nothing but death can relieve them.

Goiters are prevalent among them, and it is not uncommon to see men and women decorated with a huge bunch, as large as an orange, behind their ears.

Anæmic malaria is a constant skeleton, seen weakly shambling in a thin shroud of dead-white skin. Great numbers die from this manifestation of chronic malarial

LIFE AMONG THE PEASANTRY

poisoning. Quinine, which battles successfully against this disease, is an unreachable luxury to the poor. It has been put, by Spanish import duties, a dozen times higher in price than in the United States.

Blindness is often seen; only a very small percentage of the population may suffer from this malady, but it is impressed on the mind everywhere, in traveling the roads, for the blind beggars seem to have quite regular sentry posts from which they plead, by gesture alone, for a centavo.

There are many more diseases prevalent among the poor, but these have been touched upon in connection with other features of the island.

After a long day's toil (it might as well be, perhaps, after a day of lazy dozing, but the Puertoriqueños work when they can), the women plod home in the dying sunlight, with swaying hips and stiff necks, carrying, balanced on their heads, huge bundles of damp clothes, washed in the near-by river, which they throw in an empty corner of the hut for tomorrow's ironing. They laboriously blow the fleeting spark of a carefully-smouldered fire into a bright, glowing flame and prepare the frugal meal for the family. The tiny light sparkles on the hillside in the falling darkness, and welcomes the home-coming of a barefooted, ragged, cotton-appareled husband, who wearily climbs the narrow, winding pathway, with far more picturesque effect than does the ruddy glow of a conventional hearthstone within a luxurious home.

Preference in the choice of life is a materialistic problem and another story, but this is a picture which, for some subtle reason explained by people who look inward, appeals strongly to the emotions and sentiments of those who see the beautiful in the primitive.

The little children are already creeping into the house, to lie down in odd corners for a night of dreamless slumber, clasping some morsel of food, to be eaten or not depending on the speed of Morpheus's descending arms.

Somewhere, out among the huts, the thrum of the home-made, soft-toned guitar beats out a half-Spanish, half-Indian air; now it changes to a new rendition of the music of "After the Ball," a second instrument takes it up, and then a new sound strikes the ear; in quality it is between the rattle of a snake and the pit-a-patting of a clever shuffle-dancer on a sanded floor. The instrument is called a "guida" (weé-da), and is made from the great curved-neck gourd, the music being produced by passing a bit of wire from an umbrella frame (how the primitive and civilized are mingled!) up and down a series of notches cut from end to end on the outside curve of the gourd. There is some amplitude to the instrument, for, by playing higher or lower on the narrowing shell, some difference in tone is gained.

But there is a third cadence in the music; it is a drum, beaten, for all the world, like the drum made by the Papago and Yaqui Indians of Sonora desert in Mexico, only the peevish, fretful cries of a dying infant take the place of the wail of a coyote out in the moonlit cacti. It is of the same size and shape—three inches high and a foot in diameter—but not as crude; except that the Puerto Rican drum does not require to have the heads warmed in front of a fire before it will give forth sound, they are the same.

The music is weird, as it is wafted on the night air, and the dancing, which takes place later in the bare patch in front of a hut, by the flickering light of a wavering torch, is fantastic in the extreme. The dance has a slow and melancholy step, and the dancers shuffle round and round, with a slight bending of the knee which keeps the body bobbing, and yet they enjoy it. The funeral procession of slow waltzing, affected by some enfeebled

A PEON VILLAGE NEAR CAGUAS

LIFE AMONG THE PEASANTRY

Americans, is the nearest approach one can make to comparison.

This is the chief innocent amusement of the people who live in the country, in the " campos" ; they cannot read, and have not the printed page if they could. Reading books is not a habit of the people of the island of Puerto Rico, and the little, monarchical, printed sheets, laboring under the name of daily papers, are read assiduously by men of the cultivated classes, but, at five centavos, are an expensive luxury to the man who earns but fifty a day.

The men—the young fellows especially—all gamble with an abandon which would do credit to a seasoned gamester and higher stakes. A species of shell game is fashionable, as the paraphernalia costs nothing, and an anxious, eager circle, sitting on their heels, will imperil one another's balance to see who guessed the right cover. So much as a centavo or two is wagered, but the stakes are large in proportion to their earnings.

The life of the poor people in the towns is less simple and more vicious, just as it is with us. The men—and the women too, for that matter—become drunk on rum. They fight in the streets and kill each other now and then. There is less virtue in this class, and a great propensity for small pilfering. Beyond the facts that the cash received for labor is less than in our great cities, that here a poor man can go into the country and eat fruit, and that no great metropolitan centers exist where vice is hidden from the eye, there is small difference between their sins and those of our own desperately poor class. In fact, in the weighing, it could be shown that the advantage lies with the Puertoriqueño, in that he does not get drunk as often as a vicious American, he is less profane, and less apt to do desperate deeds. He is a mild criminal at his worst, not dominated, apparently, by the fierce, cruel, stealthy passions of his Spanish kindred, and not nearly so bad as the burly, fearless, vicious ruffian of American cities. The preponderance, in numbers, of the abjectly poor over the better class has led to an oft-expressed opinion in our American papers that the Puertoriqueños, as a people, are devoid of moral instincts, vicious, degraded, and lazy. It is not true as a generalization; they are, measured by the majority, good workers, for folk of simple mind, when labor presents itself; they are abstemious, with few exceptions, and do not paint the town red; their moral instincts are not of the highest, but they much excel our bad classes in moral feeling; immorality exists, but there are no seething seas of indecency.

The Puertoriqueño is not an anarchist or an insurrectionist, for he knows no other life and does not starve or grow cold, while the burdens of oppression are his birthright, handed down for centuries. He is, then, in spite of his wretchedness, dirt, and poverty, as we see it, a fairly-contented man; and while it may take a long time to mold this man—representing the majority—into a self-respecting, useful, franchised citizen of the United States, it can be done, for the reason that he is docile, obliging, appreciative of favors, and, best of all, possesses an inbred courtesy and politeness, and an equability of temperament, which permit him to readily absorb new ideas.

The American nation has been to him in the past the synonym of all that is just and grand and righteous, and, if we do not abuse our power, Puerto Rico may be made a twentieth-century Garden of Eden, in which the native, trained in new methods of freedom, may, for the first time in three centuries, enjoy the sweets of liberty.

CHAPTER XV

BURDEN-BEARING

A COUNTRY without roads will necessarily have a population of human burden-carriers, and generally primitive transportation methods, and nowhere is this axiom better exemplified than in Puerto Rico. It seems curious that a little island, settled as early as 1511, with a population of a quarter of a million souls two hundred years later, and with a full million near the end of four hundred years—or at the present time—should yet be in the travails of primitive methods of burden-carrying. Yet this is so. The last century, with its giant strides of machine-made progress, has only left its impress on lagging Spain reflexively, for she could not, in her senile, tottering nationality, respond to the vivifying impulses of a modern world. What progress she has made, what advances her colonies have felt, have been thrust on all from the outside bounding, hurrying civilization of other nations. Every engineering scheme, every new mechanical device and method used in her erstwhile isles of the West Indies, will be found to have emanated from foreign influences. It is not intended here, however, to discuss Spanish mediævalism, but rather to describe the methods and means of transportation in Puerto Rico, as they exist today, when America takes up the great responsibility of making new history for the island.

Spanish life, with its homes, its posing, its indolence,

its mañana, affords rare gems for the painter's brush, and, as a never-ending field of picture-possibilities to the photographer, it is superb, but it brings from the lips of the hustling business man of America—decided and demanding—just plain, ordinary profanity.

The bread-wagon is on the street somewhere; you hear the vender's high-keyed, plaintive cry rising and falling with a musical cadence. He will be before your door after a while, and in the meantime be patient, even if you are inclined to be cross before your coffee, eggs, and bread in the morning, for your human bread-wagon, with the great board or basket filled with fifty fine fresh loaves, balanced deftly on his head, must see the settlement of a misunderstanding between two scratching, biting, half-clad urchins; now he has stopped to banter a merry-eyed, dark-skinned girl, whose tattered gown discloses that she is a Venus in disguise; and heavens! he has stopped again to get a light for his inevitable cigarette. The bread is all the better when you get it, for you are hungry.

"Great Scott! I'll wring your dago neck, if you don't get around in the morning with our milk," an exasperated officer cried to the man who drove his dairy farm from door to door, but the man—not understanding—smiled his languid smile and answered, "Muchas gracias, señor!" and forthwith sat himself down on his haunches and proceeded to wring the warm lacteal fluid from the soft-eyed cow into a wine-bottle. How was he to blame that the half-starved calves, which coax the milk to flow from the walking cows, with never a good round pull from the nipple for themselves, cavorted wildly through the plaza, and had to be tied finally, neck to neck, to keep them from running amuck? "Los Americanos" are so rude!

THE BREAD-WAGON OF CAGUAS

BURDEN-BEARING

The foot-venders are so interesting, so picturesque, that one forgives them—after breakfast! Everywhere through the streets in the early morning float the cries of men and boys, in sing-song notes, calling the excellency of their wares. Here is a tall, lithe fellow, with a swinging trot, carrying on his head an immense board of fresh vegetables, and, as he comes down the street, turning his head stiffly from side to side, slowing the spinning motion of the plank with a touch of his hand, and eagerly watching the doors and windows for the beckoning finger of a customer. His deeper cry mingles with the high-pitched, shrill voice of the little black fellow, hardly waist-high, coming from the other corner with a tray, teetering on the woolly pate, filled with cocoanut and sugar dulces which his black mother has an hour before pressed into shape with her not over-clean hands.

The number and variety of things which are sold from these recklessly-balanced boards are amazing; all kinds of vegetables and fruits, dulces, candies, cakes, trinkets, and bottled, fermented cocoanut milk.

Some of the equilibrious feats are remarkable. The angle which the heavy tray may take seems to make little difference, for the bearers apparently never drop them. It is possible to turn completely around with a tray five feet long—which sets it slowly whirling by momentum—without touching hand to it, and I once saw a man, with a tray piled up with cakes and candies on his head, chase a tantalizing boy half a block, finally landing his persecutor in the gutter by a flying kick, without so much as shaking his load.

In the early morning, when the shadows creep long and slender on the ground, the roads to the cities are filled with market people from the country. The milkman is perhaps most in evidence, either driving his cows with him to milk before his customer's door—which method, by the by, should insure unadulterated milk,—or carrying a big can, decorated with dangling ladles and measures, on his head. Some of them swing along with lurching step, never touching hand to the high, ten-gallon, open-mouthed can of fluid.

The hat-weaver and the broom-maker stride unsociably behind each other toward the market-place, to sell the handiwork of a week's labor, carrying their wares on an oscillating shoulder pole. The banana and platano man moves forward under a load of two hundred pounds of green bunches of fruit as if it were a feather, while, coming out of town, are two pedlers, their baskets, piled high with cheap stuffs for the peasants, being so heavy that they must have assistance to lower them to the ground, and still they will march five miles without a rest.

In the never-flagging procession come four men, two bearing, swung to the bamboo pole on their shoulders, a rude hammock with a tented sheet screening its contents from the rapidly-heating sun. Only a poor old man going into town to die! They may take him into the poor-house, if he belongs to the church; if not, he goes to the bare room of the dead-house at the cemetery. Too sick to work; too poor to be cared for; a blessing to die!

The more opulent travel on ponies, with great loads bulging from their sides which would put a full-grown government pack-mule to the blush. Oranges are carried in great round panniers, which, when well filled, must weigh nearly three hundred pounds, and the driver, not content with all this load sawing on his little animal's back, usually seats himself astride in the center. It is no uncommon sight to see whole families go to town on one pony, the man and wife aback, and the youngsters in the baskets.

BURDEN-BEARING

Two hogs, weighing a hundred and fifty pounds apiece, are often brought to market in these big baskets, with all four feet tied together, and, through their muzzled snouts, they give forth a faint intimation of what protests they would utter if they were to slip the curb.

The bulkiness of some of these pony-loads takes the breath away; for example, one man comes to town with a load of eighteen plaited pack-saddles, two bales of grass for horse collars larger than those of compressed hay, and, on the top of all this, two new wicker baskets; even then, not satisfied with the staggering load, the master hoists himself up between these hills of grass, and placidly rides twelve kilometers into the city.

Trunks, household furniture, and in fact everything imaginable are packed over the steepest, most precipitous mountain-trails on the backs of these patient, ever-responding native ponies. One never ceases sympathizing with these sturdy little animals, which, badly treated and uncared for, struggle through life handicapped by weights far above their class.

The real gentleman—that is, the Spanish official gentleman—never rides a basket saddle: he prefers an English saddle; but the majority of mountain-living coffee- and tobacco-planters use, almost exclusively, a soft leather pad to which are attached two small, rectangular wicker baskets. The position astride is one of sitting on a stool with your legs dangling from the knees. The gait of the ponies is a quick running walk or single-foot, which is very smooth going, from the top of this broad pad; easier, in fact, than on a saddle with stirrups. All the native horse-stock is small, and many of them are hardly higher than a good-sized Shetland. Their staying qualities are marvelous, and in a day's ride over trails no American horse can stay near them. They are the horse for Puerto Rico and tropical climates generally. The stock might be improved in size, perhaps, by crossing with the hardy cayuse or cow-pony blood, but an admixture of large, blooded stock would be a doubtful experiment. The big American animal does not thrive in the climate.

The principal draft animals are oxen—fine, large, big-horned fellows, quick and active on their feet, and, when urged forward, capable of keeping up a trotting gait for miles. It is said that the use of oxen as draft animals indicates a primitive condition in the evolution of a people. The great mass of these people are primitive enough to bear out this assertion, but it must be said that the indigenous ox has been highly bred to a quicker draft animal than is ever seen elsewhere. He is an admirable institution in an agricultural country, where four yokes of animals are required to drag a plow through the heavy cane-land, and, as a draft animal, he nearly rivals the mule. The mule will probably replace him in the course of time, but the heavy horse never, as the climate and diseases are against him.

In the island, oxen are firmly yoked from the horns, in place of the loose yoke on the shoulders known to us in America. Considerable criticism has been indulged in, by the late invaders, regarding this cruel manner of handling the beasts; but, as a matter of fact, a yoke firmly lashed at the base of the horns—which is the strongest draft point on these short, heavy-necked animals—is far preferable to an open yoke which wears the shoulders into blisters at every step. They move more easily in the stiff yoke, and back admirably, which is a movement not executed with the open yoke.

It is distressing to watch the drivers goading their teams forward with sharp spikes driven in the end of light shafts, and blood is often seen flecking their necks,

OXEN—THE PRINCIPAL DRAFT ANIMALS ON THE ISLAND

BURDEN-BEARING

where the cruel barb has been wilfully thrust home. Societies for the prevention of cruelty to animals are the only remedies for such evils where man has a heart of stone toward his beast.

The ox-cart is the typical, heavy, two-wheeled, broad-tired vehicle known to every southern Californian, and on it immense loads are conveyed over the best military highways; and, during the cropping seasons of coffee, tobacco, and sugar, the strings of lumbering carts seem never to cease by day, while at night one hears the rumbling of train after train, each carrying spook-like candle-lanterns made of tin—a favorite variety being an old coal-oil can driven full of round holes, behind which the candle splutters and flickers in a fantastic way.

Every town has its scores of island-made, public carriages, of the surrey class, drawn by sore-backed rats of ponies. They are exceedingly comfortable and the rates are low, governed by municipal regulation. The Jehu is no more exemplary, however, than our own metropolitan cabby, and it is advisable to make your bargain in advance, or be willing to pay on demand, go to the alcalde's office and settle it, or walk away while your driver dances around you and talks excited Spanish.

No city except Mayaguez has yet soared to the heights of rail-riding cars. Traveling by foot, the ox-cart, the pony, and the low carriage has contented them. Mayaguez alone took a metropolitan flight and established a line of street-cars, running through the city to the water-front a mile away. They run on a track so narrow that one feels like sticking his foot out and hopping along to keep the car balanced. The little boxes hold sixteen passengers on a squeeze and are drawn by mules; though they run fifteen minutes apart, they are a comfort to the traveling public and are much patronized.

PUERTO RICO

As I sit in the growing twilight, voices are wafted to my balcony in weird, foreign cries of " Dulce! Si vende dulce!" "Agua de cocoa! Mucho fresco!" For a hundred years—yes, for two hundred years—have these voices filled the evening air and pleaded for patronage from some fair buyer on the balconies above, where idly the Spanish belle wiles away the evening in laughter, and casts longing eyes at the gay caballero promenading beneath. A generation hence and all this will have passed away, and, in the dying, a new, strong nation will have arisen; the old charming picture gone, and a new one of smoking trains, burring trolleys, blinding lights, a milkman in a wagon, and a huckster with a one-horse cart, who cries, " Fish! Fresh fish!"

CHAPTER XVI

COCK-FIGHTING

THE only real recreation of the rural Puertoriqueños seems to be cock-fighting. Bull-fights have never gained a foothold in the island, though many of the Spanish-born citizens profess a profound regret that their national pastime seems not to have met with favor. The only reason given is that the people have always been too poor to indulge in the expensive luxury of importing any of the distinguished matadors from home, such experts being indispensable when it is desired to raise bull-fighting above the level of mere brutality.

As a matter of fact, cock-mains are more reprehensible, morally, than bull-rings, since in the former is displayed a brutal fight to the death between untrained but plucky birds, while the latter call for an exhibition of skill of hand and nerves of iron on the part of the human participants.

Every town in Puerto Rico has at least one cock-pit, built and owned by some thrifty lover of the mains. They differ little in construction, consisting of an earth-floored ring some eighteen feet in diameter, surrounded by an outwardly-inclined, closely-boarded fence, with half a dozen hinged entrance gates, which may be closed fast when a fight is on. Back of this fence, board seats are built, sometimes rising three deep like circus benches, and in the ultra-fashionable places they are divided into numbered and reserved seats. Covering the ring is a square, open-sided, roofed shed, with a railed balcony having a row of benches some eight feet above the ring level. Outside of all is a high fence, built of clapboards from the great royal palm, which prevents intrusive glances.

It requires little provocation to start the inhabitants of the entire countryside to fighting their pet game-cocks. Sunday afternoon—after a hasty visit to the church in the morning—is always devoted to the island pastime, but a saint's day, a feast day, or any one of the many constantly-recurring festive holidays brings out hundreds of country folk, who trudge along the narrow trails, barefooted and lightly clad, with birds under their arms, or jog along upon the cantering-gaited ponies, with their legs hung over the wicker side-panniers from which valiant chanticleers thrust forth their heads and lift their strident voices in defiant challenge.

It is not to be supposed that game-bird fighting is followed by the entire population as a means of recreation, for the wealthier and commercial classes, while not eschewing the amusement of watching a main now and then, take no active part in the pit. The followers of the gaff are, however, not numbered entirely, as in our own country, among the tougher element, but it has as its devotees most of the poorer element, laborers or peons who work on the large plantations for hire, and have little garden plots of their own to supply their family needs. They are quiet, hard-working people, when work is to be had, who enjoy intensely their few simple pleasures, and go into ecstasies over their great sport of cock-maining.

Around the cock-pit are gathered two hundred jabbering peasants, in cotton clothes and loose blouses, with a sprinkling of the better-dressed and more opulent townsmen, clad in immaculate white duck, set off with starched

COCK-FIGHTING AT CAGUAS

COCK-FIGHTING

bosoms, collars, and small flowing ties. The ring is crowded with men carrying their pet prize-cocks under their arms, all striving to secure wagers, and vociferously proclaiming the virtues of their respective birds as fighters.

The first fight has been arranged, and the referee claps his hands as a signal for all gathered in the ring to move outside, as only the " handlers " are allowed within the enclosure. The birds are fought with their own gaffs, instead of with the metal, razor-edged blade which is strapped to the legs of cocks in the United States, and a great deal of preparatory scraping and polishing of the bone gaffs takes place, until they become needle-like in sharpness. Then all the crest or neck feathers are cut off with scissors, and sometimes the comb is trimmed low, but not often, as all the minor details of handling, so rigorously observed among our own gambling fraternity, seem here to be dispensed with.

The birds are teased into fighting humor while held in the hand, and viciously pluck at each other's heads; now they are dropped on the ground with a quick movement, and at the order of the referee they are at it. High up in the air they strike the first few plunges, and one dodges under, while the uppermost bird lands over his enemy with a surprised look, but whirls and grabs his opponent on the red comb with a strong beak, and plants his gaff fairly on the side of the other's head. A roar of approval goes up from the crowd who have backed this bird, and a counter set of suppressed *hi's* of fear rise from those wishing for the success of the other favorite. The fight is fast and furious.

At last the red cock sinks his head with blinded eyes, and the blood drips off upon the ground. His panting antagonist watches him a moment, as if not willing to take advantage of his desperate condition, and, at the lull, each owner rushes forward and grabs his bird. One takes the bloody head and neck of his pet into his mouth and sucks the congealing blood, and then breathes new life into the sinking cock from his own lungs; the other resorts to a water-bottle from which he fills his mouth and blows it on the head and neck, and under the wings of his bird until the closing eyes brighten from the refreshing spray.

Time is called! In the center of the ring lies a small square, outlined with sunken wooden sticks, and on its opposite edges the birds are set. The mongrel-spotted bird goes for his game-colored enemy immediately, and strikes him three times to the other's once. Poor fellow! his fight is over! he turns and runs away, followed by his fierce tantalizer. Once more they are rubbed into shape. One vicious gaff, as they come together, and the red bird sinks dead, the bone lance going deep into his eye and brain.

The crowd surges into the ring and the money changes hands, while the owner of the dead bird gathers up the bundle of bloody feathers with some show of tenderness.

On and on it goes for hours, until the hundred contestants have been reduced by half, and the once bright-plumaged, bragging birds, who dared each other on from the balcony as they struggled at the end of their restraining bark thongs, have changed to bedraggled, bruised fellows with hanging heads and bent legs, whose drooping eyelids tell the story of the desperate fight. They are only birds, but there is something very pathetic in witnessing their fight for life,—fighting to kill, if you prefer,—surrounded by a concourse of howling human beings who cheer on each stroke that draws another drop of vital blood. It is a brutal sport, this baiting of birds against one another, that fight with blinded, bloody eyes,

COCK-FIGHTING

not seeing their enemy at the finish, but striking wildly, unflinchingly, at the superior force as they die; but it is the one, the only amusement which these people could afford, the only one offered them by a nation which has crushed out human hearts and dwarfed human minds by three centuries of malicious officialism.

There was no drinking, no carousing among the spectators; no ugly swearing, no bad feeling engendered, and no taint of rowdyism such as we see in our own country at such gatherings. Instead, with one accord the people were out to enjoy their holiday in gay good humor, and, while excitement rose to a tremendous pitch, no harsh word was spoken and threatening looks were unknown. That the amusement was brutal and of low order seemed not to occur to anyone. They had been taught this form of pastime, and conscience did not trouble them.

Through the little entrance gate, built from the wood of the royal palm, the crowd moved from a cock-fight to a solemn Catholic ceremony to be held in the near-by cemetery, and in the lead strode a little black youngster, in one of our soldiers' cast-off campaign hats, his bare, black chest shining through the front of a dirty cotton coat; what cared he that the fight had cost him a silver piece, hardly gained by blacking the army's shoes? he was happy in the possession of a handful of copper centavos which did credit to his acumen as a bird-backer, and made him envied by his youthful playmates. His twinkling eyes and merry laugh sobered quickly to awe-stricken glance and solemn expression, as the black-garbed priest strode by.

Verily only such a mercurial race could have stood the blighting abuses of a despotic government with complacence.

CHAPTER XVII

THE PRINCIPAL CITIES

EVERYONE who intends to visit Puerto Rico asks two questions, "Which is the best town on the island?" and "Which is the best town for business?" The answers to both questions must necessarily be a trifle ambiguous, for each of the three principal cities, San Juan on the north coast, Ponce on the south, and Mayaguez on the west, possesses certain prestige, commercially, over the others, while, if the first question refers to climate, no one of the three compares favorably with many of the interior mountain hamlets.

The answer to any question regarding climate is to be found in the chapter on physiographic features. There is little difference in the temperature of the coast-lying towns, though the annual rainfall of San Juan and Mayaguez is somewhat greater than at Ponce, bringing more cool nights, which are, perhaps, counterbalanced by unpleasantness in moisture-saturated air.

As regards sanitary conditions, preference may be given to Mayaguez, then Ponce, and next San Juan, but any city which is dependent, for the removal of its sewage, upon surface drains and bullock-carts cannot be regarded as a wholly desirable place of residence, and, under a tropical sun, germ diseases will necessarily be more or less prevalent.

It will be better to portray the general characteristics

THE PRINCIPAL CITIES

of each city separately, and let the reader form his own opinions.

San Juan

San Juan, as the seat of the island government, has always been the leading city in population, and also as regards the congested condition of its populace. It boasts—naturally, as the past home of the Spanish Governor-General—the residences of the principal military, naval, and high civil functionaries, and the finest public buildings, while there have been appropriated and expended more monies for general local improvements than in any other city.

It has undoubtedly the best harbor on the island, in that it is completely landlocked, though at present it is sadly in need of dredging so that ships may have sufficient depth of water and room to maneuver in the basin. The city is entirely circumvallated by an immense seawall, and guarded on the north and east by the picturesque, antiquated, and massive forts of Morro and San Cristobal, the construction of which began in 1630 by the erection—covering eleven years—of Morro castle at the entrance of the harbor, followed by the raising of San Cristobal, a mile to the eastward, over a century later (1771), and the final adding, bit by bit, up to the middle of the present century, of the great sea-walls and masonry platforms which connect them, and pass around the landward side of the tiny island upon which San Juan is built. During the war-scare of 1897 and 1898 the old forts suddenly blossomed out, under hastily-renewed building enterprise, with several new series of gun emplacements and numbers of bomb-proof ammunition rooms of modern construction, which, in their up-to-date types of architecture and fresh cement faces, look very incongruous beside the castellated and grey-walled structures of the past.

PUERTO RICO

The population of the city and suburbs is estimated at about 30,000, and probably within the narrow confines of the town itself, which is compressed into a very limited space between the great forts on the seaward side and the battlements of the harbor, live over 20,000 souls. The principal house portion of the town consists of well-constructed—so far as the walls go—double-storied buildings, with now and then one rising to three floors. In the more squalid portions of the city (one can walk all over the town in an hour), the houses are but a story high, and in a single room an entire family—and more—eke out an existence in the semi-darkness of the one-windowed, illy-ventilated apartment. The storekeepers and business men who do not live outside the city, in the pretty little suburban towns of Bayamon, Santurce, and Rio Piedras, usually live over their stores on the second floor. A town residence with a front yard is unknown, and the only bits of green to be seen are in the gardens of the Governor-General's palace, Casa Blanca, or in the inner courtyards, measuring a few square yards, of some of the more prosperous merchants.

The streets are narrow and dark, a gloom increased by the projecting balconies of the second story, where, in the evenings, the family sit and chatter in the light, pleasant chit-chat of southern climes. The sidewalks are so narrow two people may not walk abreast, and hence the streets—which, it must be said, are well paved and scrupulously clean—are used as highways for pedestrians and vehicles in common. One wonders, with the reckless driving of the "cocheros," who race down the streets in their carriages, giving as they come a high, shrill cry of warning, that more accidents do not occur to the slow-moving foot-travelers.

There are two public plazas, one near the heart of the

THE STREET OF THE HOLY CROSS, SAN JUAN

THE PRINCIPAL CITIES

town, upon which face the City Hall and the Intendencia, and the other on the outskirts of the city, under the frowning walls of San Cristobal. The former is merely a flat, open space, cement-paved and surrounded by a thin line of young shade-trees. In the evenings, the citizens of the town closely crowd this little quadrangle and promenade, apparently in happy spirit, to the music of the band. The Plaza de Colombo is still more restricted in area, and in it stands a handsome statue of Columbus, while behind his back one may partake of the vinous beverages of Spain and the island, in a tiny wooden booth. Facing this square is the grand theater, which is not only a handsome building, but has a seating capacity of nearly 5,000. The stage is wide and deep, and the settings admirable. Some of the most noted opera-singers have sung to crowded audiences in this house. Theatrical performances, however, have been, as a rule, far apart, the French vaudeville having, oftener than anything else, brought laughter from San Juan audiences. This great opera-house has served, too, as a public meeting-place, and all vital political questions have been discussed in its auditorium, by eloquent speakers who easily pass into frenzies of meaningless rhetoric, and arouse, to the boiling-point, the enthusiasm of this mercurial people for a few short hours.

There are two clubs or casinos in the city, Spanish and Puerto Rican; in fact there are three, now that the Americans have opened their hostelry, which has a rapidly-growing membership, principally of army officers.

One small library may be found on the main plaza, filled principally with Spanish literature, though there are many old files of English magazines, and, curiously enough, it is now thronged, day and night, with American soldiers, who pore over the English reading matter or greedily scan the pictures in the Spanish books.

San Juan boasts of the most pretentious, at least, of the educational institutions, and the best-supported churches on the island, and it has an island hospital for the insane, a poor-house, a jail, the largest barracks for soldiers, and a great military hospital, which recently, under American hands, has become a model institution. The schools, churches, and charitable institutions will be treated under a separate head.

There is more of historic interest and general picturesqueness in this old place, founded by Ponce de Leon in 1511, than in any other locality, and hence the tourist and the sight-seer may have their hearts gladdened by the moss-grown and decaying architecture, though to the business man, the man who contemplates making Puerto Rico his future home, it is perhaps the least attractive spot. Its drawbacks may be summed up by saying that the city has virtually no more room to expand on the baby island, without reclaiming outlying morass; it has already a shrewd and far-sighted population of business men, Spanish, Puerto Rican, French, and German, with just a few Americans who are old residents, and they cover fully every branch of possibly profitable trade, and are perfectly competent, both by experience and accumulated wealth, to quickly seize new chances and hold closely in their grasp the old.

There are, however, two advantages—both natural—possessed by this town over the seacoast places; first, the harbor, which, by its protected position and ready accessibility from the north, will always make this a desirable port of entry, and again its position on a sloping hillside, in close proximity to the sea, which renders the problem of introducing underground drainage a compara-

THE PRINCIPAL CITIES

tively easy one, and will, when this sanitary improvement is accomplished, convert San Juan into the most healthful of towns, instead of being, as it is now, a breeding-place for periodic pestilence.

Water-Works of San Juan

Nine miles from San Juan, by the military road, near the little town of Rio Piedras, there is a piece of engineering just approaching completion which is to result in furnishing the capital of Puerto Rico with a much-needed water-supply. Aside, one is surprised that cities of the size of San Juan should have remained so many years in a primitive condition, without modern water-works, without gas, without electric light, without sewage, and without street-cars.

The awakening to the needs of modern life and the possibilities in the direction of mechanical comforts has come only in the last few years, and then principally through the instrumentality of progressive Americans.

It is calculated that within four months San Juan will be able to dispense with the questionable supply of rain-water in cisterns, to which may be attributed a portion of the sickness developed, which will be replaced by well-filtered water drawn from an uncontaminated source far up in the mountain ravines.

This has been practically accomplished by damming a mountain stream, at normal periods some thirty feet in width, by a substantial wall of masonry twenty feet high. American engineers would pronounce this portion of the work defective, in that along the low flood-plains to the left of the stream there are no extension retaining-walls, and hence all flood-waters rush around the unprotected end of the dam. The monetary loss, when the spring waters cut a new stream-bed, as they will, over the alluvial plain, will be of small moment as compared to the distress which will be caused by the temporary cutting off of the water-supply from a city whose people have become educated to the use of water from faucets.

Beyond this primary objection to the work as it stands, it may be said that the undertaking has been well and ably executed, under the direction of Spanish engineers, including, as it does, settling basins, sand filters, pumping basins, steam lifting pumps, primary receiving reservoirs, and secondary distributing reservoirs.

It is estimated that this plant is capable of raising and distributing two million gallons of water in twelve hours, with one set of pumps in action.

All the great basins have been built by throwing up a massive surrounding-wall of earth, and erecting against this a stone wall four feet in thickness, finished with a cement lining. The stone used in their construction is a fine-grained, blue limestone, brought from the mountains within a mile and a half of Rio Piedras. As a building-stone, it is said to be excellent. It is worked, however, with some difficulty, as the massive rock seems to have no general lines of cleavage. The entire eastern end of the island abounds in immense, metamorphosed sandstones, approaching quartzites, and in limestones ranging to argillites. Both make fine building-stone, and, with better roads and easier means of transportation, they will very likely come into extensive industrial use.

The water comes from the dam through a twenty-four-inch pipe to two settling basins which are used alternately, and it is here held for twenty-four hours until the major portion of the foreign matter has precipitated.

Provision is made at the lower end of these basins to flow off the water into the stream, so that the basins may be cleaned of the accumulation of mud.

THE PRINCIPAL CITIES

From the settling basins, it is flowed into great duplicate filter basins, which have a bed-covering of four feet of coarse sand; the water passes through these beds of sand into the final pumping basin.

In the event of any trouble with the filter beds, it is possible to flow the water, by side trenches with cemented walls, around the filter basin, directly into the pumping pits. The pumps are direct-coupled, and the engines are of the condensing type, manufactured by a Glasgow firm.

The primary reservoir is situated a hundred and sixty feet above the pumps, and is a work of beauty. The walls are of rough masonry, topped with a handsome stone fence. The center of this great basin, holding three million seven hundred thousand gallons, is divided by a median wall, and the valve-house is situated at one side of this division.

A twenty-inch main leads into the city, this piping having been furnished by a Belgian company.

The entire work has been planned and carried out under the supervision of Spanish engineers, though the story goes that the original plans for this plant, with estimates of cost, were presented by a Scotch engineer on the island, and, with his approval, they were mailed to Madrid for final sanction. These plans, it is stated, were then stolen from the post-office, and copies made of them under the direction of the Governor-General, who forwarded them as an original scheme. They were approved by the government at Madrid, the Scotchman getting neither credit nor money.

The total cost of the completed plant with the water in the mains, it is said, will be somewhat over six hundred thousand pesos.

PUERTO RICO

Ponce

Ponce claims, by her last census, a population of 49,000 people in her urban and rural districts of the province. In the town proper, however, the population is 15,000, or a little over; though, by including the villages of Cantera, Canas, and La Playa, which are closely connected together and lie two miles away, on the highway leading to the water-front, the number may be raised to 24,500, or quite as many people as in San Juan proper.

It may be overdrawing a trifle to say that the spirit of Ponce is American; there is no doubt, however, that there is a far more progressive air about the inhabitants than elsewhere. They court and foster enterprise, and—which is a desirable condition—the population is principally Puerto Rican, as distinguished from the conservative Spanish, over whom many years will pass before they will change their methods, or hold out the hand of frankness to Americans.

In the past there has been much jealousy between the capital and Ponce; in fact the feeling has almost amounted to hatred on the part of the Ponceños for the controlling officialism of the other town, and most of the weakly-conceived schemes of revolt and rebellion against the formerly existing government have originated in societies of native-born islanders, of strong mentality, who live in the southern district. This constant uncertainty as to what Ponce might do, if provoked too far, did much to lessen the weight of the oppressive yoke of Spanish usurers, and gave her a chance to fairly use the brains of her citizens in municipal government. Without going into detail, it may be said that Americans will here find the hand of hospitality and fraternity extended to them, in a degree not existing in the older town, and, further, the

A MARKET SCENE AT PONCE

THE PRINCIPAL CITIES

writer believes that the people will heartily coöperate in any improvements or methods which will lead to a practical betterment of the city or its laws.

An important factor to men contemplating a permanent residence in some town on the island is the possibility of extension of the corporate limits. Ponce has none of the natural barriers to expansion existing at San Juan, as it is built upon a level surface, under the edges of the rolling foothills, and at a considerable elevation above the sea. It can grow readily in almost any direction with equal facility, and it has not, at its threshold, any of the miasmic, fetid marshes so common to the coast.

The heart of the city is well built, with many brick houses, and the streets, while not paved as in San Juan, are well macadamized and wide, with sidewalks which are too narrow, yet are an advance over other towns, since two people may easily walk abreast. The outskirts of the city are rather ragged, both as to houses and people, and in this fringe the city's poor live in separated huts and houses, bad enough, but far better than the prevailing condition at the capital, where the poverty-stricken, frightfully unclean, live crowded shoulder to shoulder.

The principal plaza of the town is a park of real beauty —with the refreshing shade of its great trees—in which are situated an old cathedral, the primitive hand-pump fire department, and an open dining pavilion.

There are three hospitals, including the military, a home for the destitute poor, a few fair schools, several clubs at which Americans are very graciously received, a very pretty little theater, several hotels and cafés which are the best on the island, a library with a few rare books and many worthless ones, gas-, electric-light, and ice-plants, all too small and defective, water-works supplying an abundance of good, potable water, thermal baths of which few seem to avail themselves, and lastly the only Protestant church in Puerto Rico.

The seaport of Ponce is La Playa, two miles away, which has a resident population of some 3,500. It is the warehouse of Ponce, and is a great advance over San Juan, whose lack of storage facilities for incoming or outgoing merchandise is astounding, the materials often lying piled twenty feet high along the water-front, exposed to the weather.

The harbor proper has ample water for vessels drawing twenty-five feet to within a few hundred yards of the shore, where it shoals so rapidly that few steamers venture nearly as close in as they might. A most serious shortcoming of this port—and it applies equally well to all the others—is the lack of a wharf. It is astonishing that, with an average annual trade aggregating some thirty millions of dollars, not a wharf has ever been constructed at any water-front in Puerto Rico, or even attempted except at Mayaguez, where a partially-built and defective structure is found.

Commercially, Ponce ranks second, and, unless the trend of American enterprise should take an unexpected turn, it will, in a few years, be the greatest trading-center on the island. It has, in support of this assertion, the following elements: A good harbor, rather too open, but withal fairly protected, and wharfs can be economically constructed here, as elsewhere; the port-town is admirably suited, in its location and in the buildings already on the ground, for handling a great commercial trade; Ponce is a delightful home for the merchant and business man, probably the most healthful one on the island at the present time; it has more good wagon-roads leading out to sections rich in coffee, sugar, cereals, fruit, and tobacco than any other town, as well as a railroad connecting it with the prolific Yauco district to the west; and finally it possesses, inherent in the population, more progressive business enterprise, as measured by American standards. Ponceños have well, though perhaps egotistically, likened themselves to the brains of the island, and contemptuously slur at the capital by adding, "And San Juan is the stomach!"

Mayaguez

Mayaguez is the prettiest town, of the three large centers, in the lightness and grace of its architecture, which, in Spanish towns, is always apt to be heavy. It also has the broadest streets and the widest foot-pavements, and is situated upon rounded, rising ground which will permit of easy drainage.

The population is estimated at about 12,000, and it is said that there is a greater percentage of white inhabitants than in any other town; exactly what is meant by "a white population," in Puerto Rican significance, is difficult to determine, as few inhabitants, unless direct from Spain or aliens, are free from some trace of negro blood.

This city claims the honor of being nearest to the point where Columbus landed on island soil, and the inhabitants have, in consequence, erected a monument to his memory in the central plaza, which, in connection with the handsome stone railing surrounding the paved park, set with statuettes commemorative of this landing, forms a fitting tribute to the great discoverer. If Columbus had been a domestic man, instead of a wanderer on the face of the earth and an untiring seeker after pastures new, his shade must have long since cried out in agony against the turmoils and brawls which have kept his weary bones circulating among a quartet of graves, and caused him to press his foot—whether he would or not—upon nearly every sandy stretch of the West Indies. Three places on the island of Puerto Rico, alone, claim that there he bent his silken hose and raised his eyes to heaven in thanksgiving!

There is not, in the town of Mayaguez, the same visible evidence of poverty, in the hordes of ragged, tattered natives upon the streets, and the citizens claim that there is less distress and want; there are certainly, in the outskirts, less huts and hovels of the poor. This can be explained, to some extent, by the fact that Mayaguez is off the main artery of travel, and does not so readily catch the negroes from the little islands of the Lesser Antilles, who are each year drifting in greater numbers from their forlorn sea-homes to Puerto Rico, in the hope that it holds out more material promise; also, the great coffee districts, which reach almost to the city's edge, demand laborers for longer periods of the year; and lastly, the rate of wages has been, for the past few years, slightly higher than elsewhere,—a few centavos a day, where the usual wage is low, means a marvelous amelioration in the condition of the laboring man.

While Mayaguez ranks third commercially, and supplies very little territory with imported merchandise, industrially, or in the manufacturing of products, it leads the other cities, and gives steady employment to many men. There are four big coffee-mills, which convert the sundried coffee, brought over the trails from the Mayaguez, Utuado, and Lares districts, into a fine export article by removing the second hull, bluing, and polishing. In exportation of this product it is second only to Ponce. This town also leads in the shipment of fruit abroad, principally to the United States.

It possesses a tannery of no small proportions, where

THE PRINCIPAL CITIES

they use the native wangli bark for tanning, and turn out an excellent leather, much used by local cobblers.

There are four concerns which produce a fine chocolate, much in demand for local and Spanish consumption.

The small industries are manufacturing straw hats, weaving baskets, making the native rush pack-saddles, and polishing and cutting tortoise-shell.

Mayaguez has much the best ice- and electric-light plants on the island. Nine tons of ice a day is the maximum output. The water for the city is brought from a mountain torrent two miles away in the foothills, and is good and abundant.

Again, it is the only town which has, as its great pride, a street railway. It is very narrow gauge and the cars are tiny affairs, but it does excellent service.

The harbor has the misfortune of having a wide-open mouth seaward; in fact, it is no more than a great indenture in the coast-line, protected, to some extent, by a series of immense coral reefs, acting as a giant sea-wall and embaying the inner waters. Some years ago the construction of a steel wharf was begun, but, as before stated, it has never been completed; it is said that some eighty thousand pesos were expended in putting up what there is of the shaky structure, and, if this be true, the project has much the air of a steal, as the ironwork and labor could not have cost, in America, over twenty thousand dollars.

The municipal and other prominent buildings of the town are the alcalde's office, a fine barracks for soldiers, a substantial hospital for the military, the cathedral on the main plaza, a delightful little opera-house, and an excellent home for the aged and infirm. It has two fairly good hostelries, and a market-place which is ahead of those of the other towns in architecture and spaciousness. In the

PUERTO RICO

lower part of the city, near the theater, is a fascinating little park, with an ornamental fountain, gorgeous foliage, and flowering plants, the whole being set off with royal palms. The charm of this town, which altogether is the most desirable of any as a place of residence, is much enhanced by the magnificent ceiba trees which tower from behind the white-porticoed houses, with far-reaching branches and leaves, and by the mass of flowering vines which overgrow the heavy masonry walls, or guard fantastic wicket-gates, with their clinging sprays of white and pink flowers.

There are several casinos, and in most of them Americans will be welcome, though the Spanish club still holds aloof, the haughty spirit of its members having been somewhat wounded, perhaps, by the way in which General Schwan scared their brave soldiers, and sent them cantering through the city to the mountain wildernesses beyond.

Other Cities

From a purely business standpoint, it is doubtful whether there are other cities on the island which are of any special interest to Americans, unless they intend to engage in the enterprises of tobacco-growing and coffee-raising, or the buying of these products. Caguas and Cayey, on the great military road, are now the largest tobacco towns and lie in the heart of the tobacco district. The entire product is handled by Spaniards, who can be easily displaced by Americans understanding the business, as their shiftless, careless methods have rather retarded than built up an industry which should be only second to coffee.

Caguas is a dirty, unpleasant town of some five thousand people, including the hundreds of inhabitants of

THE PRINCIPAL CITIES

squalid, outskirting, palm-thatched huts, whose filth and degradation are hidden away behind groves of waving plantains. There are no conveniences whatever which would tend to make a residence here desirable; the sanitary condition of the streets is fearful, and the majority of the houses are infested with abominable creeping life. Spanish sentiment is also strongly against Americans.

Cayey, on the other hand, while not being much in advance of Caguas, either in convenience or sanitation, is, from a distance, one of the most picturesque of towns, and its elevation of nearly two thousand feet causes the climate to be delightful. The best cigars are made here, by half a dozen Spanish firms. This is one of the places which will, through the possession of general advantages in location, climate, and fertile soil, develop into a strong commercial city, and become a stopping-place for pleasure-seeking winter tourists. The town is really a half-way point between the two cities of San Juan and Ponce, and either is easily reached over the fine military road. The problems of sewage and water-supply may easily and economically be solved, as the town lies high in the hills, while many mountain torrents are near at hand, coming from still greater altitudes.

The only other interior town, which stands out in the mind of the writer as deserving of mention, is Lares, high in the mountains in the western end. It is almost inaccessible from the coast, as it lacks connection therewith except over execrable trails. A highway or military road reaches out from Mayaguez toward it, but the macadamized portion gives out after thirteen kilometers, and the road, in full width, stops at Las Marias, twenty-two kilometers from Mayaguez and about sixteen kilometers from Lares, so that it is reached only by a trail of which the mind without experience could only conceive in nightmare. It has an alleged wagon outlet toward Arecibo, through which nothing but a bull-cart, with three or four yoke of oxen, can wallow. Lares is a busy, thriving little coffee town, of some two thousand inhabitants, and its very isolation seems to have warmed the hearts of its people to acts of hospitality toward the stranger who comes their way. It is in the very center of a great coffee district, and many of the richest haciendas on the island are clustered in a radius of ten miles, tucked away in beauty-spots of mountain wilderness and tropical luxuriance. Senseless, malicious native bandits, imbued with the turbulent spirit of insurrection, so common among the poverty-stricken of Spanish-Americans, have, in utter wantonness, burned and pillaged dozens of fine estates pending the advent of our army, and, in wandering over the trails, one meets everywhere the desolated ruins of once happy homes and large coffee-works. In consummation of revenge, they have, through their blind hatred of Spain and her once loyal citizens, only succeeded in taking the bread from their own mouths and those of their children. There is perhaps no more desirable town in which to embark in the coffee business, and certainly no better region, all things considered, in which to become the owner of coffee-land.

Most of the other coast towns and principal interior cities have been mentioned in other articles, but those which have been here described are the most desirable, in varying degree, as regards accessibility to harbors, business, and residence. Yauco, the coffee town on the south, Arecibo, a large coffee town on the north coast, Guayama and Humacoa, sugar towns of the southeastern portion, with poor ports four miles away, Fajardo, on the east coast, with a good harbor, Aguadilla, on the west above Mayaguez, and many interior towns might all be dis-

THE PRINCIPAL CITIES

cussed specifically, but, while many of them will no doubt, in years to come, develop into commercial towns of note, under the progressive methods of hustling Americans, they do not at present possess the attractiveness of the places described.

CHAPTER XVIII

SCHOOLS, CHURCHES, AND CHARITABLE INSTITUTIONS

ONE approaches the subject of the schools, churches, and charitable institutions of Puerto Rico with many misgivings, so palpably bad has been the Spanish administration along these lines.

Schools

The island " Budget " for 1897-98 shows an appropriation of 69,776 pesos for Public Instruction, which was allotted, ostensibly, to the eight districts in varying proportion, based upon their relative importance and population, but which in practice, it is said, had use found for most of it in the city of San Juan. It is not to be supposed that this insignificant amount represents the entire school fund for the island, as each municipality provides for its own school taxes in its annual estimate of expenses for the district.

It may be pointed out that the district of Ponce—which, by the way, rather leads in money expended upon common-school education—appropriated in 1897-98 the sum of 34,000 pesos. Assuming that Ponce secures a share of the government fund to the amount of 8,000 pesos, her total appropriation would be raised to 42,000 pesos to be annually expended in a district with a total population of 49,000 souls.

It is difficult to say, by reason of the lack of accurate

AT THE INDUSTRIAL SCHOOL, SAN JUAN

SCHOOLS

census, what proportion of the population are children between the ages of six and eighteen years, but they probably compose as many as two-fifths of the people in this island of rapid births and early deaths. If this is true, there should be somewhere in the neighborhood of 20,000 children in the district who should be going to school.

The census of the Ponce district, for 1897, gives 14,394 persons as the number who can read and write or read alone, or $29\frac{87}{100}\%$ of the population. In the last ten years illiteracy in this section has been reduced some $5\frac{1}{2}\%$, but, granting that 30 % of the people receive some education, there would remain, among the 20,000 children of school age, at least 25 %, or 5,000, who attend either public or private schools, in securing an education. As a matter of fact, a majority of the children of the more well-to-do people go to private institutions, under paid tuition, and hence even the above estimate of attendance must be cut down, by possibly a thousand, to represent those who actually derive benefit from the public-school fund.

With 4,000 children and 42,000 pesos available for education, the cost per child would reach the really liberal rate of over $10 a year—more than twice as much as Alabama expends on a child, and about two and a half times less than is required to educate a little one in New York state. If a compulsory school law were in effect, however, and the 75 % of the waifs of the poor, who go hungry, unclean, and in tatters all through childhood and youth, and emerge into man's estate in the densest ignorance and without mental capacity to ever raise themselves above the fifty-centavos-a-day rate of wages, were forced to secure some education, it will readily be seen how utterly inadequate would be the present school appropriation, as it would average then but $1.35 a year for each scholar in Ponce, which city and San Juan are the centers of education. In the outlying country districts not above a few cents per possible scholar are appropriated.

The school fund of Ponce district is not wisely or economically expended; 8,690 pesos of the local fund are annually spent in the rental of schools, which, for the most part in the country, are miserable little shacks, with a single room so small that not above fifty scholars can sit, at one time, within the badly-lighted space, on plain unbacked benches, while in the town some of the places selected for schools in the narrow streets are wholly unsuitable—unsanitary, dark, upon the ground floor, and within close seeing and hearing distance of the traffic of a busy thoroughfare. Five thousand pesos go for books, writing materials, and to caretakers of school buildings, while only 20,580 pesos raised by Ponce are used for teachers' salaries.

It may interest the reader to see the salary list:

1 Principal for High School for boys..................	$1,200
4 Teachers, Elementary, 1st class, $720..............	2,880
1 Teacher, Elementary School at La Playa...........	720
2 Teachers, Elementary, 2d class, $540..............	1,080
3 Teachers, Auxiliary, Coto, Canas, and Machuelo Abajo, $360..	1,080
19 Teachers, rural schools, at $300..................	5,700
1 Principal for High School for girls................	1,200
1 Teacher, Elementary, 1st class, for girls...........	720
5 Teachers, 2d class, for girls, at $540..............	2,700
3 Teachers, Auxiliary, at $360.....................	1,080
40	$18,360
For teachers for the school for the poor, and salaries for special branches................................	2,220
	$20,580

It need hardly be pointed out that the teachers who receive 300 pesos a year are not intellectual giants, and

THE TUNGILLO CHURCH, NEAR CAROLINA, BUILT IN 1813

SCHOOLS

that the methods adopted in teaching are careless, slovenly, and lacking in system. To the hardship of insufficient salary is added the mortification of having your avocation looked down upon as degrading, for mediævalism has not yet been rooted out, and the office of the scribe is considered a menial one.

If fifty teachers are allowed for the district, which assumes that another 1000 pesos are paid from the year's appropriation, each of the teachers will be compelled to instruct some 90 pupils. Alabama with her 41 % illiteracy has a teacher for every 45 scholars, while New York with but $5\frac{1}{2}$ % illiteracy gives a teacher for every 33 pupils.

In point of fact, one-half of the ninety scholars to a teacher are never on hand at once, as the attendance is constantly broken by the necessity, or pretext, that the little ones must assist the parents to earn a living. Child-labor is so universal among the poor (95 % are poverty-stricken), and, under tropical suns, it is so much easier for indolent parents to command the children to bear the brunt of the daily work than to do it themselves, that it is only by the persevering effort of the children themselves, who look upon school as a happy recreation, that they ever get within the doors of the educational edifices. Under these harrowing conditions a child may learn to read and write in a few years, but the great majority of them never acquire more than the merest smattering.

The system of teaching pursued in the elementary schools is largely an oral one, in which the children chant their lessons, as a unit, after the teacher. Tests of individual knowledge are seldom made, and competition, and merit systems, which are the soul of school advancement, are unknown.

The higher branches of a common-school education are taught to very few, and the darkness in which Spanish races dwell, with regard to the natural sciences, is glaringly manifested in all their works of public engineering and mechanics.

San Juan, Ponce, and Mayaguez each supports a school for the grown-up poor, and it is said they have met with considerable success.

San Juan has an industrial school, under the protecting wing of the church, where some two hundred boys are taught, in slipshod fashion, various branches of industrial mechanics and physics.

The support for this school, the island Insane Asylum, and the Deputaccion Provincial was derived from a monthly lottery held in San Juan, in which it is said a clear profit of some twenty thousand pesos was made.

With a view to giving some conception of the illiteracy which exists on the island, it may be said that, in a total population of 806,708 (census 1887, thought to be very defective), only 14 % of the people can read and write or read only, or there are 695,328 persons who are compelled to make their mark, and to whom a printed page is wholly unintelligible. The educated people are gathered in the large cities, and hence the percentage of illiteracy is much smaller in the towns, while that of the country is more profound, until in some rural districts a pall of utter ignorance envelops the people which could not be greatly exceeded even in the heart of Africa. In the Ponce district, where the claim is made that the least illiteracy obtains, there are three barrios, with a combined population of 5,500 souls, where but 6 % of the people can read or write, and 8,000 more in one barrios where but 8 or 9 % read the words upon a printed page.

While the condition of ignorance is far-reaching in the island today, it may be said that the Puerto Rican youngster possesses the inherent ability to learn readily and looks forward to schooling as a pleasure. Under a proper school system, the intellectual tone of the island population may be raised in a generation, from an almost bestial condition to a point where the people will become average thinking citizens of the United States. Illiteracy possesses the advantage—for us as administrators of Puerto Rico's future affairs—that we at least will not have to overcome deep-rooted race prejudices, either political, social, or religious; the mass of the people lie dormant and unthinking, hating only mildly the Spaniard's oppressive yoke which has ground them down to serfdom in the past, and watching with pathetic eyes for that amelioration of hardship, promise of which is held out to them by their ideal savior, America.

Churches

The clergy of the island say that Puerto Rico is a godless country; that her people live without hope or desire of elevation. The people, upon the other hand, retort that the holy cloth has been, from time immemorial, disgraced and prostituted in the representatives of the church, whom Spain has hired and forced upon them.

There is probably truth in the assertions of both claimants, but the real weakness in the ecclesiastical system of the island, and the one which has led up to the discords of the past, and has fostered vice in the church itself—if it does exist—lay in the fact that the church and state leaned upon one another in close association, the state supporting the church financially, and using her oftentimes as a political lever to further the ends of grasping civil officials. Purity in the administration of holy institutions may not be expected where their representatives are directly dependent upon a civil government for their support, and the laity, in a country where every politician

PUERTO RICO

is looked upon as a trickster, will view the veriest saint with suspicion.

There are seventy-one cathedrals on the island, one in every town of consequence, constructed and paid for by the central government with taxes collected from the people.

The total appropriation for the church in 1897–98 was 194,000 pesos, in round figures, or nearly five per cent. of the total revenue of the island; the salary roll for some 250 men, including a bishop at 9,000 pesos, a dean and an archdeacon at 5,500, 11 parochial clergymen at 1,500 each, 17 curates at 1,000, 58 at 700, 31 assistant curates at 600, 85 sacristans at 150, and several priests in charge of hermitages and special churches, amounts to 168,000 pesos, while the remainder of the appropriation goes for "materials."

It will be noted that the average government support for each church is over 2,000 pesos per annum, and also that the lowest salary paid, excepting that of the caretakers, is 600 pesos a year. The average salary for school teachers, who are so badly needed, is but half this amount.

Beside the salaries paid the clergy, the church fees for marriages, burial services, rituals, etc., serve to augment the total revenues.

The life of the clergy seems to have been one of idleness and almost complete indolence in the past; they have never been active factors in an effort to ameliorate the depressed condition of the people; they have never been educators, and, as spiritual advisers, their relation to the people has apparently been purely perfunctory. There have been, of course, exceptions to this rule; good, earnest, honest men, who soon outlived their usefulness, if not compliant with the wishes of civil functionaries. There are many tales of how Puerto Rican politicians and

THE CHURCH AT LAKES

DISSOLUTION OF MARRIAGES

Spanish officials have used the church to foster political ends, and many more unpleasant relations, by men who are enemies of the church government as it exists, of general viciousness, immorality, and grasping for material possessions on the part of priests. Some of these stories are unfortunately too true, but many of them have been made up out of whole cloth. The result has been, however, to almost wholly separate the people from the church; a church in which "we dare not send our daughters to confession," said one bitter layman. Most of the population profess religious sentiments, but church attendance is restricted to a few women and girls, and, whether the opprobrium heaped upon the clergy be deserved or not, the stigma cannot now be removed without a complete remodeling of the organization, perhaps by the church of America. Under the American régime which has set in, the church appropriations have already been cut off, and reconstruction now rests in the hands of the people themselves, as the future support of the church is dependent upon the generous spirit of the populace.

Dissolution of Marriages

There are no civil courts in Puerto Rico in which the bonds of marriage may be dissolved. Under the old Spanish law, marriage is held to be a holy function pertaining to the church alone; and under the church laws, while separation of husband and wife may be granted for specified reasons, neither party may again enter into the marriage relation so long as both parties live.

Adultery and maltreatment are punishable under the provisions of the criminal code, and may be made a basis for separation proceedings before an ecclesiastical tribunal composed of church authorities, the chief of whom is the Archbishop of San Juan.

PUERTO RICO

Ecclesiastical or canonical law provides for declaring marriage null and void in each of several cases, viz.: First, where one of the parties may not legally marry, *e. g.*, a priest; second, where the canonical rules for carrying out marriage have not been complied with, *e. g.*, when the banns have not been properly published; third, where marriage has been consecrated, but not consummated through the physical incapacity of one of the parties.

Separation has been resorted to, that a division of property might be made by law, and the proper support be given the wife by a recalcitrant husband.

Charitable Institutions

A most prodigious amount of suffering and disease exists among the poor of the island, and, in comparison with the number of poverty-stricken and needy people, little is done in a public way to relieve the misery and suffering.

At San Juan, Ponce, and Mayaguez there may be found small houses for the destitute poor, aged, and infirm, also poor and military hospitals, and physicians to the poor; but beyond this, with one or two exceptions, it can hardly be said that active measures have ever been taken to relieve the sickness and distress visible on every side throughout the island.

Ponce carries an item in her city " budget " of about 34,000 pesos for charities, and San Juan spends annually some 28,000 pesos for the same purpose, or quite as much as for school purposes. The homes for the extremely poor in these three cities are rather attractive places from the outside, but are very barren of interior decorations, comfortable furniture, and other necessities which, to the American mind, should be present to make the fleeting hours of the poor outcasts less burdensome.

The few charitable organizations seem to exist more in

THE CATHEDRAL AT HORMIGUERO

CHARITABLE INSTITUTIONS

name than in the activity of their patrons, and no systematic attempts are made to distribute clothing and food among the needy; though it may be pointed out, incidentally, that lack of clothing in a tropical climate does injury to the modesty of the spectator, rather than hurt to the victim of rags. Hunger, though, particularly in the larger towns, gnaws the vitals of hundreds of peasants every day of their lives, and the enfeebled condition of half the populace is due to a constant diet of fruits, which are naturally the cheapest foods.

Along the roadsides and military highways throughout the island, one passes mendicants with supplicating hands outstretched; covered with sores, grotesque in swollen limbs of elephantiasis, carrying huge goiters protruding from the neck, sightless from unmentionable diseases, or wan and wasted from anæmic malarias.

The writer never saw a Spaniard pass one of these creatures without throwing toward the shriveled hand a copper coin, and yet the almsgiver may be the alcalde of the near-by town, where, in the dark confines of a foul cell in the city hall, two men lie dying upon the damp, green-coated bricks, rolled in their own filth. Nothing is done for them; what need? They are there to die; better so. This pictured contrast is no feat of imagination, for, in almost every interior town on the island, one may usually find a number of wretched objects lying upon brick floors in the basements of the town buildings, without covering or pillows, suffering from racking fevers or frightful disorders, brought there by friends or relatives almost equally as poor, and left to die in the hands of the city authorities, who, while they have no money to save an ebbing life—and no doctor will come without his fee, —do bury the pauper dead in the cemeteries, without coffin and without ceremony.

PUERTO RICO

Assurances are always given that these dying people are fed, yet, at Aguas Buenas, for eighteen hours no one went near a poor old man lying, with a crust of hard bread clutched in his dying hand, upon the floor, in a foul atmosphere, beneath the city judge's office, until an American officer made an investigation and threatened to put all the city officials under arrest. It was in this same town that sleeping American soldiers were given nightmares by the terrible cries for water of a man who was in the last stages of some dropsical affection, and yet locked into a windowless cell in one of the town buildings.

At Caguas, as many as four men were seen at one time in the mortuary house outside the cemetery gate, unkempt, uncared for, and dying by inches; two, beyond recovery, lay on the brick floor, one on a bench, and the fourth on the gruesome white slab of the dead-house. The sexton placidly awaited their demise, and said no doctor could be had, as they did not have money to employ one.

It is difficult to understand what instinct inclines a man to distribute alms upon the street, and yet lets him, with callous soul, gaze with unlifted, unassisting hand upon wretched scenes like these; but the same bland, polite, obsequious man will be found throughout the island, who distributes his coppers in public, will go to any pains to serve his foreign equal, but will stare unmoved upon such human miseries. It is here we discover the inherent, the inbred, brutality of Spain.

There is a broad, deep field in Puerto Rico for American charitable societies, and limited assistance of the poor will be more far-reaching in its effects, over a given area, than in the United States, at the same time doing more to win the undying gratitude of the great army of the down-trodden, and firm alliance with America, than years of liberal legislation.

A CEMETERY IN PUERTO RICO

CHAPTER XIX

BURIALS AND CEMETERIES

THE last journey to the grave is always replete with sadness, but nowhere does one feel the deep pathos of funeral scenes as in Spanish - American countries. There goes some poor fellow down the glaring, sunlit street, all his troubles o'er in silent death, borne in his rude coffin on the shoulders of four barefooted, ragged-clothed, trotting men; or perhaps it is a slip of a girl, born to penury and hardship, reared to young-womanhood with never a day that she knew a full meal; and yet in life her black eyes smiled and she was happy in her simple pleasures. Yes, it is the girl; for the meager, black-cotton shroud, tacked closely to the unlidded coffin, clingingly molds her upturned face and childish, budding form.

Going to her last resting-place, down the dusty, white-hot street, under the lazy scrutiny of corner loungers, past the little stores where, in moments of great happiness in life, she had spent her few centavos on a checkered handkerchief; it was in there, where the tiny panniered horse stands patiently and with hanging head before the door, that Lorenzo once bought her the little tawdry heart she wears on her cold breast today. What matters it now! Lorenzo loves another girl, but it was such a happy moment when he—great strong fellow that he was—called her " corazon mio."

No one seems to care; she is dead, they will bury her,

that is all there is to it. No, not all, for a wrinkled, weazen-faced old woman sits in the darkest corner of her tiny, palm-thatched hut, and rocks back and forth, with heavy, hot tears dropping on her withered, enfeebled hands, and behind the coffin, which rises and falls like a last lullaby, under the rhythmic step of the bearers, a boy—her little brother—stumbles blindly along, trying not to cry, for fear the grown-ups will think him less a man, though his eyes are hot and red with straining.

She is to be buried within the enclosure of the great brick wall of the cemetery, not in any of the beautiful tombs and niches, with their garlands of rare porcelain roses; not under the clustering, flowering bushes, or near the slender funereal tree, where she had thought, in her childish way, that it would be so sweet to lie at rest, but out in the pauper half, among the trampled weeds and in the earth sown with gruesome bones and skulls. It is a horrid place, under the festering sun, covered with rotting bones of dead long gone, heartlessly dug up by the keepers—the graveyard ghouls. And yet they are not to blame, for two centuries of poor dead lie buried in this little plot. Two years, two whole years, they have the right to remain unmolested in their shallow, muddy beds, pelted by the torrential rains and fiercely burned by the shimmering heat, and then;—well, the newly dead must go under ground, and old bones offer no resistance to a spade.

The boy lies prone on the rough clods—not a man now—heartbroken and convulsed, and his hands, working nervously in the rank weeds, dislodge the whitened fragment of a skull. The rude pine box, slatted below and uncovered above, rests unevenly on the ground beside him, for they thought her such a little girl they dug the grave short by two inches. They lower her now on coarse

A PAUPER BURIAL

ropes of grass, and the sexton picks up a clod of earth, with bowed head presses it to his lips, and it falls rudely on her sheeted face as he casts it from his hand, muttering, "God rest you, little one." The shovels rasp and scrape against each other for a little and it is done. The boy never moves, even when the shingled board bearing her name is thrust into the soft, new mound.

The ineffable sadness of these pauper funerals, as they pass hurriedly through the streets day after day—one might almost say hour after hour—wrings the heart of the onlooker, and forces tears to the eyes in spite of oneself. Yet the multitude of Puertoriqueños see nothing in them to rouse even a fleeting sigh that life should be so narrow, so confined, for the poverty-stricken, so little at its end. Perhaps, after all, it is wasted sentiment, for death brings the poor release from many, many hardships.

One sees on the island, in any town, a hundred funerals where the coffin is hurriedly carried through the streets on the shoulders of men, without mourners, to be buried in the pauper's plot, without ceremony and without clergy, to one where the priests move down the narrow street in funeral march, chanting the requiem before the slowly-moving hearse, drawn by caparisoned horses, and followed by weeping relatives.

I have seen, in Caguas, three burials of paupers in one day, where even the rude box, consisting of four boards, slatted on the bottom and without top, was denied the dead as a last resting-place, and the body was calmly turned out of its narrow confines to drop heavily, face downward, in the four-foot hole.

A Catholic Puertoriqueño, poor though he may be, must rest within the brick-walled enclosure of some one of the seventy-one city cemeteries of the island. If the creed differs or he be a freethinker, outside the holy gates he lies, buried behind the wall, obscure, unknown. All dead in the cities or in the country must be buried at these places, and it is no uncommon sight to watch, high on the slippery trails, reliefs of men trudging through the mud toward town, bearing laboriously a dead body. No municipal provision is made for defraying pauper burial-expenses, and the transporting must needs be a work of love. The graves are dug by sextons, who are paid minute salaries and eke out an existence by small fees and tips given them by the owners of sarcophagi and niches. To be buried within the enclosure requires a certificate from the parish priest, stating that the deceased was a Catholic.

Some of the funerals of the wealthy are functions of great solemnity and ostentation. In a magnificent funeral of this kind, the body is carried in state from the house to the cathedral, with chanting, black-skirted fathers accompanying the hearse. At the church, a solemn ceremony takes place, which is deeply impressive, and then the march to the grave proceeds, to the murmuring chant and the dirgeful tolling of bells. At the grave is gathered half the city, and employed orators extol the virtues of the deceased, and thank the assembled multitude for the goodness of heart which prompts them to do honor to the dead.

For church services, a funeral costs from fifteen to one hundred pesos, controlled by the amount of chanting done, whether it takes place during the march from the house to the cathedral, from the cathedral to the cemetery, or both. At the funeral of the young, a band is often secured.

The price of lots in the cemeteries varies in different towns; at Ponce, they sell for twelve pesos a square meter. The niches, which are built along the brick walls

MORTUARY DECORATIONS AT PONCE

BURIALS AND CEMETERIES

in tiers of four or five, are owned by the municipalities and rented for a term of years, or sold outright. A hundred pesos buys one for eternity, twenty-five pesos insures a peaceful rest for five years, but Providence must take care of the bones after this, if relatives fail to advance the next instalment, for the city won't, and deliberately hauls the skeletons from the vaults and casts them into brick pits made for the purpose, in the corners of the yard. It is a hideous collection of heterogeneous, disarticulated vertebræ which has accumulated in these corners during past years; crumbling to fine dust at the bottom, and fed constantly by new specimens at the top.

The mortuary decorations are unique in these cemeteries, consisting of wreaths of French porcelain flowers among the handsomest, and frosted metal ones in the cheaper. Often the photograph of the deceased graces the front of his crypt, in a metal frame. Images of Mother Mary, crucifixes, and doves form another series. Fresh-cut flowers are seldom seen, but rare foliage plants, of gorgeous color, vie with flowering, climbing vines and beautiful tropical shrubbery.

Most of these cemeteries—whose limits were determined by the San Juan government—have long since become cramped and inadequate quarters for the dead, and, in some places, they might even be designated as noisome pest-holes, dangerous, in their infectious exhalations, to the living in the close-by towns. It takes less than three years at Ponce to make the round of digging new graves, from end to end of the pauper lot, and consequently this hallowed ground is strewn with human bones.

Some provision for the decent burial of paupers, and immediate enlargement and removal of cemeteries to greater distances from the cities, are questions which need prompt attention at the hands of American authorities.

CHAPTER XX

THE MONEY OF THE ISLAND

PUERTO RICO has been the financial plaything of Spain in the past. Many different monetary schemes have been foisted on the unresisting island, which—unlike its sister province Cuba—has never had the courage to revolt against the outrages and impositions of political machinations.

The financial system has always been on a silver basis, though it is said that thirty years ago an exceedingly small amount of gold coin was in circulation.

Prior to 1874, the silver coin of the United States was the standard and current medium of exchange, but in that year a trick was played on poor Puerto Rico by a French banking firm, headed by a man named Hermua. The slaves of the island were freed by a governmental edict, and indemnity bonds were issued by Spain to the former slave-holders, payable upon presentation, at a definite amount per black head. Then, as now, the land-holders—very few in proportion to the total population—held the major portion of the money in the island, the slave getting nothing for his labor, and the poor man practically living from hand to mouth.

To meet this bond issue the Spanish government resorted to a cash-raising scheme, by which an arrangement with the French banker Hermua and a few of his banking friends was effected; this firm agreeing to pay off the

THE MONEY OF THE ISLAND

slave indemnity in silver coin. What nation's silver currency was to be the medium was not stated in the contract, and consequently Mexico's silver dollars were used, which possessed actually more weight in silver than the United States silver dollars, though worth only some sixty-two cents. The result was the flooding of Puerto Rico with depreciated Mexican silver, through which an immense profit was secured by the French firm, and possibly by the official circles of the lawmakers of Spain.

The steps which naturally followed were the paying for all labor in cheap Mexican silver, by the limited number of large money-holders in the island, the hoarding of American silver, and its ultimate exchange for Mexican silver, which to all intents and purposes expanded, for the time being, the currency of the island, and made it possible for landowners to pay all their debts in Mexican silver, at an apparent profit to themselves.

Little thought seems to have been given to the complications which would arise in foreign exchange, but for that matter it is hardly probable that the tide of cheaper money could have been stemmed, as the natural law is for dearer money to disappear by hoarding, or in exchange with foreign countries. It is said that many United States silver pieces were punctured to prevent their leaving the island, but it is difficult to see what beneficial result could arise from recourse to such a scheme. In two years' time the silver of Puerto Rico had changed from the United States to the Mexican silver basis.

For twenty years the Mexican silver reigned supreme. There was a subsidiary copper currency, which was Spanish, but aside from this, all money was Mexican silver. By 1894 the Spanish government had evolved a new financial intrigue which was to produce results advantageous to the official machine. All Mexican silver was

PUERTO RICO

called in by the home government and a temporary paper exchange-note was issued, payable in a new silver currency to be called the Puerto Rican peso. It was claimed to be distinctly honorable and patriotic for the treasury department of Spain to desire a silver piece for her colonies which should bear the stamp of the ruling country.

In round numbers, six million Mexican dollars were called in, and six million pesos were issued from the re-minting. The outrage lay in the fact that instead of each coin weighing as much as the original piece turned in, the new peso was almost a sixth lighter in weight, making a rake-off for the Spanish government of over a million, not counting the few odd hundred thousand dollars which were never paid. The uncomplaining islanders meekly accepted the new coin, without even a formal protest.

It was then made a penal offense to import the Mexican dollar to Puerto Rico, and the few remaining pieces had to be carefully examined as to date before being accepted in commercial exchange.

For four years the peso has been the sole money of the island, but a new crisis has been reached today, by the advent of the American army in the island, and by the change of government. The new problem has perturbed the native population from end to end of the island, and a condition of unrest exists, never before apparent during the many money jugglings which have hitherto been perpetrated.

A few days after General Miles had landed his troops on the southern coast of Puerto Rico, he passed a mandatory order, as military commander, that the prevailing rate of exchange should be two to one—that is, two Puerto Rican pesos for one American silver dollar—on the assumption that a peso was worth in bullion value less than half of one dollar, backed by a gold reserve in

THE MONEY OF THE ISLAND

our Treasury. This was an apparently easy solution of the currency problem of Puerto Rico, unbacked as she was and is now by a superior money, but the righteousness and wisdom of such short cuts in intricate financial tangles remain to be proven.

The six million silver pesos on the island have never, to any extent, found their way into foreign exchange, but have been confined solely to the island, representing, for many commodities, a definite purchasing power quite on a par with American silver. This unique condition of affairs is largely due to the lack of a banking system approved by the Spanish government, and to a system of differential duties which favored Spain in every transaction, causing the people of Puerto Rico to import from Spain practically all the necessities of life, while the export trade from the island to other countries was paid in bills of exchange on the Spanish bank. It was a wheel within a wheel—taxation from the home government was quite sufficient to balance the profitable export trade with the imports from Spain in such a way that silver pesos never got farther away than the bank of Spain, from which they were placed in circulation again by the payment of the army and officials on the island, and by road, harbor, and fortification improvements carried on for the benefit of military and naval operations. Within the last few months the Puerto Rican peso has been honored for the first time by Spain—from necessity—as the returning Spanish army has carried home, in wages and plunder, an unknown but large quantity of this silver, and further the bank of San Juan, which was a repository of private funds and island municipal and school reserves, has been milked by Spain's officials. Ponce alone has lost, it is said, some sixty thousand pesos which were withdrawn and carried to Spain without due warrant.

PUERTO RICO

The amount of actual money was so weighty in character and so limited in Puerto Rico, that the banks of San Juan and Ponce, by permission of the respective municipal authorities of these towns, issued paper notes, negotiable and redeemable upon demand, with which the local business might be transacted. Neither of these paper issues had any protection from the government, and they were accepted hesitatingly or not at all by people residing outside of these cities. A false inflation of the paper currency of either bank was presumably prevented by a municipal law which demanded a monthly statement of the assets, liabilities, and outstanding paper money. As any suspicion that these banks were using all their available funds, and not holding sufficient reserve in silver to meet the outstanding paper, would have resulted in a disastrous run upon them, it is difficult to understand what advantage the issue of paper obligations possessed, above the convenience of supplying a portable certificate in place of the weighty silver piece. One, five, and ten pesos were the usual issues, though at Ponce larger paper certificates, in the nature of a bond issue, transferable, but drawing an annual interest of one-half of one per cent., were held by the larger depositors.

I am told by native financial authorities that when, for specific purposes, the peso came, from time to time, to be exchanged for gold, the accepted rate was one hundred and fifty in favor of gold, though at times it has been as low as one hundred and twelve. Again, it is said that today, since the honoring of the peso in Spain, it is possible, by shipping the silver peso to the United States, to arrange a draft exchange for Spanish gold at one hundred and fifty, with an added five per cent. commission, creating thus an exchange rate of one hundred and fifty-five. If this is strictly true, then the rate arbitrarily set

THE MONEY OF THE ISLAND

by General Miles would seem to be unfair, and likely to prove a dire hardship to a million of helpless people, to whom we are holding out the promise of future prosperity, and the happiness of a broad-gauge government, such as they have never before known.

In spite of the edict and the fact that all the custom-houses on the island in the hands of military collectors of customs, as well as the new post-office, hold that a peso, paid in duties and postage, is only half the value of an American dollar, the business men of the island have been able to run this rate down as low as one hundred and fifty, and refuse to give in return for an American dollar more than one peso and a half Puerto Rican.

Many interesting complications have arisen, due to this varying exchange. For example, Ponce, which is perhaps the most Americanized city on the island in ways and means, led the crusade against two to one, and has set 150 as the prevailing rate. San Juan, the capital, on the northern side, was slower in scaling down, and paid, for a week after the evacuation, 180 for American gold, 175 for all kinds of our paper certificates, and 165 for our silver. Why they should discriminate against one form of our currency more than another in San Juan remains to be explained. The rate there today has been reduced to a uniform 160, or 10 centavos more is paid at the capital than at Ponce for the American dollar.

At Caguas the military commander demanded 175, notifying the alcalde that all stores would be closed unless this rate was allowed, and so it was paid under protest, until about November 1st. The merchants all rightly insisted that they were injured by being forced to buy their supplies and to exchange their American money in San Juan at the rate of 160, while their selling-price had been unjustly lowered some 10 % by their having to accept American silver at 175 upon demand. Colonel Eddy of the Forty-seventh New York has ordered the alcalde of Caguas to see that the same form of exchange is maintained, based on the precedent set by the Fourth Ohio and the First Kentucky, but the order has not been enforced, and the prevailing rate has become 160.

At the island of Vieques, the exchange has been kept at two to one, by the order of volunteer captains in charge of single companies, though the natives of this island are obliged to purchase in cities like Ponce and San Juan, at a high rate, and sell at home to Americans at a loss of 25 %.

These varying exchanges, pulled down by commercial natives and forced up by military orders, have caused a deep and pervading condition of unrest in the native's mind, as he has no stable medium of exchange, and cannot have one until the Congress of the United States shall have settled this problem.

The money-holder of the island desires that his silver shall remain as near as possible at a par with American silver; the few natives with large debts to pay wish that two to one might be the prevailing rate until the liquidation of their liabilities. Every American soldier is glad to get two pesos for a single dollar, and the postmaster grumbles because American silver is paid in for postage stamps with greater frequency than hitherto, and, in consequence, he is no longer able to pay his board bills in Spanish money, at a decided saving to himself.

It is possible that criticism and scandal may arise from the present monetary condition of the island, and unfortunately the most upright of men in public places are in a position to be questioned as to their disinterestedness and integrity. As an example, it may be said that some 15,000 pesos were placed in the hands of a well-

THE MONEY OF THE ISLAND

known firm of brokers doing business in Puerto Rico, who were selected by the President as Treasury agents, and as a repository of customs collections. This firm agreed to favor all army officers, upon demand, with an exchange of two to one. This they did for several days, and then posted a notice that hereafter 160 would be the rate, explaining to military men that the original amount of Puerto Rican silver deposited with them had become exhausted. It is quite likely that this was true, but if it was not, then this firm, which is only under obligation to return either the sums deposited with them in the original coin or their equivalent — half the amount in United States currency,—has made by the transaction forty centavos on every dollar deposited.

The collectors of customs have kept long lists of names of military officers who desired to take advantage of the two-to-one valuation, and have personally disbursed their funds in exchange for American notes. Much complaint is heard in the ranks that a favored few are receiving this exchange, while the majority are forced to accept the rate set by the native tradespeople. Every customs official and every postmaster is open to the ugly imputation that he is conducting a brokerage business on his own behalf. There is nothing to prevent his doing so.

The prices of many commodities have risen in Puerto Rico, probably owing to the fact that the shopkeepers feel the need of protecting themselves against the new exchange in some way; it may be because of their ability to get more money out of the freer-handed Americans. Both reasons are given by the soldiers who have lived on the island since the occupation, and it is further said that two prices exist, a higher one for the American and a lower one for the native, but the storekeepers deny both assertions.

PUERTO RICO

While it is probably true that the natives desire to reap as great a harvest of money as possible from the American curio-hunter, the matter of supply and demand is naturally controlling the situation. Never before has the demand for almost everything produced in Puerto Rico been so great. The Spanish soldier got eight pesos a month—when he was paid—while the ordinary private in our army gets a little over $15, or, at the prevailing rate of exchange, three times the salary of the Spaniard, and it is paid regularly and spent freely. The Spanish officers received smaller salaries than our officers, and besides had the habit—most disastrous to their tradesmen—of ordering on credit and never paying; on the other hand, our officers are better livers, demand larger meals, and buy everything they see which is new and unique, paying promptly as they go.

The solution of this difficult money problem lies with Congress, and, by quick and decisive action, our legislators may relieve a condition which is fast making the people of our new province dissatisfied.

It may be pointed out that a serious injury would be done the Puertoriqueños if Congress were to legislate upon the financial situation from a standpoint of bullion value. The peso is a little lighter than our dollar, and it is said that it is of less fineness, while its actual bullion value is said to be about 46 cents at the present time. It differs from our dollar, however, weight for weight, fineness for fineness, only something like 10 %.

If the bullion value alone were to be allowed, the money of Puerto Rico would be suddenly contracted by one-half; that is, a people today possessing six million silver pieces, with which they purchase their comforts and pay the laborer his daily wage, would tomorrow be reduced to three million dollars. Men who now are fairly

THE MONEY OF THE ISLAND

well off would then be poor, with but one-half their accumulated savings.

It may be argued that a financial readjustment must be passed through in Puerto Rico, and that prevailing prices will increase or decline to meet changes in money values, but the fact that Puerto Rico has had but six million pesos to carry on the commercial transactions of a population of a million souls, of which amount one-half is held by two banks, should not be lost sight of. The dearth of money has been the curse of the island, and among a large proportion of the poorer element, the primitive method of exchanging commodity for commodity has been resorted to, whereby the poor man suffered, as usual, being forced to take, in return for his agricultural products, whatever might be offered him, in manufactured articles, by his more opulent neighbor, the tradesman.

Under such circumstances, any policy which tends to still further decrease the purchasing power of their silver, or contract their circulating medium, must do a serious injustice to the natives of this island, to whom we offer the protection of a liberal government. It also means the crushing out of commercial activity among the indigenous population, and the aggrandizement of every monied American who may desire to invest his capital in this rich and fertile region.

As financiers, are we willing to further oppress a people who have suffered much already at the hands of rapacious rulers? Rather, as generous Americans, we should seek to so legislate as to supply the needs and insure the commercial success of these new wards of our nation.

An equable solution of the problem, and one which may be reached with no particular generosity on the part of our country, lies in reminting, as soon as possible, the Puerto Rican pesos into silver dollars bearing the American eagle. Allowing 386 grains of silver for the Puerto Rican peso and 412½ grains for the American dollar, there is a difference of some 8 %. A fair mintage charge could hardly bring the difference between the two pieces up to more than 15 %. If such a proposition were to be considered and such a law enacted, Puerto Rico would suffer a 15 % depreciation of her currency in remintage, securing in exchange a stable financial system endorsed by the government of the United States.

Unless we repudiate Puerto Rico's silver, any plan which is adopted must necessarily result in the ultimate absorption of the present currency of the island by the United States Treasury. This money will be returned to our Treasury, through the custom-houses and post-offices, at the present high rate of profit to our government —which now receives, through an arbitrary ruling, two pieces of their silver in exchange for each one of its own, though, value for value in bullion, their respective values differ but a few cents—or it will be returned after brokers and bankers and speculators have each secured a margin of gain.

Spain has been held to be a robber because, in 1894, she recoined the Mexican silver dollar in current circulation into a lighter piece bearing her stamp, appropriating the margin for her own enrichment. What argument can be advanced to defend our government against the severest criticism for having, through military power, set an arbitrary rate of exchange, whereby every peso collected at fifty cents by our Treasury may be reminted, after the addition of five cents' worth of silver, into one of our own silver dollars ?

CHAPTER XXI

REVENUES AND TAXES

A CURSORY glance at the revenue system of Puerto Rico, and a comparison of the annual amount raised with the population, would not lead one to believe that the island inhabitants were heavily taxed, but careful study of the commercial and economic condition of affairs reveals the fact that the lightness of the burden is only apparent.

In 1897-98 the " Official Budget " of the island shows a gross revenue of almost 4,000,000 pesos, and an expenditure of something over 3,500,000, or a surplus of nearly 500,000 pesos. Granting the population to be over 800,000 people, the actual central government tax (exclusive of district and municipal taxes) is less than five pesos per capita, as against over $7 per capita in the United States in 1898. It must be remembered, however, that the earning capacity of the poorer 80 per cent. of our citizens is nearly five times as great per capita as in the same proportion of Puerto Rico's population, where the average annual wages are little above 75 pesos. The money in circulation, per capita, in the United States was $24.66 in 1898, while in Puerto Rico, for the same year, it was but seven and a half pesos. We import, of dutiable articles (principally luxuries, purchased by the wealthy), but $5.66 per capita, and pay with these imposts, in normal times, one-third of our federal expenses. In 1896, Puerto Rico imported dutiable commodities (mainly necessities of life) amounting to twenty-two and a half pesos per capita, and paid one-half of the island expenses, or four times as much per head, in money valuation, with only a gain of a proportionate one-sixth in defraying the expenses of the government. We pay the rest of our government expenses principally by internal revenues, except in war times, on luxuries, while the island raises hers by direct taxation on property, personal and real.

As the form of taxation in Puerto Rico and her relation to the home government were similar, in some phases, to those in vogue in our own states, we may compare her revenue proportionately to that of our wealthiest state, New York.

The state tax in New York averages, for state, county, and municipality, about $5 per capita—her state tax alone is about $2.50 for each person. The San Juan district of Puerto Rico, in 1897, raised 598,483 pesos, while the Ponce district collected 287,754 pesos, and Mayaguez a little more than the latter. The writer is informed that, in round numbers, the revenue from the eight districts and seventy-one municipalities is nearly 2,000,000 pesos, which, added to the general revenue already mentioned, brings the total taxation up to 6,000,000 pesos, or some seven and a half pesos per capita. It should be remembered that Spain demanded, for the support of the central government, twice as much money as it takes to support the cities and districts, while in New York the state requires but 14 per cent. for the total expenses, and the remainder is devoted to cities and counties.

Apparently the average yearly tax per head in New York ($15) is double that of the Puertoriqueño (seven and a half pesos); but, to prove the greater tax-paying capacity of New Yorkers, it may be shown that one per-

REVENUES AND TAXES

son in every ten is employed in manufacturing industries alone, as laborer or skilled artisan, and receives an average yearly wage of $600, or $50 a month. For over eight-tenths of the population of Puerto Rico there is now no industrial opportunity, except as agricultural laborers at the low wage of fifty or sixty centavos a day, and then but five months' work in the year. Of this proportion, which represents about 650,000 men, women, and children, not over two-fifths can earn this wage of seventy-five pesos a year. In New York, one-tenth of the population supports one-fourth of the population, with an aggregate wage of about $330,000,000, while in Puerto Rico a little less than one-third of the population supports over three-fourths of the population, with a total wage of 19,500,000 pesos. It is difficult to imagine a more pitiable commercial and industrial condition.

One hundred and fifty thousand people pay the direct taxes of the island and the major portion of the imposts, the very poor people contributing their share only in a head tax, a market tax, and in the purchase of imported cottons and quinine. Less than 50,000 estate-owners probably shoulder one-half the burden of the annual revenue, which would be nearly sixty pesos per capita.

Now as to the items in the island " Budget ": In 1897-98, 1,252,377 pesos were required for the Army; 222,668 pesos for the Navy and Marine; 423,818 pesos for Church and Justice; 878,178 for Public Works; 260,800 for Hacienda, and 498,501 for General Obligations—a total of 3,536,342 pesos. The total revenue was 3,939,500 pesos.

The Army, Navy, and Church cost the people 1,668,-655 pesos (193,610 pesos went to the Church), or nearly one-half the expenses of the island, while for public improvements—for a country in direst need of good roads, better harbors, and transportation facilities—but 878,178 pesos were appropriated, while even then a commensurate expenditure is not evident, the major portion having been expended upon the few military roads, in the salaries of caretakers and laborers. Included in Puerto Rico's obligations were expenses, divided proportionally among the colonies, for supporting the " Ultra Mar " or Colonial Ministry Department at Madrid, and, in recent years, a share of the expenses for carrying on the war with Cuba.

It is difficult to see that the taxes drawn from the sinews of the island were ever of any benefit to her people, the beneficiaries being a great corps of Spanish officials, clerks, soldier police (Orden Publico and Guardia Civil), and priests, who, when their pockets were silver-lined and opportunity offered, returned to the mother country. It is true that the greater portion of the money was spent again in the island by the government's servants, but, even granting this as desirable, there yet remains the fact that the tax-paying public was supporting a vast army of rapacious, shiftless, and often vicious men, whose espionage was rather to be deplored, since it usually led to greater personal hardships.

About one-half the island tax was derived from customs duties, the remainder from a stamp duty on all legal paper (which was sold by authorized officials), and legal documents, such as papers of legislation, corporation, and all official business; a tax on transfers and sales of property and mortgages—one and a half per cent. on sales, one per cent. on mortgages; also a tax on wills running from one-fourth to eight per cent., depending on the relationship between testator and heirs. It may be said here that the recorder of deeds had vested in him power of censorship, which permitted him to deter-

REVENUES AND TAXES

mine whether transfers of property could be legally made. Opponents to the old methods insist that it was a common thing for recorders to grow wealthy in a few years, as it required a bribe with an elastic scale to secure the sanction of the recorder to a sale and transfer of real estate.

The postal and telegraph systems were in the hands of the government, and the collected tariff formed part of the revenues, but the expenditures for maintaining these departments have always been greatly in excess of the receipts, as their principal value seemed to lie in furnishing a host of clerical positions for agents of the government, who acted as spies and kept a close scrutiny over messages and mail matter.

Next there was a direct tax of five per cent. on real estate, the appraising of values being done at San Juan; this valuation also served as a basis for assessing the local district and municipal tax, which amounted to from seven and a half to ten per cent., and lastly a " Cedula Personal," or certificate of identity, which every person was required to have, and which ranged in price (depending upon official or civil position, business, and income) from twenty centavos for peons to twenty-five pesos for those with an income of over 20,000 pesos per annum.

The municipal taxes were raised by fees for licenses on all commercial and industrial pursuits; an " Arvitrios," or charge for market-houses, butchering, and city property; fees on the insurance of public certificates, water rents, public dances and functions, theatrical performances, fines, etc.; also an " Octroi " or duty on consumption—every article used for food, beverage, or fuel was taxed, and the fees paid by the seller. This tax worked a great hardship to the peasant who brought in a few pesos' worth of produce to the markets from his little garden patch in the hills. If the above taxes were not sufficient to meet district and municipal expenses, a final and direct tax on personal and real estate was permissible, up to any percentage necessary to meet the deficiency.

Each municipality had to contribute to the support of an island organization of administrative character, known as the "Deputaccion Provincial," an amount determined by the Governor-General, and apportioned among them according to their population and importance—Ponce's share was, in 1897, 14,326 pesos. This organization had charge of some public works of small importance; the civil institute (a sort of high school, the best on the island), the island insane asylum, an industrial school recently established in connection with an asylum for orphans at San Juan, and the jails; it also had authority to advise the Governor-General on all administrative problems. The major portion of the expenses of this "Deputaccion" and the institutions controlled thereby was met by a government lottery scheme, which, without force, drew forty thousand pesos a month, principally from the pockets of those who could ill afford it.

The cost of gathering the revenues was greatly augmented by a system of separate collection for state and municipal taxes; the state's share being secured by one set of collectors and the town's by another.

At the present time (1898) there is much complaint among island citizens, for the reason that, though the Spanish Orden Publico (common police) of some 2,000 men, and the Guardia Civil (civil guard), who numbered 4,000, ceased to exist as paid organizations at the raising of the United States flag, and the church is no longer supported, the taxes have not been reduced by the new American masters. There will be justice in this criticism when we are able to withdraw our 6,000 soldiers—as we

REVENUES AND TAXES

should do so soon as quiet civil administration intervenes —who are now doing police duty on the island and who cost us, for their support, fully as much per annum as the old Spanish appropriation provided.

The reader who has followed the windings of Puerto Rican taxation will most likely feel, with her citizens, that the burden, compared with the commercial activity and prosperity of the island, has been excessive, and that, when the meager benefits which have accrued to the population in improvements during the past are taken into consideration, they may well claim to have struggled under a galling yoke of oppression.

It is the right of every taxed community to demand that it shall receive, in return for its support of the government represented by an expenditure of sinew and labor, security of person and property and a commensurate advance in ease of living through internal improvements carried on for the good of the most people. None of these blessings have Puertoriqueños ever received at the hands of the parent government, except, perhaps, during a short period at the beginning of the century when, to induce colonization, liberal laws and little taxation prevailed. Instead, the revenues have, for several generations, been almost wholly absorbed in supporting a totally disproportionate civil list, in which almost every position was a sinecure, and a military organization, including common soldiers, Guardia Civil, and Orden Publico, numbering at times over ten thousand men—an army ten times as large in proportion as that which we contemplate in our new army of one hundred thousand men.

CHAPTER XXII

COURTS

AN appreciation of abstract justice has never been cultivated in the Spanish mind, and, in truth, it would be remarkable if there remained more than a rudimentary process in the brain of a colonist of Spain, which responded to impressions of impartial fair play, after laboring under centuries of despotic military government, in which the courts of justice have been used constantly to subserve the ends of governors-general by ridding them of their enemies and in freeing their friends who have lucklessly brought upon themselves popular odium.

The judicial systems of Spain and some other European countries are faulty to the point of viciousness, in that there are no tribunals of law which take precedence over military and civil jurisdiction, vested in the authority of one man who possesses power to appoint and dismiss such judges and court officials as he may see fit. While in Puerto Rico it was possible, in certain cases, to take an appeal to the highest court in Madrid, the obstacles which might be placed in the way of the plaintiff were tremendous, as the Governor-General not only controlled the action of the courts on the island, but was in close and active touch with the government of the mother country.

The island administration of justice was and will be carried on—until Congress acts—by three courts, subject

COURTS

to such modifications in the old plan, by the President, as may best meet the needs of the changed conditions. The first is known as the Justice of the Peace Court, " Juez Municipal," with one in each of the seventy-one municipalities. The judge in this court had jurisdiction over all civil questions in which the matter involved represented 200 pesos or less; in criminal matters authority was limited to the trying of petty offenses, and violation of city ordinances, the maximum penalty which might be imposed being thirty days' imprisonment or a fine of twenty-five pesos. An appeal might be taken from this court to the next higher one, " Juez de Instruccion," whose decision was final.

The justice of the peace was also in charge of the civil registry—the registration of births and marriages. His salary was paid in fees alone, and nominally did not exceed fifty pesos a month, though the office was estimated by outsiders as being worth, under the old régime, from three to five thousand pesos annually.

The second court was presided over by a district judge, " Juez de Primero Instancia y de Instruccion "— " Primero Instancia " relating to civil matters and " de Instruccion " meaning the instruction in criminal matters. The positions were somewhat like our country judgeships.

All suits involving above 200 pesos were tried before this tribunal. The plaintiff must be represented by an attorney and a " Procurador." From the decision an appeal might be taken to the " Audiencia Territorial " at San Juan.

In criminal matters, this court had jurisdiction over all violations of law, but the judge's power was limited to instituting merely summary proceedings, and his finding, with the evidence, must be sent to the higher court,

"Audiencia de la Criminal," as he had no authority to render a verdict or convict. The salary was 3,600 pesos a year.

There were three courts under the designation of "Audiencia de la Criminal," one at San Juan, another at Ponce, and the third at Mayaguez. Each court was composed of three members, a presiding and two associate judges. These courts rendered decisions and could convict in all criminal cases; appeal from them could only be made to Madrid. Trials were public, there was no jury, and in fact a jury is unknown in Spanish law. The legal groundwork was the depositions made before the lower court, though new evidence might be introduced and witnesses summoned. If the evidence was not sufficient in the opinion of the court, the case was quashed. The salary of the presiding judge was 4,000 pesos and that of the associates 3,500 each.

The final appeal in both civil and criminal matters was to the Court of Reviews, "Tribunal de Cassacion," at Madrid. This was done by forwarding all records and depositions. There were five members, and a public prosecutor made all the charges.

Previous to the autonomical decree, all court officials were appointed by the Madrid government or the Governor-General of the island, but, under the autonomy which was granted Puerto Rico in February, 1897, the mantle of patronage fell upon the shoulders of the Provisional Minister of Justice, selected by the Crown. As either power was supreme to appoint or dismiss the men who administered decisions in the courts of law, the system was meretricious in the extreme, and, under these conditions, it is little wonder that influential Puertoriqueños looked upon their courts with contempt, as institutions open to knavish influences, corruption, and bribery;

COURTS

while the poor man trembled with fear lest he fall victim for another's sins, and disappear forever in the dungeons of San Juan. It was possible, under legal rulings, to detain a man in prison, without hearing, indefinitely—"prison prevention," as it was known—with a bail so high that neither he nor his friends could meet it, and to pigeonhole all evidence in the case. Unless powerful friends could be produced at the court in Madrid, a political enemy might thus be buried for the rest of his natural life.

Perhaps the worst example of despotic power ever witnessed in Puerto Rican law was the court known by the misnomer of "Court of Military Justice," established in January, 1891. The ostensible function of this court was to determine criminal offenses of civilians who should be subjected to military trial. Most of the cases tried before this tribunal were founded on alleged insults to individuals in the military organizations, the army, navy, and Guardia Civil. It gave an excellent opportunity for officers to settle old grudges against civilians and not to settle their bills, it being a universal practice for officers to run up store bills which they never paid, and which the tradesman dared not attempt to collect, unless he had a "pull," through fear of summary imprisonment.

The press was also held in check by this court, and it was no uncommon thing for an editor to suffer imprisonment for the slightest offensive allusion to the army; it is asserted by some that, through its aid, systematic bulldozing of private citizens was indulged in, and, when politicians could not reach their enemies by other means, it was easy, by crossing palms with gold, to have them spirited away by the soldiers. The real function of this court was to try cases of incendiarism, brigandage, sedition, and taking up arms against the government.

An example of the working of the district courts in Puerto Rico came under the personal observation of the writer at Utuado, where a man had been arrested, at the instance of an American officer, for obtaining goods under false pretenses. The prisoner—a town marketman—had been furnishing fresh beef to the American soldiers, under contract; the cattle he had obtained from a poor native, and refused to pay for them upon presentation of the poor man's bill, stating that they were for the United States government and the meat had to be furnished free. The cattle-owner, an illiterate man, learned later that he was entitled to compensation and presented a bill the second time, when the butcher, with a few friends, intimidated him by threatening to have him arrested and sent to the prison at San Juan—a threat which kept the victim's lips closed for some weeks. In conversation with American soldiers later, he was not only assured that he was entitled to pay for goods delivered, but advised to report to the officer commanding the garrison. The result was the arrest of the butcher, and the matter came up before the local Spanish judge. Upon the day of the trial, the butcher came into court with the money to liquidate his debt, and with friends who were willing to swear that " he was a good man." The judge immediately declared the case settled, and, when the American officers protested that the man was guilty of an offense against the law, whether he tardily made reparation or not, replied that if a man paid his debt he could no longer be held guilty. For so long has just this method been in vogue, of making men pay under pressure, and considering the case closed when the debt, with added judicial fees, has been settled, that the moral guilt of the situation is not comprehended. Men known to be guilty are held innocent, provided they have suffi-

COURTS

ciently powerful friends to testify that they are " good men." It will take years to eradicate the inherent Spanish trait of considering that any means justifies an end, and to teach our new people the ethical principles upon which law and justice are founded.

CHAPTER XXIII

PAST POLITICAL METHODS

THE word of law, as read in royal decrees and sanctioned by the Spanish Cortes, for the government of Puerto Rico, is as mild as summer zephyrs, and, in the translation of the tender, solicitious, equable edicts voiced by Mother Spain to her child of the western isles, one hears only the dulcet tones of a brooding parent, and expects to find only the nursing hand, guiding the little one toward the full vigor of complete manhood.

The American understands not, or comprehends with difficulty, that the written laws of Spain are but meaningless vaporings, frank only on their surface, created by minds skilled in the euphony of language, and craftily subtle in methods which bastardize the essence of truth. We have of late, however, become extremists in our wholesale denunciation of the Spaniard, and search for scathing, opprobrious adjectives by which we may further revile him.

In point of fact, while for centuries Spain's rule, both at home and in her foreign possessions, has been practically synonymous with all that is vicious in preconcerted and perverted officialism, the little island of Puerto Rico has been free from much of the insatiable oppression which has wrung, from the people of other provinces, a sweat of gold, for the personal enrichment and aggrandizement of unscrupulous officers.

PAST POLITICAL METHODS

In the early periods of active discovery, two and three centuries ago, the Spanish seekers after renown and fame and riches were carrying conquest into the mainland of the western hemisphere, blotting out gentle civilization by the sword, with a hilt of the cross of Christ, in their greed for gold alone. They passed Puerto Rico by as being barren and destitute of rushing waters with a glint of yellow, and devoid of gem-laden aboriginal kings, dwelling in castles veneered with precious metals; it was only a region fair to look upon, and hence, for the past two centuries, little progress has been made in colonization, beyond the killing off of the half-million poor Indians to whom the island had been a happy home.

A government with definite official reports from its administrative departments did not exist in Puerto Rico until after the beginning of the present century. No intelligible returns were made of the custom-house and revenue receipts of the island, though both import and revenue laws were in vogue.

The population in 1778 was roughly estimated to be some eighty thousand people, and it was generally admitted that their needs from the outer world were supplied by contraband traffic. The Governor-General, the military and the civilian officers, were supported by taxes levied on Mexico until 1810, when that country permanently rebelled. The little island was looked upon with very little interest until the day Spain found herself, by repeated revolts of her American colonies, left in possession of only Cuba and Puerto Rico.

In the early years of the century, the island enjoyed broad-gauge laws, in that a royal decree of 1815 fostered emigration by free grants of land to colonists, the area being determined by the number of slaves owned by the settler. He was not subjected to taxation for ten years,

PUERTO RICO

and paid neither import duties on agricultural machinery nor export duties on the products of the soil.

The general laws governing the municipalities and districts were exceedingly liberal, and the inhabitants, instead of being overtaxed, were, to their own detriment and to the future harm of the state, undertaxed, which engendered a spirit of discontent in the people, as greater revenues were demanded from them in after years, proportionate to the public improvements, the population, and the complexity of life.

This wide-open invitation for colonists had the desired effect of relieving the heretofore dormant condition of the island, and, in a space of fifteen years, the population had more than doubled itself, or reached nearly 400,000 souls.

At no time during fifty years, from 1775 to 1825, were the revenues ever adequate for the support of the local government, as the customs duties were unblushingly diverted to the pockets of office-holders; neither could Spain now mulct other possessions to meet the salaries of the military branch of the island, and consequently the poor soldiers often—as in recent times—went unpaid and half-rationed. In 1825 his Majesty the King of Spain found an honorable Governor-General in Don Miguel de la Torre, and, for the first time in the history of the island, it became self-supporting, and the troops were regularly paid and fed.

Smuggling, which was almost universal, was much reduced by the aid of the army, and thieving from the government strong-box, which had been practised with open effrontery and mutual connivance, was curtailed to limits of decency and modesty. While it has been possible, since that time, for officials to grow rapidly rich, so long as they are in power, the undisguised and flagrant abuses have been discontinued.

PAST POLITICAL METHODS

As almost supreme power has been at all times vested in the Governor-General of the island, appeals to the home government against abuses, by those outside the official circle, were freighted with personal danger and were seldom resorted to, as an untoward result might mean the quiet disappearance of the complainant. From 1825 to 1870, abuses slowly became greater—not that taxes in the main became higher per capita, but that discrimination was practised in the levies to such an extent that a once rich landholder in official disfavor might, within a few years, become poverty-stricken, through the machinations of the government machine, which worked as a unit, not with a view to fairly upholding good printed law, but to ruining its enemies and winning the mantle of a fleece of gold.

During the provisional republican government which existed in Spain after the revolution which deposed Isabella II. in 1868, and continued until 1874, when the Queen's son Alphonso was declared king, Puerto Rico enjoyed, under the Moret law, a very liberal scheme of government, vesting in the municipalities civil rights never before possessed by them. In 1875, the light of populistic participation in the affairs of the island again went out, and another law, known as the " Elduayen " (Minister of the Colonies) promulgation, went into effect. The centralization of power was more severe than had hitherto been known, and, while this decree was ostensibly only provisional in character, it continued in force until 1897, when what was termed the Canovas reform scheme was given birth.

Spain at last was becoming frightened at the misbehavior of Cuba, and, fearing that the grumblings of her smaller child, Puerto Rico, might end in still greater disaffection, tried hard to pacify her by promises of self-government. The new laws did not in actuality confer a whit broader field on the governed, for, as before, each municipality was directly dependent for every privilege upon the "Deputaccion," a monarchical organization of island authorities at San Juan, who approved or disapproved municipal action.

The agitators in Puerto Rican legislation recognized their power during Spain's crisis with rebellious Cuba, and, under the plea of sincere loyalty to the home government, but with covert intimations of a possible uprising of the people against existing law, sent a commission, late in 1896, to Madrid to sue for autonomy and home rule.

The members of this commission were its president, Señor Gomez Brioso, leader of the Puerto Rican party, Señor Sabero, leader of the autonomical party in Spain, Señor Matienzo, an island judge, Señor Degetan, and Señor Muñoz Rivera, who was in close touch with the Governor-General.

The Canovas ministry was in power, and from them it was impossible to secure further concessions. Señor Sagasta, however, promised them that, if they would recognize his own party, the Liberals, and work for its future elevation, he would, when in power, give to Puerto Rico the autonomy she so earnestly desired. Several ends were to be subserved by this arrangement; it divided the political opinions of the island between the Conservatives and the Liberals; kept down any impending revolution by throwing the Autonomists into the Liberal party, and finally gave Sagasta a lever upon the island which he had not hitherto possessed. The proposition was agreed to by a majority of the committee of five, though Sabero and Degetan protested against selling themselves to the opposite party in Spain, instead of

PAST POLITICAL METHODS

holding out firmly for recognition of the autonomistic party of Puerto Rico.

Upon the return of this commission to Puerto Rico, an immense mass-meeting was held in the theater at San Juan, a building which is used for all great public demonstrations. Feeling ran high, and fervid, eloquent speeches for and against accepting the Sagasta proposition followed each other in quick succession, the outcome being the dividing of the house against itself and the forming of two parties—one, known as the Liberals, to further the Sagasta interests, and the other antagonistic, the members of which called themselves "Autonomista Puros." The Liberals insisted, with some truth, that the Puros represented only the disgruntled rabble, led by a handful of men who had been given political positions, while the Puros could not find sufficiently strong vituperative epithets by which to express their feelings against men who had again sold, body and soul, a million people who desired to be free, into the sordid clutches of Spain, for the paltry gift of temporary political and material advancement.

The autonomistic scheme contemplated universal suffrage in the election of a Lower House or Legislature, to be composed of thirty-two members representing the eight districts of the island; an Upper Chamber of fifteen Senators, seven of them to be chosen by the Crown and eight of them by popular vote; the Governor-General remained the representative of the Crown, with a Cabinet of six men, which number was afterward reduced to four: the President of the Senate, the Minister of Justice, the Secretary of Finance, and the Secretary of State.

In November, 1897, both Cuba and Puerto Rico were granted autonomy by the Madrid government, and the four cabinet ministers were " provisionally " selected for

Puerto Rico by the Crown, and empowered to organize and put in working order as rapidly as possible, the new laws.

One often hears, in confidential post-prandial talks among American politicians, of clever manipulative tricks on the part of leaders (many of them should make us blush) by which they carry the people with them and undermine their opponents; but the spirit of fair play usually predominates, and, when defeat comes, it is, to all outward appearances, taken gracefully. Not so among Spanish-speaking races, in whose brains and nerves and hearts the spirit of political strife is one of bitter turmoil, engendering hatred so intense, so vile, that it stops short of nothing in unprincipled trickery, and reaches, often, the bitter end in underhand assassination of human impedimenta which block the way to party success.

For centuries the population of Puerto Rico had accepted quietly the dictates of monarchical power as inevitable; the struggle among the populace had been one of individuals after government positions, with their recognized but unlawful perquisites—and, failing in this, hope at least remained of securing friendly recognition which might absolve them from all but nominal taxation, and perhaps from direct persecution—rather than a fight for communal recognition. Autonomy, when it was finally sprung on them, was a veritable firebrand which made a bonfire of all reason among the native Puertoriqueños, who possessed no influence with the government and hated Spaniards—the exemplification of tyranny,—and their few native brethren with official positions, as typifying souls sold for gain. Every native, whether he was high or low, if he could read and write, saw only in the prospective change a chance at last to feed from the government trough, and not the higher principle involved, which might

PAST POLITICAL METHODS

mean the solidarity of a community, whereby, with united purpose, they might act for the betterment of the masses.

It is not likely that the Spanish government meant that the remnants of her colonies should ever control themselves by universal suffrage, and it was distinctly evident, in the preliminary narrowness of the Liberals, that the government still reigned. From the seat of the island control at San Juan, the monarchical representatives began their campaign by solidifying their ranks through the appointment of Liberal alcaldes and councilmen throughout the seventy-one municipalities, giving a few minor positions to Autonomists who weakened in their cause, and were willing to be led blindly in the King's interests.

The Autonomists, however, had awakened, and, taking courage in numbers, dared to begin a crusade of their own. It should be remembered that but sixteen per cent. of the 800,000 inhabitants of the island can read or write, and that the great unlettered mass cared nothing about the new movement, beyond the fact that the illiterate always feel an ill will toward the governing class, and that they hated Spaniards and wealthy men as representing the taskmaster. Their dormant feelings could therefore, if fired at all, be inflamed against the Liberals, and upon this mass the Puros worked, delivering open-air speeches, lurid in the pyrotechnics of language.

It became evident to the Governor-General that something must be done to pacify and placate the Puros. The leaders of the opposition party were called together and given public positions, with the understanding that they were to bring their party into line and coalesce it with the Liberals. This was accomplished and harmony seemed so assured that the now Union party held a great festal gathering on the 11th of February, 1898, which was known as " Glory Day."

PUERTO RICO

The Puros, who had been led to believe that they should be allowed to share the patronage throughout the island, now made demand for representation in the various municipal councils, but Señor Rivera, the Liberal leader, in impassioned speeches exhibited how absurd it would be to distract the public attention at the present time from the patriotic issue at stake, and again disturb the balance in a now united party, which was cemented by the bond of fraternity, and whose eyes were cast forward as one man toward the long-sought goal of individual freedom. The Puros, in their desire for pecuniary aggrandizement, had defeated their own ends.

Two delegates were sent from every municipality to elect permanent secretaries of the cabinet, and it is said by the Puros that these delegates were to be equally divided in sentiment, Puros and Liberals; but, whether this be so or not, the paper ballot which was cast in the convention was overwhelmingly Liberal, and this party had scored the first victory for the Madrid government.

The whole scheme of autonomy and faction fights came to a sudden end at the landing of the American forces at Guanica, and never got farther than the selection of the cabinet. It is said that the convention assembled became panic-stricken, on hearing the news that our soldiers were advancing toward San Juan, and adjourned *sine die*.

No attempt has since been made to resurrect this infant, autonomy, who died in the borning, except at the city of Ponce, which is always progressive. When General Wilson reorganized the municipality of Ponce, the Ponceños were assured that they should have complete control of municipal administration, and, acting upon this assurance, the Board of Councilmen presented a memorial to General Henry, who was at that time the

PAST POLITICAL METHODS

military head of the southern district, setting forth the privileges which were to be granted them under the contemplated autonomy, and prayed approval. On September 29, 1898, General Henry endorsed the memorial favorably and Ponceños were happy; but on October 18, 1898—only twenty days later—General John R. Brooke, in military control of the island, cast a gloom over the sunny landscape of promising reform, by issuing his General Order No. 1, in which he said, in Article ix.: "The provincial and municipal laws . . . will be enforced unless they are incompatible with the changed conditions of Puerto Rico, in which event they may be suspended by the Department Commander. They will be administered substantially as they were before the cession to the United States." This order, emanating from a higher military authority than General Henry, relegated them to pre-existing Spanish law, and it was carried out, though Ponce commissions waited upon the Commanding General, and sued for approval of their plan of municipal autonomy. The Alcalde and Board of Councilmen resigned. The situation was complicated by the fact that General Brooke had around him, as his chief advisers, the former alleged autonomistic cabinet, who represented, in reality, Spain's interests, but who had, under the changed conditions, espoused the American cause, and become ardent workers and sympathizers in the new régime.

The question which arises in the American mind is whether or not the people of Puerto Rico are fitted, at the present time, for the acceptance and fulfilment of the duties involved in universal suffrage. Are they capable of governing themselves, and is their mental and moral condition such as to justify their entering into statehood? There are many opinions, pro and con, upon this subject,

PUERTO RICO

but the majority of the answers, among the inhabitants of the island themselves, are in the negative. There are over 800,000 people, eighty-four per cent. of whom can neither read nor write; men, women, and children who, in generations dead, have never taken the slightest interest in public affairs, and in the living generation cannot, in the depth of their ignorance, comprehend the primary elements of self-government. Of the 100,000 left who can read and write, less than one-half are said to possess, by deed of title, almost the entire island. At least one-third of these have, at different times, held government offices, either municipal or central. None of them, except the scattered few who have been educated in the United States, have ever been in intimate contact with the working of republican forms of government, while every man who has held a Spanish position is conversant and thoroughly imbued with the spirit of a spoils-system combination so extensive that it puts to shame the most halcyon days of metropolitan aldermen in America.

The writer has no wish to discredit the earnest, honest men of the island, who look forward to American methods as a saving grace, and incidentally it may be remarked that the majority of the educated population, whether they have or have not hitherto been identified with Spanish methods, recognize the inherent weakness which existed under the old administration, and consider the change for the better. It must be plainly stated, however, that there is not today a sufficient proportion of the population versed in the administration of republican forms of government to warrant the extension of universal suffrage.

It may be pointed out that, in the late autonomical elections, the registration numbered less than 100,000, though both Liberals and Puros exerted every effort

PAST POLITICAL METHODS

toward securing allies, and that, at the election, less than fifty thousand votes were polled, or less than one-fourth of the number entitled to franchise.

The primary lessons in control of affairs by popular voice, which will lead finally to complete statehood, must begin in the municipality. Ponce made a good start, which was nipped in the bud. It has been said that those in city power desired but to sell franchises with perquisites to themselves. Even so; we are familiar, in this country, with corporate deals which feathered nests with as many millions as Ponceños would secure thousands in the installation of industrial enterprises. If decent municipal purity cannot be secured in Puerto Rico within the next decade, we have indeed shouldered for America a sodden load.

Ten years of public-school education—compulsory if necessary—should reduce illiteracy to fifty per cent. ; ten years of American capitalization of island enterprises and immigration to foster the industries should add a hundred thousand Americans to the population, fitted to instruct, if not control, future legislation. Possibly then we may speak of the state of Puerto Rico and add another star to our flag.

CHAPTER XXIV

HISTORICAL SKETCH

HISTORIANS differ as to the actual date of the landing of Columbus on the shores of Puerto Rico, and they also differ as to the spot upon which he first set his foot; suffice it to say, however, that, upon his second voyage in 1493, to newly-discovered America, he found the little island and landed, either upon the northern coast near San Juan, or at Aguadilla on the northwest coast. It is related that, not finding the natives friendly, he set sail again and proceeded farther to the westward.

Don Juan Ponce de Leon accompanied him on this expedition, and was much impressed with the beauty of the island, returning finally in 1508, after many wanderings, to take possession of Puerto Rico. In 1510 the first town, called Caparra—now known as Pueblo Viejo,—was built near the present site of San Juan, and in 1511 the towns of Aguada and San German were started.

The Indians—who were estimated at 600,000 souls under a chief, Caciqui Agueynaba—were at first very friendly, but Spanish oppression and desire for gold and slaves soon caused them to turn against their "immortal" conquerors in serious revolt, and for a while it looked as if the colonists would be blotted out of existence. Superior arms and military science finally prevailed, and, a century later, these simple aboriginal folk, driven like

HISTORICAL SKETCH

oxen under the yoke and ravaged by disease, had become nearly extinct.

Puerto Rico has been the theater of many fierce attacks by foreign powers, all of which were repelled—with greater or less success—up to the period of American occupation, and it is a mooted question whether our first army of occupation would not have been wiped out, if it had not been for the timely arrival of notice of the protocol, before any attempt was made to capture the Spanish positions at the impregnable passes of Aybonito and Guayama. In 1519, Sir Thomas Pert and Sebastian Cabot harried these Spanish possessions; in 1529, the French privateers destroyed the town of San German; Hawkins, Raleigh, and Drake—freebooters and slavers under royal commissions of England—plundered and sacked Spanish colonies at every opportunity during the latter part of the sixteenth century; and in 1595, Drake made an onslaught on San Juan resulting in the almost complete destruction of the town. The great fortifications of Morro were, after this, hastily carried to completion. The Earl of Cumberland, in 1598, captured the castle and city of San Juan, but an epidemic of tropical fever broke out among his men, and he was forced to release his hold. The Dutch, in 1615, played a part in invasion, under General Baldwin Henry, but were driven away with considerable loss and without capturing Morro castle.

For a quarter of a century, between 1625 and 1650, pirates and filibusters worked great havoc to the early Spanish colonies, and in consequence many of the colonists returned to Spain. The British again, in 1678, attacked San Juan, but their fleet was almost wholly destroyed by a storm which drove the vessels upon the rocky coast. In 1702, another British squadron landed at

Arecibo, but was repelled, and, in 1797, the most formidable British invasion yet attempted was set on foot, when Sir Ralph Abercrombie, with 10,000 men, laid siege to San Juan and Aguadilla; but Morro castle and the great stone defenses at the capital had been completed and could not be taken. Since Abercrombie's repulse, no warlike demonstration had been made before San Juan, until the bombardment by our navy in 1898.

APPENDIX

EXTRACTED FROM

"TRADE OF PUERTO RICO." BY FRANK H. HITCHCOCK, CHIEF, SECTION OF FOREIGN MARKETS, U. S. DEPARTMENT OF AGRICULTURE, 1898

AGRICULTURAL IMPORTS OF PUERTO RICO IN 1894 AND 1895

ARTICLES IMPORTED.	CALENDAR YEARS.			
	1894.		1895.	
	Quantities.	Values.	Quantities.	Values.
ANIMAL MATTER.				
Animals, live:				
Asses..................number	62	$1,496	....	....
Cattle................... do	38	1,232	....	....
Horses.................. do	9	1,448	1	$241
Total........................	....	4,176	....	241
Animal products:				
Bristles and hair..........pounds	1,140	209	291	53
Dairy products—				
Butter...................pounds	298,129	57,418	365,835	70,459
Cheese................... do	1,322,351	347,289	1,286,178	337,790
Total.................. do	1,620,480	404,707	1,652,013	408,249
Feathers—				
For ornament...........pounds	141	926	141	926
Other .... do	655	960	743	1,089
Total................. do	796	1,886	884	2,015
Glue and albumens.........pounds	27,044	3,433	19,330	2,454
Grease.................... do	14,061	616	37,908	1,660
Gut, dried................ do	1,448	9,510	752	4,936
Hides and skins............ do	6,781	593	....	....

PUERTO RICO

ARTICLES IMPORTED.	CALENDAR YEARS.			
	1894.		1895.	
	Quantities.	Values.	Quantities.	Values.
ANIMAL MATTER—*Continued.*				
Meat products—				
Bacon, hams, pork, and lard, pounds	8,678,006	$1,139,554	9,706,556	$1,274,618
Jerked beef............do	1,037,496	63,578	2,272,249	139,245
Meat, pickled..........do	33,426	2,194	90,769	5,960
Poultry and game......do	251	33	....	....
Other................do	1,016,464	88,985	1,281,230	112,163
Total................do	10,765,643	1,294,344	13,350,804	1,531,986
Wool, raw..........pounds	392	144	309	122
All other animal products.......	....	315	....	322
Total animal products........	....	1,715,757	....	1,951,797
Total animal matter..........	....	1,719,933	....	1,952,038
VEGETABLE MATTER.				
Breadstuffs:				
Cereals—				
Wheat..............bushels	....	....	11	17
Other..............pounds	1,171,068	20,504	237,182	4,152
Total....................	....	20,504	....	4,169
Flour—				
Wheat ....barrels	238,794	1,434,075	170,460	1,023,694
Other................do	17,785	76,292	1,347	5,779
Total................do	256,579	1,510,367	171,807	1,029,473
Bread, biscuits, pastes for soups, and all other preparations of, used as food..............pounds	1,691,138	151,196	1,359,874	110,375
Total breadstuffs.............	....	1,682,067	....	1,144,017
Canned goods..........pounds	563,373	221,938	453,199	178,536
Chocolate and sweetmeats.....do	437,143	153,076	212,620	74,454
Cocoa, or cacao..............do	108,214	28,420	87,561	22,996
Fibers, vegetable:				
Cotton.............pounds	41,057	4,673	14,811	1,686
Hemp, and tow of ....do	7,425	455	2,562	157
Manila, jute, and other vegetable fibers..............do	....	....	4,076	143
Total.................do	48,482	5,128	21,449	1,986
Forage and bran..........pounds	11,605	152	27,862	366
Fruits....................do	1,039,970	45,521	975,776	40,781
Indigo and cochineal........do	110	72	46	31
Madder, etc..............do	221,558	14,547	328,718	21,583
Malt liquors and cider:				
In bottles..........gallons	135,497	103,940	139,803	107,243
In other receptacles......do	2,479	1,359	....	....
Total................do	137,976	105,299	139,803	107,243
Oils, vegetable:				
Cocoanut, palm-nut, and other heavy oils..............pounds	9,356	736	6,876	541

APPENDIX

ARTICLES IMPORTED.	CALENDAR YEARS.			
	1894.		1895.	
	Quantities.	Values.	Quantities.	Values.
VEGETABLE MATTER—*Continued*.				
Olive—				
In bottles................pounds	53,173	$9,310	28,188	$4,935
In other receptacles....... do	2,018,552	194,382	3,496,161	336,672
Total.................. do	2,071,725	203,692	3,524,349	341,607
Other.....................pounds	323,096	38,185	307,558	36,349
Total vegetable oils..... do	2,404,177	242,613	3,838,783	378,497
Opium, jalap, resin, and scammony, pounds	291	732	86	216
Rice........................... do	72,674,540	2,226,763	74,145,046	2,271,819
Saffron.................... do	459	4,416	1,078	104
Seeds:				
Oleaginous................pounds	11,916	469	9,751	384
Other..................... do	9,777	128	72,078	947
Total.................. do	21,693	597	81,829	1,331
Spices, not including saffron...pounds	126,442	27,684	190,911	42,080
Spirits, distilled:				
Alcohol and brandy........gallons	4,426	3,234	6,088	4,448
Liqueurs, cognac, and other compound spirits—				
In bottles..............gallons	47,977	70,102	28,522	41,674
In other receptacles...... do	77,849	73,937	44,657	42,413
Total.................. do	125,826	144,039	73,179	84,087
Total distilled spirits.... do	130,252	147,273	79,267	88,535
Starch, dextrin, and glucose...pounds	173,437	9,110	67,838	3,564
Tea........................ do	247	254	262	270
Tobacco, leaf................ do			38,261	8,709
Vegetables, including pulse:				
Pulse, dried...............pounds	5,356,911	152,413	3,595,528	102,299
Vegetables, pickled or otherwise preserved..................pounds	770,349	134,878	555,824	97,317
Other..................... do	12,711,566	222,563	11,482,525	201,044
Total.................. do	18,838,826	509,854	15,633,877	400,660
Wines:				
Champagne or sparkling.....gallons	1,243	11,350	486	4,437
Still wines—				
Made from grapes—				
In bottles............... do	19,142	69,924	9,128	33,345
In other receptacles..... do	49,297	90,037	15,732	28,733
Other -				
In bottles............... do	19,354	21,209	41,640	45,632
In other receptacles..... do	1,050,758	345,547	971,498	319,389
Total wines............ do	1,139,794	537,967	1,038,484	431,536
Total vegetable matter.........		5,963,463		5,219,314
Total agricultural imports......		7,683,416		7,171,352

PUERTO RICO

NON-AGRICULTURAL IMPORTS OF PUERTO RICO IN 1894 AND 1895

	Calendar Years.			
ARTICLES IMPORTED.	1894.		1895.	
	Quantities.	Values.	Quantities.	Values.
	Pounds.		*Pounds.*	
Cotton fabrics	5,498,534	$2,932,921	3,791,411	$2,070,667
Fish and shellfish, fresh, salted, and otherwise preserved	26,046,046	1,591,865	30,339,905	1,918,107
Wood, and manufactures of	....	1,391,766	....	840,511
Leather, and manufactures of	....	877,153	....	711,417
Tobacco, and manufactures of	466,143	409,617	790,317	692,333
Iron and steel, and manufactures of	13,541,931	769,860	11,884,866	658,413
Fabrics of hemp, flax, jute, manila, etc.	1,982,765	412,549	2,364,135	408,974
Machinery and apparatus	3,227,002	296,629	3,350,354	344,879
Soap	4,858,822	212,679	5,678,817	248,571
Paper and pasteboard, and manufactures of	3,680,280	305,043	2,376,014	196,197
Mineral oils, crude and refined	5,630,004	122,776	11,355,094	169,629
Cotton yarn and thread	166,610	145,856	177,013	154,964
Woolens	181,218	262,648	107,574	154,947
Paraffin, stearin, wax, spermaceti, and manufactures of	1,422,513	223,795	970,121	151,995
Glass and glassware	2,734,836	152,430	2,503,617	125,688
Coal and coke	37,715,180	90,797	51,729,658	124,536
Silk fabrics	28,925	202,850	15,009	98,786
Hats and caps	....	155,551	....	82,855
Chemicals, drugs, and medicines	1,867,335	85,283	1,452,829	79,379
Marble and other stone, cement, lime, and plaster	4,305,693	64,590	4,738,646	70,061
Dyes, dyestuffs, and varnishes	793,169	92,336	543,847	64,206
Earthen-, stone-, and chinaware	1,792,894	100,122	2,244,228	58,520
Copper, brass, and bronze, and manufactures of	106,523	40,545	101,084	34,096
Books, music, prints, maps, engravings, etc.	89,404	33,128	65,016	25,380
Carriages, cars, and other vehicles	....	10,993	....	8,841
Fans	8,534	8,196	6,945	6,660
Ships and boats	....	22,612	....	1,158
All other non-agricultural imports	....	388,330	....	162,331
Total non-agricultural imports	....	11,402,920	....	9,664,101

APPENDIX

AGRICULTURAL EXPORTS (DOMESTIC) OF PUERTO RICO IN 1894 AND 1895

ARTICLES EXPORTED.		1894. Quantities.	1894. Values.	1895. Quantities.	1895. Values.
ANIMAL MATTER.					
Animals, live:					
Cattle	number	4,306	$166,212	3,674	$141,816
Horses	do	56	1,081	52	1,004
Sheep	do	46	266	....	....
Game-cocks	do	54	104	188	363
Total		....	167,663	....	143,183
Animal products:					
Hides	pounds	762,197	63,389	646,884	53,799
Honey	do	....	....	2,679	587
Horns	do	6,118	134	661	20
Meat scraps	do	....	....	9,994	219
Tallow	do	66,800	2,924	20,492	897
Total animal products		....	66,447	....	55,522
Total animal matter		....	234,110	....	198,705
VEGETABLE MATTER.					
Breadstuffs: Maize	bushels	56,205	68,885	56,633	69,410
Cocoa, or cacao	pounds	12,425	2,175	11,202	1,961
Coffee	do	50,507,159	11,496,082	40,243,693	9,159,985
Fruits and nuts:					
Fruits—					
Mangoes	number	300	3	....	....
Oranges	do	47,000	114	1,444,038	3,484
Pineapples	do	4,242	287	35,224	2,380
Preserved, in sugar or otherwise,	pounds	1,579	553	999	386
Total fruits		....	957	....	6,250
Nuts: Cocoanuts	number	516,817	9,974	239,889	4,630
Total fruits and nuts		....	10,931	....	10,880
Ginger	pounds	....	....	2,429	106
Hedionda *	do	....	....	1,087	47
Oil, bayberry	gallons	24	347	95	1,390
Peanuts	pounds	....	....	2,535	111
Pulse, dried	do	....	....	12,707	362
Spirits, distilled:					
Anisette brandy	gallons	264	251	....	....
Bay rum	do	7,913	4,047	12,544	6,414
Rum	do	6,585	2,406	11,938	3,052
Total	do	14,762	6,704	24,482	9,466
Starch	pounds	....	....	42,121	1,844
Sugar and molasses:					
Molasses	pounds	15,957,253	244,466	35,219,823	539,571
Sugar	do	106,723,699	3,169,895	132,147,277	3,905,741
Total	do	122,680,952	3,414,361	167,367,100	4,445,312
Tobacco, leaf	pounds	3,369,616	619,474	3,665,051	673,787
Total vegetable matter		....	15,618,959	....	14,374,661
Total agricultural exports		....	15,853,069	....	14,573,366

* A small bean used as a substitute for coffee.

PUERTO RICO

QUANTITY AND VALUE OF MERCHANDISE IMPORTED IN FIVE YEARS END
AGRICULTUI

ARTICLES IMPORTED.	1893.		1894.	
	Quantities.	Values.	Quantities.	Values.
ANIMAL MATTER.				
Animals, live (other than cattle, horses, and sheep)...................................	....	$3	....	....
Animal products:				
Beeswax......................pounds	....	....	....	....
Feathers and downs, crude................	....	....	....	....
Honey......................gallons	380	266	550	$205
Total animal products.............	....	266	....	205
Total animal matter................	....	269	....	205
VEGETABLE MATTER.				
Chocolate, other than confectionery and sweetened chocolate.......................pounds	....	....	....	....
Coffee................................. do	91,906	23,814	372,427	81,226*
Fruit plants, tropical and semi-tropical........	....	220	....	....
Fruits and nuts:				
Fruits—				
Bananas...........................	....	....	....	4
Oranges...........................	....	1,563	....	10
Prepared or preserved fruits..........	....	23	....	648
Other fruits ‡.......................	....	5,948	....	981
Total fruits.......................	....	7,534	....	1,643
Nuts—				
Cocoanuts.........................	....	20,680	....	14,192
Other nuts........................	....	....	....	....
Total nuts.......................	....	20,680	....	14,192
Total fruits and nuts.................	....	28,214	....	15,835
Oils, vegetable:				
Fixed or expressed, except olive...........	....	....	....	....
Volatile or essential................pounds	458	1,162	....	....
Total...............................	....	1,162	....	....
Plants, trees, shrubs, vines, etc............	....	....	....	....
Seeds (except linseed or flaxseed)............	....	634	....	....
Spices, unground (except pepper, black or white, and nutmegs)................pounds	18,800	496	2,658	243
Spirits, distilled:				
Brandy......................proof gallons	....	....	....	....
Other............................ do	15	27	35	46
Total....................... do	15	27	35	46

* Not separately stated. ‡ One year only—1893.

APPENDIX

JNITED STATES FROM PUERTO RICO DURING THE
30, 1897
:TS

1895.		1896.		1897.		Annual average, 1893–1897.	
Quantities.	Values.	Quantities.	Values.	Quantities.	Values.	Quantities.	Values.
....	....	....	....	....	$10	....	$3
....	....	....	....	80	19	16	4
....	....	....	....	....	10	....	2
....	....	....	....	225	113	231	116
....	....	....	....	....	142	....	122
....	....	....	....	....	152	....	125
....	....	....	....	94	23	19	5
66,782	$11,724	159,649	$24,101	133,083	22,489	164,769	32,671
....	*	....	*	....	*	....	†220
....	....	....	....	....	47	....	10
....	5,472	....	2,442	....	5,711	....	3,040
....	21	....	58	....	212	....	192
....	2,027	....	381	....	486	....	1,965
....	7,520	....	2,881	....	6,436	....	5,207
....	8,390	....	7,571	....	14,321	....	13,030
....	....	....	....	....	19	....	4
....	8,390	....	7,571	....	14,340	....	13,034
....	15,910	....	10,452	....	20,796	....	18,241
....	....	....	....	....	40	....	8
....	155	....	....	....	438	92	351
....	155	....	....	....	478	....	359
....	142	....	....	....	....	....	28
....	....	....	....	....	....	....	127
....	....	....	750	71	2,743	50	4,990	172
7	17	....	....	....	....	2	3
5	10	....	34	28	2,507	1,257	519	274
12	27	....	34	28	2,507	1,257	521	277

‡ Including nuts, free of duty.

PUERTO RICO

QUANTITY AND VALUE OF MERCHANDISE IMPORTED IN FIVE YEARS END
AGRICULTU1

ARTICLES IMPORTED.	1893.		1894.	
	Quantities.	Values.	Quantities.	Values.
VEGETABLE MATTER—*Continued*				
Sugar and molasses:				
Molasses............gallons	2,502,666	$708,905	2,554,265	$630,370
Sugar—				
Not above No. 16, Dutch standard—				
Beet sugar............pounds	....	....	....	....
Other............ do	99,578,182	3,227,522	75,484,143	2,392,514
Above No. 16, Dutch standard, do	39,729	1,411	61,887	1,537
Total sugar............ do	99,617,911	3,228,933	75,546,030	2,394,051
Total sugar and molasses............	....	3,937,838	....	3,024,421
Tobacco, leaf, not suitable for cigar wrappers, pounds	....	....	...	....
Vegetables:				
Pickles and sauces............	....	....	....	....
Other, in their natural state............	....	5	....	....
Total............	....	5	....	....
Wines other than sparkling:				
In bottles............dozen	4	39	1	12
In casks............gallons	....	....	141	58
Total............	....	39	....	70
Total vegetable matter............	....	3,992,449	....	3,121,841
Total agricultural imports............	....	3,992,718	....	3,122,046

APPENDIX

'HE UNITED STATES FROM PUERTO RICO DURING THE
UNE 30, 1897—*Continued*
RODUCTS—*Continued*

1895.		1896.		1897.		Annual average, 1893–1897.	
Quantities.	Values.	Quantities.	Values.	Quantities.	Values.	Quantities.	Values.
2,277,346	$460,129	2,256,073	$520,275	2,639,134	$470,532	2,445,897	$558,042
....	....	238	10	....	....	48	2
56,352,522	994,073	81,582,572	1,707,308	86,607,317	1,577,911	79,920,947	1,979,866
432	11	....	....	....	....	20,409	592
56,352,954	994,084	81,582,810	1,707,318	86,607,317	1,577,911	79,941,404	1,980,460
....	1,454,213	....	2,227,593	....	2,048,443	....	2,538,502
....	....	....	....	2,390	450	478	90
....	....	....	....	....	3	....	1
....	....	....	....	....	....	....	1
....	....	....	....	....	3	....	2
....	....	2	8	30	132	7	38
....	....	....	....	123	46	53	21
....	....	....	8	....	178	....	59
....	1,482,171	....	2,262,253	....	2,094,167	....	2,590,576
....	1,482,171	....	2,262,253	....	2,094,319	....	2,590,701

PUERTO RICO

QUANTITY AND VALUE OF MERCHANDISE IMPORTED INTO YEARS ENDED

NON-AGRICULTURAL

ARTICLES IMPORTED.	1893.		1894.	
	Quantities.	Values.	Quantities.	Values.
Articles, the growth, produce, etc., of the United States, returned (except distilled spirits)...	....	$1,399	....	$4,512
Books, music, maps, engravings, etc...........	....	25	....	196
Brass, and manufactures of.....................	....	8	....	....
Chemicals, drugs, and dyes:				
Gums..	....	....	....	231
Other..	....	3,629	....	2,005
Total	....	3,629	....	2,236
Clocks and watches: Watches, and parts of...	....	40	....	....
Coal, bituminous.......................tons	181	450	....	....
Coal tar, crude, and pitch of coal tar....barrels	5	30	....	....
Copper, pigs, bars, ingots, old, and other unmanufactured.............................pounds	....	....	....	....
Fertilizers: Guano......................tons	1	11	....	....
Glass and glassware: Bottles, vials, demijohns, carboys, etc , empty and filled...............	....	4	....	....
Household goods and personal effects and wearing apparel in use............................	....	300	....	101
Iron and steel, and manufactures of:				
Scrap iron and steel, fit only to be remanufactured............................tons	6	71	....	....
Manufactures of iron and steel—				
Machinery, n. e. s.....................	....	....	....	30
Other.................................	....	....	....	500
Total	6	71	....	530
Metals, metal compositions, and manufactures of n. e. s., except bronze.......................	....	....	....	....
Paper, and manufactures of.......................	....	....	....	50
Perfumery, cosmetics, and all toilet preparations..	....	8,654	....	5,447
Salt.....................................pounds	....	....	....	....
Shells of all kinds, unmanufactured.............	....	....	....	411
Stamps...	....	*	....	*
Straw, manufactures of.............................	....	....	....	....
Wood, and manufactures of:				
Unmanufactured—				
Cabinet wood, other than mahogany..	....	*	....	*
Other unmanufactured................	....	1,062	....	80
Manufactures of—				
Cabinetware or house furniture.........	....	....	....	....
Other manufactures of.................	....	222	....	....
Total wood, and manufactures of...	....	1,284	....	80
All other articles...................................	....	....	....	25
Total non-agricultural imports......	....	15,905	....	13,588

* Not separately stated.   † Annual average, 1896 1897.

APPENDIX

THE UNITED STATES FROM PUERTO RICO DURING THE FIVE JUNE 30, 1897—*Continued*
PRODUCTS

1895.		1896.		1897.		Annual average, 1893–1897.	
Quantities.	Values.	Quantities.	Values.	Quantities.	Values.	Quantities.	Values.
....	$5,162	....	$18,982	....	$76,231	....	$21,257
....	50	....	165	....	....	....	87
....	....	....	381	....	....	....	73
....	....	....	....	....	....	....	46
....	1,192	....	2,727	....	1,113	....	2,133
....	1.192	....	2,7·7	....	1,1·3	....	2,179
....	....	....	....	....	....	....	8
195	488	....	....	5	18	76	191
....	....	....	....	....	....	1	6
....	....	1,000	70	....	....	200	14
....	....	....	....	....	....	....	2
....	....	....	....	....	4	....	2
....	250	....	523	....	50	....	245
....	....	....	....	....	....	1	14
....	....	....	....	....	....	....	6
....	....	....	617	....	20	....	228
....	....	....	617	....	20	1	248
....	85	....	....	....	22	....	21
....	....	....	....	....	....	....	10
....	11,476	....	8,784	....	7,459	....	8,364
1,200,000	1,613	....	....	....	....	240,000	323
....	2,072	....	1,747	....	1,205	....	1,087
....	*	....	10	....	4	....	†7
....	....	....	48	....	....	....	10
....	937	....	149	....	539	....	‡542
....	....	....	....	....	40	....	236
....	655	....	....	....	....	....	131
....	111	....	197	....	....	....	106
....	1,703	....	346	....	579	....	798
....	250	....	....	....	....	....	55
....	24,341	....	34,400	....	86,705	....	34,988

‡ Annual average, 1895–1897.

PUERTO RICO

QUANTITY AND VALUE OF DOMESTIC MERCHANDISE RICO DURING THE FIVE YEARS
AGRICULTURAL

ARTICLES EXPORTED.	1893.		1894.	
	Quantities.	Values.	Quantities.	Values.
ANIMAL MATTER.				
Animals, live:				
Horses....................number	....	....	....	....
Mules........................ do	....	....	....	....
Other, including fowls............	....	$24	....	$30
Total................................	....	24	....	30
Animal products:				
Dairy products—				
Butter....................pounds	63,835	9,780	139,774	21,456
Cheese...................... do	244,884	28,721	130,545	16,568
Milk........................	....	544	....	605
Total................................	....	39,045	....	38,629
Glue......................pounds	1,142	142	1,623	225
Grease, grease scraps, and all soap stock...	....	354	....	345
Hair, and manufactures of............	....	21	....	....
Hides and skins, other than furs....pounds	....	293	....	34
Honey..............................	....	332	....	....
Meat products:				
Beef products—				
Beef, canned...........pounds	4,045	354	6,166	509
Beef, salted or pickled..... do	80,360	3,894	79,300	4,159
Beef, other cured.......... do	....	....	....	....
Tallow.................. do	11,100	778	3,305	171
Total................................	....	5,026	....	4,839
Hog products—				
Bacon...................pounds	180,341	14,090	230,976	19,038
Hams...................... do	801,868	99,754	799,812	98,695
Pork, pickled.............. do	3,318,600	282,980	4,480,400	360,684
Lard...................... do	3,239,094	306,809	3,979,784	343,573
Total................................	....	703,633	....	821,990
Oleomargarine, or imitation butter, pounds	43,670	5,458	76,534	10,182
Other meat products.................	....	10,895	....	17,723
Total meat products............	....	725,012	....	854,734
Oils, animal, not elsewhere specified—				
Lard oil...................gallons	289	180	210	154
Other, except whale and fish... do	154	120	739	425
Total................... do	443	300	949	579
Total animal products..............	....	765,499	....	894,546
Total animal matter.................	....	765,523	....	894,576

APPENDIX

:PORTED FROM THE UNITED STATES TO PUERTO
;DED JUNE 30, 1897
ODUCTS

1895.		1896.		1897.		Annual average, 1893–1897.	
Quantities.	Values.	Quantities.	Values.	Quantities.	Values.	Quantities.	Values.
7	$1,125	11	$1,570	19	$4,590	7	$1,457
....	....	....	....	1	300	....	60
....	....	....	92	....	....	....	29
....	1,125	....	1,662	....	4,890	....	1,546
102,914	12,448	20,655	2,754	33,525	4,009	72,141	10,090
25,319	3,038	25,404	2,946	26,478	3,022	90,526	10,859
....	667	....	737	....	729	....	656
....	16,153	....	6,437	....	7,760	....	21,605
970	115	2,521	353	2,685	323	1,788	232
....	564	....	603	....	278	....	429
....	....	....	....	....	....	....	4
5,465	336	1,800	145	....	....	....	162
....	....	....	....	....	....	....	66
1,584	123	2,112	163	2,496	192	3,281	268
35,625	1,781	32,925	1,606	61,100	2,905	57,862	2,869
....	....	....	....	86,000	4,055	17,200	811
3,990	234	7,591	411	4,565	256	6,110	370
....	2,138	....	2,180	....	7,408	....	4,318
399,222	29,001	295,396	19,186	618,015	33,233	344,790	22,910
680,411	70,967	985,718	92,549	888,945	79,369	831,351	88,267
3,285,200	221,848	4,495,550	343,311	3,450,200	152,411	3,805,990	252,247
3,414,798	243,148	4,027,501	244,467	4,572,985	228,051	3,846,832	273,209
....	564,964	....	599,513	....	493,064	....	636,633
110,515	13,540	18,440	1,738	....	....	49,832	6,183
....	12,025	....	17,092	....	19,474	....	15,442
....	592,667	....	620,523	....	519,946	....	662,576
60	36	194	102	150	82	181	111
169	120	230	165	805	372	419	240
229	156	424	267	955	454	600	351
....	609,991	....	628,328	....	528,761	....	685,425
....	611,116	....	629,990	....	533,651	....	686,971

265

PUERTO RICO

QUANTITY AND VALUE OF DOMESTIC MERCHANDISE RICO DURING THE FIVE YEARS

AGRICULTURAL

ARTICLES EXPORTED.	1893.		1894.	
	Quantities.	Values.	Quantities.	Values.
VEGETABLE MATTER.				
Bread and breadstuffs:				
Barley..........................bushels	....	....	....	....
Bread and biscuit................pounds	432,075	$22,768	338,445	$16,959
Corn (maize)....................bushels	23,874	14,614	17,449	9,141
Corn meal........................barrels	14,847	43,065	28,414	77,409
Oats............................bushels	4,003	1,847	5,315	2,286
Rye flour.........................barrels	6	23	57	172
Wheat..........................bushels	....	....	....	....
Wheat flour......................barrels	167,053	733,308	200,813	734,443
Other breadstuffs, and preparations of, used as food...........................	....	21,431	....	30,764
Total...........................	....	837,056	....	871,174
Broom-corn...........................	....	1,072	....	715
Coffee and cocoa, ground or prepared, and chocolate...........................	....	77	....	17
Fruits and nuts:				
Fruits—				
Apples, dried...................pounds	....	....	50	6
Apples, green or ripe...........barrels	744	2,134	470	1,923
Preserved fruits—				
Canned........................!	....	2,622	....	2,050
Other.........................	....	848	....	577
All other green, ripe, or dried fruits...	....	269	....	408
Total fruits........................	....	5,873	....	4,964
Nuts...............................	....	....	....	44
Total fruits and nuts................	....	5,873	....	5,008
Grasses, dried...........................	....	*	....	....
Hay.............................tons	4	58	....	....
Hops...........................pounds	2,953	518	2,167	434
Malt liquors:				
In bottles.....................dozen	4,850	8,254	2,639	4,361
In other receptacles...........gallons	....	....	....	....
Total...........................	....	8,254	....	4,361
Oil cake and oil-cake meal:				
Cotton-seed....................pounds	} 8,050	129	16,500	208
Flaxseed or linseed................do				
Total.................. do	8,050	129	16,500	208
Oils, vegetable:				
Cotton-seed....................gallons	171	120	450	225
Linseed.........................do	5,526	2,643	1,844	889
Volatile or essential, except peppermint...	....	358	....	725
All other...........................	....	106	....	56
Total...........................	....	3,227	....	1,895

*Not separately stated. † Annual average, 1894–1897.

APPENDIX

(IM)PORTED FROM THE UNITED STATES TO PUERTO (RICO)
(EN)DED JUNE 30, 1897—*Continued*
(PR)ODUCTS—*Continued*

1895.		1896.		1897.		Annual average, 1893–1897.	
Quantities.	Values.	Quantities.	Values.	Quantities.	Values.	Quantities.	Values.
....	....	21	$12	....	....	4	$2
194,729	$10,431	399,687	19,930	673,128	$29,787	407,613	19,975
1,200	714	595	276	1,200	433	8,864	5,036
2,417	6,665	355	886	897	1,698	9,386	25,945
1,217	601	1,692	657	896	288	2,625	1,136
2	10	2	7	4	13	14	45
....	....	....	....	9	8	2	2
118,617	382,676	129,021	486,482	126,933	516,188	148,487	570,619
....	9,707	....	13,107	....	13,083	....	17,618
....	410,804	....	521,357	....	561,498	....	640,378
....	1,050	....	1,265	....	2,062	....	1,233
....	240	....	337	....	330	....	200
						10	1
225	752	494	1,525	697	1,478	526	1,563
....	1,656	....	1,774	....	2,187	....	2,058
....	10	....	191	....	....	....	325
....	294	....	22	....	458	....	290
....	2,712	....	3,512	....	4,123	....	4,237
....	....	....	....	....	....	....	9
....	2,712	....	3,512	....	4,123	....	4,246
....	....	....	30	....	28	....	†15
....	....	3	52	2	30	2	28
2,488	294	3,929	423	2,505	266	2,808	387
857	1,479	1,350	2,173	1,425	2,264	2,224	3,706
....	....	....	....	300	90	60	18
....	1,479	....	2,173	....	2,354	....	3,724
600	6	2,000	21	....	....	‡867	‡9
11,400	115	7,500	100	15,000	200	‡11,300	‡138
12,000	121	9,500	121	15,000	200	12,210	156
1,060	308	1,784	449	170	46	727	230
450	267	764	400	291	119	1,775	863
....	278	....	1,262	....	415	....	608
....	....	....	5	....	258	....	85
....	853	....	2,116	....	838	....	1,786

‡ Annual average, 1895-1897.

PUERTO RICO

QUANTITY AND VALUE OF DOMESTIC MERCHANDISE RICO DURING THE FIVE YEARS

AGRICULTURAL

ARTICLES EXPORTED.	1893.		1894.	
	Quantities.	Values.	Quantities.	Values.
VEGETABLE MATTER—*Concluded.*				
Plants, trees, and shrubs................	....	*	....	....
Rice...................................pounds	*	*	....	....
Roots, herbs, and barks, not elsewhere specified.	....	$125	....	$86
Seeds.....................................	....	547	....	393
Spirits, distilled:				
Brandy.....................proof gallons	....	....	....	....
Whisky, rye.................... do	15	48	6	21
Total..................... do	15	48	6	21
Starch...............................pounds	15,283	636	34,083	1,280
Sugar, refined....................... do	3,450	182	5,310	272
Vegetables:				
Beans and peas..................bushels	16,691	23,685	30,976	44,105
Onions........................... do	40	44	127	130
Potatoes......................... do	1,547	1,559	655	569
Vegetables, canned...................	....	514	....	489
All other, including pickles and sauces....	....	167	....	73
Total................................	....	25,969	....	45,366
Vinegar............................gallons	300	62	....	....
Wine, unbottled.................... do	....	....	233	115
Total vegetable matter..............	....	883,833	....	931,345
Total agricultural exports...........	....	1,649,356	....	1,825,921

* Not separately stated.

APPENDIX

.TED FROM THE UNITED STATES TO PUERTO
) JUNE 30, 1897—*Continued*
:TS—*Concluded*

1895.		1896.		1897.		Annual average, 1893–1897.	
Quantities.	Values.	Quantities.	Values.	Quantities.	Values.	Quantities.	Values.
....	$11	....	$1,970	....	$7	....	†$497
....	....	9,700	194	....	....	†2,425	†49
....	....	....	26	....	....	....	47
....	89	....	133	....	327	....	298
5	10	....	....	....	....	1	2
....	....	....	....	3	15	5	17
5	10	....	....	3	15	6	19
16,185	673	25,489	985	31,630	1,093	24,534	933
450	12	....	....	1,486	72	2,139	108
5,289	7,338	36,522	44,244	44,849	57,550	26,865	35,384
....	....	386	369	....	....	111	109
1,770	1,240	2,769	1,675	8,969	5,707	3,142	2,150
....	210	....	307	....	152	....	334
....	109	....	274	....	61	....	137
....	8,897	....	46,869	....	63,470	....	38,114
....	....	....	....	....	....	60	12
200	91	1,270	343	446	163	430	142
....	427,336	....	581,906	....	636,876	....	692,259
....	1,038,452	....	1,211,896	....	1,170,527	....	1,379,230

† Annual average, 1894–1897.

PUERTO RICO

QUANTITY AND VALUE OF DOMESTIC MERCHANDISE RICO DURING THE FIVE YEARS
NON-AGRICULTURAL

ARTICLES EXPORTED.	1893.		1894.	
	Quantities.	Values.	Quantities.	Values.
Agricultural implements:				
Mowers and reapers, and parts of...........	....	....	....	$688
Plows and cultivators, and parts of.........	....	$2,631	....	5,359
All other, and parts of.....................	....	539	....	1,463
Total......................................	....	3,170	....	7,510
Art works: Painting and statuary............	....	740	....	265
Blacking...................................	....	1,681	....	1,301
Books, maps, engravings, etc................	....	4,950	....	2,809
Brass, and manufactures of..................	....	2,181	....	3,161
Bricks:				
Building...........................M	....	....	....	....
Fire.......................................	....	1,711	....	1,673
Total......................................	....	1,711	....	1,673
Brooms and brushes.........................	....	4,408	....	4,990
Candles............................pounds	88,027	8,384	98,500	9,718
Candy and confectionery.....................	....	2,603	....	1,939
Carriages, horse-cars, and vehicles, n. e. s., and parts of.............................	....	10,351	....	13,819
Cars, passenger and freight, for railroads, and parts of................................	....	....	....	....
Celluloid manufactures......................	....	*	....	....
Charcoal....................................	....	*	....	29
Chemicals, drugs, dyes, and medicines:				
Acids......................................	....	1,586	....	'2,801
Dyes and dyestuffs.........................	....	17	....	3
Medicines, patent or proprietary...........	....	13,152	....	10,490
Other......................................	....	38,691	....	41,890
Total......................................	....	53,446	....	55,184
Clocks and watches:				
Clocks, and parts of.......................	....	1,609	....	890
Watches, and parts of.....................	....	517	....	135
Total......................................	....	2,126	....	1,025
Coal and coke:				
Anthracite.........................tons	319	1,364	122	510
Bituminous........................... do	17,990	48,065	15,179	41,252
Coke................................. do	*	*	*	86
Total......................................	....	49,429	....	41,848
Copper, and manufactures of:				
Ingots, bars, and old...............pounds	....	....	882	128
Other......................................	....	1,566	....	1,504
Total......................................	....	1,566	....	1,632

* Not separately stated.   † Annual average, 1894-1897.

APPENDIX

XPORTED FROM THE UNITED STATES TO PUERTO
NDED JUNE 30, 1897—*Continued*
RODUCTS

1895.		1896.		1897.		Annual average, 1893–1897.	
Quantities.	Values.	Quantities.	Values.	Quantities.	Values.	Quantities.	Values.
....	....	....	....	....	....	....	$138
....	$2,023	....	$3,372	....	$3,215	....	3,320
....	705	....	3,595	....	1,024	....	1,465
....	2,728	....	6,967	....	4,239	....	4,923
....	168	....	211	....	75	....	292
....	964	....	2,093	....	2,512	....	1,710
....	6,785	....	2,381	....	5,250	....	4,435
....	3,162	....	4,059	....	3,738	....	3,260
4	28	....	....	....	....	1	6
....	1,615	....	6,835	....	1,663	....	2,699
....	1,643	....	6,835	....	1,663	....	2,705
....	1,898	....	1,393	....	1,323	....	2,802
61,000	4,975	44,750	4,188	13,865	1,276	61,228	5,708
....	959	....	1,006	....	459	....	1,393
....	6,780	....	7,879	....	9,430	....	9,652
....	....	....	....	....	810	....	162
....	....	....	28	....	....	....	†7
....	....	....	53	....	4	....	†22
....	1,881	....	1,626	....	1,410	....	1,861
....	13	....	9	....	30	....	14
....	7,397	....	12,001	....	10,339	....	10,676
....	32,406	....	42,522	....	36,661	....	38,434
....	41,697	....	56,158	....	48,440	....	50,985
....	743	....	1,201	....	1,054	....	1,100
....	30	....	457	....	652	....	358
....	773	....	1,658	....	1,706	....	1,458
100	420	99	419	888	3,003	306	1,143
30,152	76,762	30,752	78,206	21,897	55,974	23,194	60,052
14	70	145	560	....	....	‡53	†179
....	77,252	....	79,185	....	58,977	....	61,338
....	....	....	....	....	....	176	25
....	1,969	....	2,477	....	1,718	....	1,847
....	1,969	....	2,477	....	1,718	....	1,872

‡ Annual average, 1895–1897.

PUERTO RICO

QUANTITY AND VALUE OF DOMESTIC MERCHANDIS[E] RICO DURING THE FIVE YEAR[S]
NON-AGRICULTU[R]A[L]

ARTICLES EXPORTED.	1893.		1894.	
	Quantities.	Values.	Quantities.	Values.
Cotton, manufactures of:				
Cloths—				
Colored..........................yards	63,749	$3,486	196,578	$7,975
Uncolored.......................do	76,007	5,632	69,855	4,557
Wearing apparel....................	....	1,447	....	620
All other..........................	....	5,179	....	8,132
Total............................	....	15,744	....	21,284
Cycles of all kinds, and parts of............	....	*	....	*
Dental goods.....................	....	*	....	1,113
Earthen- and stoneware............	....	381	....	167
Emery, and manufactures of:				
Emery...........................	....	*	....	....
Manufactures of—				
Emery cloth....................	....	*	....	31
Emery paper...................	....	*	....	....
Emery wheels..................	....	*	....	164
Total emery, and manufactures of...	....	*	....	195
Fertilizers.............................tons	253	6,976	321	8,176
Fish:				
Fresh, other than salmon..........pounds	....	....	....	....
Dried, smoked, or cured—				
Codfish, including haddock, hake, and pollock....................pounds	58,580	2,139	20,030	1,009
Herring........................do	69,407	2,026	135,554	3,784
Pickled—				
Mackerel......................barrels	111	1,284	34	478
Herring........................do	92	358	....	....
Other..........................do	25	125	....	....
Salmon—				
Canned.......................pounds	1,004	128	1,248	137
Other, fresh or cured..................	....	482	....	304
Canned fish other than salmon............	....	....	....	151
Shell-fish—				
Oysters............................	....	342	....	412
Other..............................	....	75	....	17
All other fish........................	....	....	....	11
Total fish.......................	....	6,959	....	6,303
Flax, hemp, jute, etc., manufactures of:				
Bags..............................	....	15	....	....
Cordage........................pounds	147,480	12,383	258,077	16,515
Twine............................	....	185	....	113
All other..........................	....	1,284	....	1,420
Total............................	....	13,867	....	18,048
Ginger ale.....................dozen quarts	....	....	....	....

* Not separately stated. † Annual average, 1896–1897.

APPENDIX

(PORTED FROM THE UNITED STATES TO PUERTO
IDED JUNE 30, 1897—*Continued*
ODUCTS—*Continued*

1895.		1896.		1897.		Annual average, 1893-1897.	
Quantities.	Values.	Quantities.	Values.	Quantities.	Values.	Quantities.	Values.
175,329	$6,691	371,241	$11,785	60,880	$2,467	173,555	$6,481
32,182	3,055	123,743	8,663	49,818	4,590	70,321	5,299
....	1,134	....	551	....	957	....	942
....	3,600	....	5,544	....	3,988	....	5,289
....	14,480	....	26,543	....	12,002	....	18,011
....	*	....	7,929	....	4,120	....	†6,025
....	3,363	....	1,707	....	1,004	....	‡1,797
....	159	....	309	....	137	....	231
....	*	....	20	....	....	....	†10
....	53	....	264	....	54	....	‡101
....	7	....	....	....	....	....	‡2
....	16	....	38	....	25	....	‡61
....	76	....	322	....	79	....	†200
123	3,945	184	5,335	255	6,689	227	6,224
....	....	....	....	85	10	17	2
12,527	618	9,210	375	21,330	651	24,335	958
118,411	2,596	48,641	981	50,169	952	84,436	2,068
* 25	293	* 47	627	* 785	6,977	200	1,932
	*		*		*	‖ 46	‖ 179
565	2,305	49	261	128	650	153	668
240	30	982	101	432	41	781	87
....	395	....	2,396	....	1,766	....	1,069
....	....	....	....	....	99	....	50
....	223	....	177	....	165	....	264
....	85	....	73	....	267	....	103
....	....	....	....	....	....	....	2
....	6,545	....	4,991	....	11,578	....	7,275
....	....	....	69	....	47	....	26
220,000	11,176	326,547	16,458	179,681	8,395	226,357	12,985
....	88	....	181	....	102	....	134
....	977	....	1,789	....	1,038	....	1,302
....	12,241	....	18,497	....	9,582	....	14,447
20	35	....	....	....	....	4	7

‡ Annual average, 1894-1897.   ‖ Annual average, 1893-1894.

PUERTO RICO

QUANTITY AND VALUE OF DOMESTIC MERCHANDIS
RICO DURING THE FIVE YEAI
NON-AGRICULTUR,

ARTICLES EXPORTED.	1893.		1894.	
	Quantities.	Values.	Quantities.	Values.
Glass and glassware:				
Window glass....................	....	$88	....	$72
All other........................	....	12,013	....	12,065
Total......................	....	12,101	....	12,137
Gunpowder and other explosives:				
Gunpowder..................pounds	1,070	350	2,060	544
Other...........................	....	391	....	935
Total......................	....	741	....	1,479
India-rubber and gutta-percha, manufactures of:				
Boots and shoes....................pairs	407	188	499	229
All other........................	....	2,053	....	2,301
Total......................	....	2,241	....	2,530
Ink, printers' and other................	....	1,725	....	2,273
Instruments and apparatus for scientific purposes, including telegraph, telephone, and other electric............................	....	4,142	....	5,650
Iron and steel, and manufactures of:				
Pig iron.........................tons	....	....	15	225
Bar iron....................pounds	6,950	139	37,510	586
Manufactures of—				
Car-wheels...............number	....	....	200	600
Castings, n. e. s.................	....	14	....	311
Cutlery........................	....	1,104	....	408
Firearms.......................	....	140	....	....
Locks, hinges, and other builders' hardware...................	....	10,768	....	13,622
Machinery, n. e. s...............	....	56,389	....	31,373
Nails and spikes—				
Cut...................pounds	162,854	3,222	104,900	2,080
Wire, wrought, horseshoe, etc., and tacks..............pounds	23,325	1,360	33,179	1,589
Plates and sheets—				
Of iron..................pounds	....	....	....	....
Of steel..................do	....	....	....	....
Printing-presses...................	....	1,940	....	475
Railroad bars or rails, of steel.....tons	....	....	....	....
Saws and tools....................	....	11,486	....	16,471
Scales and balances...............	....	8,016	....	7,169
Sewing-machines, and parts of.......	....	4,618	....	3,534
Steam-engines, and parts of—				
Fire engines ....number	....	*	....	*
Locomotive engines....... do	1	4,408	1	2,400
Stationary engines........ do	6	4,291	7	4,046
Boilers, and other parts of engines.	....	5,770	....	4,105
Stoves and ranges, and parts of.......	....	1,425	....	564
Typewriting machines................	....	*	....	*
Wire......................pounds	1,073,142	28,891	1,401,182	31,607
All other manufactures of iron and steel.	....	15,321	....	29,025
Total iron and steel, and manufactures of..........................	....	159,302	....	150,190

* Not separately stated.

APPENDIX

.TED FROM THE UNITED STATES TO PUERTO
) JUNE 30, 1897—*Continued*
:TS—*Continued*

1895.		1896.		1897.		Annual average, 1893–1897.	
Quantities.	Values.	Quantities.	Values.	Quantities.	Values.	Quantities.	Values.
....	$109	....	$69	....	....	....	$68
....	7,394	....	12,108	....	$8,160	....	10,348
....	7,503	....	12,177	....	8,160	....	10,416
1,300	222	....	....	....	....	886	223
....	1,081	....	1,599	....	690	....	939
....	1,303	....	1,599	....	690	....	1,162
144	119	354	232	400	250	361	204
....	2,510	....	2,828	....	2,899	....	2,518
....	2,629	....	3,060	....	3,149	....	2,722
....	1,934	....	1,871	....	1,814	....	1,923
....	5,350	....	17,866	....	22,801	....	11,162
2	32	....	....	5	90	4	69
10,357	120	10,046	156	....	....	12,973	200
....	....	....	....	12	88	42	138
....	212	....	158	....	264	....	192
....	600	....	327	....	327	....	553
....	460	....	....	....	....	....	120
....	7,491	....	8,925	....	8,216	....	9,804
....	56,642	....	44,524	....	69,462	....	51,678
91,400	1,354	79,040	1,551	51,960	992	98,031	1,840
30,413	1,238	27,218	1,258	30,115	1,425	28,850	1,374
....	....	....	....	15,930	375	3,186	75
....	....	....	....	6,660	123	1,332	25
....	1,092	....	46	....	1,143	....	930
71	1,795	47	1,394	....	....	24	638
....	7,881	....	12,496	....	7,083	....	11,083
....	4,975	....	7,209	....	6,781	....	6,830
....	2,230	....	2,953	....	2,242	....	3,115
1	4,000	....	....	....	....	....	800
....	....	....	....	3	26,296	1	6,621
3	3,000	2	1,265	4	2,141	4	2,949
....	10,115	....	5,670	....	10,796	....	7,291
....	385	....	707	....	814	....	779
....	*	....	*	....	590	....	† 590
677,000	13,476	1,077,900	21,251	813,485	15,719	1,008,542	22,189
....	18,408	....	23,743	....	25,519	....	22,403
....	135,506	....	133,633	....	180,486	....	151,823

† 1897 only.

PUERTO RICO

QUANTITY AND VALUE OF DOMESTIC MERCHANDISE RICO DURING THE FIVE YEARS
NON-AGRICULTURAL

ARTICLES EXPORTED.	1893. Quantities.	1893. Values.	1894. Quantities.	1894. Values.
Jewelry, and manufactures of gold and silver..	....	$18,377	....	$10,472
Lamps, chandeliers, etc., for illuminating purposes	....	5,716	....	5,336
Lead, and manufactures of....................	....	1,107	....	1,519
Leather, and manufactures of:				
Leather—				
Buff, grain, splits, and all finished upper leather......................	....	66	....	870
Patent or enameled....................	....	820	....	233
Sole..........................pounds	3,830	752	750	120
All other.............................	....	706	....	1,069
Manufactures of—				
Boots and shoes..................pairs	1,414	1,286	710	698
Harness and saddles..................	....	4,005	....	3,731
All other.............................	....	1,656	....	1,682
Total leather, and manufactures of..	....	9,291	....	8,403
Lime and cement:				
Lime............................barrels	988	2,266	2,067	4,109
Cement............................ do				
Total...................... do	988	2,266	2,067	4,109
Marble and stone, and manufactures of:				
Unmanufactured........................	....	535	....	676
Manufactures of, all except roofing slate...	....	3,063	....	6,338
Total.............................	....	3,598	....	7,014
Matches....................................	....	....	....	....
Musical instruments:				
Organs......................number	1	69	1	300
Pianofortes....................... do	1	450	....	....
All other, and parts of...................	....	97	....	383
Total	....	616	....	683
Naval stores:				
Rosin..........................barrels	383	801	1,157	2,300
Tar............................. do	435	947	200	478
Turpentine and pitch.............. do	103	256	155	350
Turpentine, spirits of.............gallons	9,789	3,635	7,933	2,737
Total.............................	....	5,639	....	5,865
Notions, n. e. s............................	....	*	....	6,789
Oakum....................................	....	*	....	....

* Not separately stated.

APPENDIX

EXPORTED FROM THE UNITED STATES TO PUERTO
ENDED JUNE 30, 1897—*Continued*
PRODUCTS—*Continued*

1895.		1896.		1897.		Annual average, 1893–1897.	
Quantities.	Values.	Quantities.	Values.	Quantities.	Values.	Quantities.	Values.
....	$3,747	....	$8,698	....	$3,786	....	$9,016
....	3,941	....	6,039	....	3,615	....	4,928
....	1,816	....	1,731	....	3,729	....	1,980
....	325	....	1,876	....	582	....	744
....	650	....	261	....	234	....	440
682	103	....	....	7,102	1,255	2,473	446
....	75	....	367	....	23	....	448
116	120	810	1,049	768	725	764	775
....	3,573	....	4,800	....	3,040	....	3,830
....	454	....	986	....	1,509	....	1,257
....	5,300	....	9,339	....	7,368	....	7,940
267	437	92	156	....	....	685	1,397
				12	18		
267	437	92	156	12	18	685	1,397
....	450	....	704	....	204	....	514
....	2,174	....	2,637	....	2,286	....	3,299
....	2,624	....	3,341	....	2,490	....	3,813
....	....	....	7	....	....	....	1
....	....	....	500	....	500	....	74
....	....	1	5	1	45	1	290
....	180	....	....	....	....	....	142
....	180	....	505	....	545	....	506
442	891	881	1,768	159	318	604	1,216
133	325	295	650	266	573	266	595
56	100	61	102	98	154	95	192
9,104	3,107	7,239	2,392	9,890	3,174	8,791	3,009
....	4,423	....	4,912	....	4,219	....	5,012
....	2,588	....	3,415	....	3,492	....	†4,071
....	....	....	....	....	393	....	†98

† Annual average, 1894–1897.

PUERTO RICO

QUANTITY AND VALUE OF DOMESTIC MERCHANDISE RICO DURING THE FIVE YEARS

NON-AGRICULTURAL

ARTICLES EXPORTED.		1893.		1894.	
		Quantities.	Values.	Quantities.	Values.
Oils:					
Animal—					
Whale........................	gallons	....	....	10	$8
Fish........................	do	80	$56	40	15
Mineral, crude................	do	509,987	34,555	514,995	37,325
Mineral, refined—					
Naphthas..................	do	300	58	445	112
Illuminating..............	do	480,390	40,927	171,446	16,565
Lubricating...............	do	4,100	1,191	20,589	4,457
Total oils..................		....	76,787	....	58,482
Paints and painters' colors..............		....	6,506	....	6,370
Paper, and manufactures of:					
Paper hangings....................		....	163	....	41
Writing-paper and envelopes.............		....	1,399	....	1,680
All other.......................		....	19,145	....	16,630
Total		....	20,707	....	18,351
Paraffin and paraffin wax	pounds	26,473	1,496	19,193	3,362
Perfumery and cosmetics...............		....	2,501	....	2,844
Photographic materials................		....	*	....	*
Plaster............................		....	....	....	....
Plated ware........................		....	2,950	....	2,712
Quicksilver........................	pounds	90	47	90	48
Sand..............................		....	....	....	....
Silk, manufactures of.................		....	....	....	....
Soap:					
Toilet or fancy..................		....	386	....	424
Other...........................	pounds	404	19	930	42
Total		....	405	....	466
Sponges...........................	pounds	*	*	40	27
Stationery, except of paper.............		....	7,319	....	4,350
Stereotype and electrotype plates.........		....	....	....	64
Straw and palm-leaf, manufactures of......		....	753	....	313
Teeth, artificial.....................		....	*	....	....
Tin, manufactures of..................		....	1,883	....	1,223
Tobacco, manufactures of		....	....	....	45
Toys..............................		....	831	....	566
Trunks, valises, and traveling-bags........		....	1,252	....	4,335
Varnish...........................	gallons	1,790	1,988	1,665	2,271

* Not separately stated.

APPENDIX

EXPORTED FROM THE UNITED STATES TO PUERTO
ENDED JUNE 30, 1897—*Continued*
PRODUCTS—*Continued*

1895.		1896.		1897.		Annual average, 1893–1897.	
Quantities.	Values.	Quantities.	Values.	Quantities.	Values.	Quantities.	Values.
....	....	....	....	....	....	2	$2
....	....	....	$14	2,552	$646	544	146
518,100	$43,546	708,008	68,080	623,958	59,676	574,992	48,637
110	31	320	76	612	100	357	75
323,700	32,605	241,692	30,732	268,020	30,713	297,050	30,308
11,569	3,914	9,352	3,460	7,563	2,562	10,635	3,117
....	80,096	....	102,362	....	93,697	....	82,285
....	4,173	....	3,395	....	2,390	....	4,567
....	34	....	12	....	17	....	53
....	430	....	1,073	....	1,028	....	1,122
....	12,038	....	14,338	....	12,796	....	14,990
....	12,502	....	15,423	....	13,841	....	16,165
6,290	250	13,410	556	25,637	939	18,201	1,321
....	1,946	....	1,987	....	1,680	....	2,192
....	*	....	88	....	854	....	†236
....	....	....	*	....	47	....	‡47
....	1,784	....	1,890	....	2,013	....	2,270
....	....	....	....	....	....	36	19
....	....	....	....	....	15	....	3
....	....	....	10	....	....	....	2
....	343	....	365	....	164	....	336
4,000	200	5,350	255	10,450	338	4,237	171
....	543	....	620	....	502	....	507
....	....	186	98	26	7	†63	†33
....	3,164	....	5,765	....	5,257	....	5,171
....	52	....	13	....	18	....	29
....	....	....	579	....	1,033	....	536
....	289	....	241	....	248	....	†195
....	1,396	....	786	....	1,139	....	1,285
....	6	....	....	....	53	....	21
....	444	....	458	....	235	....	507
....	2,185	....	958	....	590	....	1,864
1,733	1,840	2,322	2,653	1,922	1,878	1,886	2,126

† Annual average, 1894–1897.   ‡ 1897 only.

PUERTO RICO

QUANTITY AND VALUE OF DOMESTIC MERCHANDISE RICO DURING THE FIVE YEARS

NON-AGRICULTURAL

ARTICLES EXPORTED.	1893.		1894.	
	Quantities.	Values.	Quantities.	Values.
Wood, and manufactures of:				
Lumber—				
Boards, deals, and planks......M feet	8,295	$133,341	10,353	$161,697
Joists and scantlings........... "	1,199	15,731	826	11,105
Hoops and hoop-poles..............	....	8,183	....	10,040
Shingles........................M	65	125	893	2,605
Shooks, box.........................	....	5,301	....	11,364
Shooks, other.............number	46,410	71,430	59,413	95,796
Staves and headings...............	....	28,311	....	18,516
All other lumber...................	....	4,605	....	9,470
Timber—				
Sawed......................M feet	3	46	....	....
Logs, and other timber.............	....	340	....	....
Manufactures of wood—				
Doors, sash, and blinds............	....	2,320	....	....
Moldings, trimmings, and other house finishings......................	....	143	....	340
Hogsheads and barrels, empty......	....	2,151	....	326
House furniture....................	....	25,624	....	22,521
Woodenware........................	....	941	....	577
All other...........................	....	3,955	....	2,869
Total wood, and manufactures of....	....	302,547	....	347,226
Wool, manufactures of:				
Carpets.......................yards	....	....	....	....
Wearing apparel....................	....	239	....	....
Other...............................	....	67	....	....
Total..............................	....	306	....	....
Zinc, manufactures of:				
Pigs, bars, plates, and sheets.......pounds	....	....	....	....
All other............................	....	94	....	32
Total..............................	....	94	....	32
All other articles not elsewhere enumerated....	....	7,525	....	....
Total non-agricultural exports......	....	853,432	....	879,725

* Not separately stated.

APPENDIX

:PORTED FROM THE UNITED STATES TO PUERTO
IDED JUNE 30, 1897—*Concluded*
ODUCTS—*Concluded*

1895.		1896.		1897.		Annual average, 1893-1897.	
Quantities.	Values.	Quantities.	Values.	Quantities.	Values.	Quantities.	Values.
9,245	$134,587	8,235	$117,186	9,403	$122,524	9,106	$133,867
501	7,450	*	607	183	1,986	663	8,607
*	*	*		*	*	....	† 9,112
803	1,707	140	446	609	1,188	502	1,214
....	6,711	....	12,107	....	3,097	....	7,716
77,301	106,031	64,224	101,458	43,553	72,810	58,180	89,505
....	11,855	....	14,127	....	9,360	....	16,434
....	4,915	....	5,000	....	2,506	....	5,299
310	3,300	....	....	6	60	64	681
....	....	....	....	....	....	....	68
....	24	....	....	....	....	....	469
....	212	....	64	....	201	....	192
....	421	....	518	....	349	....	753
....	18,120	....	16,518	....	15,700	....	19,697
....	397	....	547	....	497	....	592
....	2,510	....	4,897	....	3,759	....	3,598
....	298,240	....	279,631	....	234,037	....	292,336
50	40	....	....	....	....	10	8
....	....	....	150	....	30	....	84
....	107	....	45	....	27	....	49
....	147	....	195	....	57	....	141
....	....	....	....	601	39	120	8
....	16	....	236	....	20	....	79
....	16	....	236	....	59	....	87
....	800	....	16	....	168	....	1,702
....	781,751	....	868,504	....	794,323	....	835,547

† Annual average, 1893-1894.

INDEX

A

Adjuntas—the population of ; coffee-raising the principal industry, 45

Aguadilla, a town on the west coast, 96

Aguas Buenas—on the military road; scenery like Arizona and New Mexico ; hillside huts, 57 ; a cosmopolitan town ; elusive Spanish measure, 58

Antillean mountain-range—characteristics of ; the immense depth of water, 27 ; speculations concerning the early geological formation; second period of subsidence, 28 ; coral terraces ; geological formations of today ; variation in quality and color of limestone ; fine for building purposes, 29 ; excellent material for road-making ; minerals, 30

Appendix—trade of Puerto Rico ; agricultural imports in 1894 and 1895, 253 ; agricultural exports in 1894 and 1895, 257 ; quantity and value of imports into United States in 1897, 260 ; exports from the United States, 270

Arecibo—a city attractive to the eye, 13 ; a large coffee town on the north coast, 196

Arroyo, an open roadstead, 11

Arvitrios, a dealer's license, 229

B

Bay rum, the manufacture of, could be expanded into a large commercial enterprise, 77

Bay-tree, luxuriant growths of, 77

Bricks—rude machinery for making ; manner of making ; price of ; fine qualities of clay abundant, 81

Burden-bearing—the bread-wagon ; serving milk from the cow, 168 ; a vegetable - carrier ; hucksters' commodities served from planks carried on their heads; remarkable equilibrious feat, 169 ; banana-venders ; orange-venders ; a pony-load, 170 ; marvelous staying quality of the pony ; oxen the principal draft animals, active and fast travelers ; manner of yoking ; cruelty of the drivers ; structure of the ox-cart ; spook-like lanterns ; island-made carriages comfortable and cheap ; narrow-gauge street-cars, 173 ; evening cries, 174

Burials and cemeteries—the last journey to the grave ; absence of sympathy, 209 ; the potter's field, 210 ; service of the burial of the poor ; a happy release ; burial without coffins, 211 ; no burial in the cemeteries without a certificate from the priest ; cost

INDEX

Burials and cemeteries—*Continued* of church service for the dead, 212; wall niches, the cost of; disposition of the bodies on failure of the next instalment; mortuary decorations; cramped quarters; noisome pest-holes; in the pauper lot bodies are thrown out every three years, 213

Butter—the importation of; price of, 74

C

Caguas—on the great military road; one of the largest tobacco towns; an opening for Americans, 194

Carrosones, or sugar-apples—fruit looks like inverted Swiss cheeses; very palatable, 138

Cattle-raising—bright future for; no need for hay-making; succulent green bunch-grass the year round; exportation of cattle and hides, 72; like the famous long-horned cattle of Texas; a paradise for; abundance of food and water, 73; cost of cattle-raising land, 74

Cayey—a great tobacco center; hotbed of Spanish sympathizers, 37; shiftless business methods of the Spanish tobacconists, 194; a most delightful climate; best cigars on the island are made here; fine sanitary possibilities, 195

Cedula Personal—a certificate of identity which everyone was compelled to take out; the expense of, 229

Cheese—a ready market for; quality of the native product, 74

Chino, a sweet green orange, 133

Climate—general character of; favorable to the troops, 15; temperature in summer; dangers of fever; the dry season, 16; temperature in winter; differences between sunlight and shade; causes of pneumonia; rainfall; the rainy season, 17; summer heat, 19; character of, on the southern coast, 20; the most salubrious, in the western hemisphere, within the torrid zone, 26; sudden changes of temperature, 50; in winter everything that a tourist or invalid could desire, 83; favorable for tobacco culture, 117

Cock-fighting—the only real recreation of the rural Puertoriqueños; bull-fighting never gained a foothold; every town has at least one cock-pit; construction of, 175; Sunday afternoons are always devoted to this pastime; all classes at the mains, 176; birds fight with their own gaffs; manner of handling the birds, 177; manner of reviving the birds between rounds, 178; an orderly crowd, 179

Coffee—primitive coffee-breaker, 59; first in importance as an industry; no special training required to raise it, 85; tree shelter required to protect it from the sun; "Yauco" brand for the French; price of good coffeeland, 86; cost of transportation over the hills, 87; cost of starting a new plantation, 88; profits from, 89; lack of system in planting; character of the shade-trees, 90; the berry-pickers, 91; wage of, 92; "side-issue" coffee; man-

INDEX

Coffee—*Continued*
ner of preparing the berry, 93; polishing process; manner of transplantation; drying by machinery, 95; machinery of American make; manner of sorting the berries; hand-picking the berries, 96; song and labor; prime coffee, price of; lower grades; quantity exported, 97; infancy of the industry; France the heaviest purchaser; its fine flavor, 98; growth of the industry, 99

Compañia de la Ferrocarriles de Puerto Rico—length of road, 68; badly-laid road; inefficient service; speed of; revocation of the franchise, 69

Corn—scarce and high-priced; difficulties of raising it; the crop; average price of, 75

Cotton, cannot be raised to compete with the foreign article, 76

Court of Military Justice, a place where private grudges were settled, 235

Courts—faulty judicial system; military autocracy, 232; Juez Municipal, one of the three principal courts; Juez de Instruccion, the next highest; Madrid the final appeal; jury system unknown in Spanish law; the courts hotbeds of corruption and bribery, 234; imprisonment without a hearing; prohibitive bail; settling old grudges; tradesmen imprisoned who importuned officers for store bills; muzzling the press; systematic bulldozing of private citizens, 235; swindling methods; payments under pressure; the usual way of settling a case, 236; any means justifies an end, 237; the laws of the island a farce, 238

Customs duties, proportion of revenue from, 228

D

Dairy-farming — drawbacks to; milking time; difficulties of keeping the milk; prices, 74

"Dark Cave"—a rival to Mammoth Cave, 56; a beautiful entrance, 60; odoriferous torches; a spider to be avoided; millions of bats, 61; the roar of their wings; crab-hunting, 62; a weird sight; character of the rock; lost in the cave; a tough scramble; color of the stalactites; two thousand feet above the sea, 64

Deputaccion Provincial—board of public works; its duties and its functions, 230

Dyewoods—forests abound with them; among them being, the brazil-wood (*Cæsalpinia echinata*); fustic (*Maclura tinctoria*); dividivi (*Cæsalpinia coriaria*); mora (*Morinda cetrifolia*); annotto (*Bixa orellana*), 143

E

Eastern shore—fine natural advantages; protected harbors; coming possibilities; innumerable coral reefs, 12

Edible fruits, 22; nature's abundance, 38

INDEX

Eggs—limited quantity; price controlled by "age"; impossible to keep them, 75

Electricity, needed for light, heat, and power, 70

El Yunque, the highest point on the island, 60

Evacuation of Puerto Rico—formal release from Spain; date of withdrawal; the night before, 2; the last Spanish bugle-call; annihilation of happy homes, 4; crowds waiting for the signal, 5; raising of the stars and stripes, 6; officers who raised the flags, 7

F

Fajardo, a town on the east coast, 196

Floriculture, the island a glowing flowering mass in the spring, 128

Frijoles, a Spanish red bean, 151

Fruit-raising—sometimes four crops a year; the country a mass of fruit blossoms in the early spring, 128; planted, for fruition, several times a year; varieties of oranges and lemons grow wild, 129; soil superior to Florida or California; almost every tropical and semi-tropical fruit grows to perfection, 130; exports to the United States in 1898; plantains and bananas the principal articles of diet; varieties of, 131; profits of plantain culture, 132; possibilities of the future culture; shaddock, 133; limes, delicate odor of the blossoms; pineapples, famous for their delicious flavor; the most inviting investment for Americans, 134; cocoanuts in abundance; tree very hardy and prolific; cocoanut oil; the cocoa-tree; cocoa and chocolate, the price of, 135; guava flowers have a delightful fragrance; pomegranates, fine in quality, but little demand for, 137; date-palm grows to magnificent proportions; figs raised in small quantities; tamarind reaches a high degree of perfection; pawpaw, fruit in bunches like squashes, flavor like muskmelon, valuable for indigestion and gastric troubles, 138; mayama, too acrid for the average taste; granadilla, a species of passion-flower, the fruit of which has a delightful flavor and aroma; breadfruits and breadnuts in quantities; manner of cooking, 139; would please the American palate, 140

Fruta del pan, a species of large breadfruit, 139

Fuel, scarcity of, 70, 78

G

Garbonzas, a succulent pea, not unlike a cooked chestnut in flavor, 151

Gedianda—a bushy weed bearing a narrow pod; a substitute for coffee; said to have great medicinal virtues; preferable to chicory, 141

Gondinga, a hash made of chopped kidneys and liver seasoned with garlic and split olives, 151

Guanica—beautiful harbor of, 10; its commercial deterioration traced to political discrimination in San Juan, 11

INDEX

Guida, a simple musical instrument made of a gourd, played by scraping the etched sides with an umbrella wire, 164

Gums and resins — guaiac gum, from the lignum-vitæ tree; from the seeds and leaves of the Indian shot (copey); balsam of copaiba from the *Copaifera;* algarroba, which produces a gum known as catechu, used for dyeing and tanning; cashew, from which a varnish is made, 144

H

"Heart of the Black Hand" country, 42; insignia on the doorways of houses, 45

Hillside homes—palm-made huts, 47; "clinging to the hillsides in defiance of the laws of gravitation," 157, 158

Historical sketch — the island visited by Columbus on his second voyage; Don Juan Ponce de Leon takes possession of the island, 250; a century later the aboriginal folk nearly all destroyed; the many attacks on San Juan; captured by the Earl of Cumberland in 1598, but from that time until the American flag was hoisted in 1898, none but the Spanish flag ever floated over the island, 251

Home-life—a hospitality seasoned with garlic and sweet oil; a cordial welcome to Americans, 145; power and prosperity confined to the few; hands stretched out with joy at their emancipation, 146; a handful of malcontents; simplicity of home-life; house decorations; chiefly cane-seated furniture, 147; rare antiques; absence of taste in arrangement; artistic beds of brass and metal, 148; scarcity of toilet articles; the kitchen a place to be avoided; methods of cookery, 149; cordial relations between the Ohio regiment and the natives; marked hospitality to American officers, 150; disastrous effect of meat diet; a rich planter's dinner; queer dishes; garbonzas and frijoles; deviled land-crabs, 151; good bread resembling the French; table decorations; table napkins; abstemiousness of the people; the morning meal, 152; the hearty meal of the day; position of honor at table; evenings at home; not a reading people, 153

Hotels—quality of; every roadside hut an eating-place; fine opening for enterprising Bonifaces, especially for winter patronage, 82

Humacoa, a sugar town in the southeastern portion of the island, 196

Hurricanes—destructive in the past; puny affairs compared with the cyclones on our prairies, 19; prevailing winds, 20

I

Ice-plants, the need for, 72
"Isle of the Gate of Gold," 9

J

Jobos, fine harbor with ample searoom, 11

INDEX

Jobos de la India—a kind of plum, fine in flavor and as large as a lemon; a powerful mucilage is made from the exudations of the tree, 137

L

Land—the cost of cattle pastures, 74; price of good coffee-lands, 86; of tobacco-lands, 122
La Playa—the seaport of Ponce; population about 3,500, 190
Lares—a coffee town; Spanish in sentiment, 51; the approach to, 52; cost of timber at, 78; almost inaccessible from the coast; can only be reached by execrable trails, 195; the very heart of the coffee district, 196
Las Marias, a dirty, unkempt village, 54

M

Manufactures, will depend largely upon the action of Congress, 80
Market-gardening, a responsive soil for, 77
Mayaguez—only city with street-cars, 173; one of the three large centers; population about 12,000; architecture light and graceful, 191
Medicinal trees, shrubs, and herbs grow in great abundance, 142
Military road—a feat of engineering skill; by whom constructed, 32; character of; character of branch roads and trails, 33; destroyed villas; gorgeous scenery, 35; impregnable positions on, 36; a dream of fairyland; the reality; coffee plantations on, 37; a journey to be remembered, 40; the only feasible road for travel, 84
Minerals—possibilities of the island yet unsolved; iron of good quality; scarcity of coal; gold in the mountain streams, 30; manner of obtaining it; copper, lead, garnets, quartz crystals, and agates, in small quantities, 31
Money of the island—the financial plaything of Spain; meeting the bond issue of the Spanish government, 214; change of legal tender; complications in foreign exchange; the reign of the Mexican dollar, 215; temporary paper money; change of standard; effect of the introduction of American money, 216; no banking system approved by the Spanish government; the floating capital of the country; municipal and school reserves milked by the retiring Spaniards, 217; local bank notes redeemable on demand; not guaranteed by the government; interest on deposits, 218; rates of exchange a possible hardship; scaling the rates; premium on American money; rates at Vieques; criticism and scandal are possible outcomes, 220; sharp practice of the Treasury agents; miscellaneous brokerage; rise of prices, 221; Americans paying as they go; solution of the money problem; effect of establishing a bullion value alone, 222; dearth of money the curse of the island; the usual results of barter; a decrease in the purchas-

INDEX

Money of the island—*Continued*
ing power would result in disaster, 223; necessity for reminting the Puerto Rican peso; arbitrary ruling, 224
Mosquito plague, 19
Mountain traveling—difficulties of, in the spring months, 18; rough roads, 34; knife-edged ridges, 58; a corduroy road; feats of stair-climbing, 59

N

Nispero, a delectable fruit with an indescribable nectar flavor, 136

O

Octroi, a duty on every article of food, beverage, or fuel, and fee paid by the seller, 229
Orchids—found in great variety; in forms that make one silent with wonder, 144

P

Pawpaw, a tree bearing bunches of fruit like squashes, taste like muskmelon of fine flavor, 138
Peasant life—its squalor and filth; contagious diseases; nature's supply of food; scant clothing, 155; average wages, 156; house-rent an almost unknown quantity; garden spots free in exchange for labor, 157; hillside houses; the staple article of food, 158; the early life of the children; short lives of the children; simple house construction, 159; sleeping accommodations; rag-baby saints; simple playthings for the children, 160; cooking utensils and service; primitive marriage forms; the church an obstacle to marriage, 161; common-law marriages; constancy and devotion the rule; chronic diseases common; goiter, elephantiasis, anæmic malaria, 162; quinine an unreachable luxury; blindness common; blind beggars have regular posts, 163; music of the peons; the dancing step, 164; illiteracy of the peons; immorality in the towns; preponderance of the abject poor; a possible Garden of Eden, 166; bringing the poor into town to die, 170
Physical ailments, 22; hygienic precautions; malarial affections; preventive measures; causes of; ability of the native doctor, 23; the "tropic liver"; malaria the worst foe; change of climate necessary, 24; high cost of medicine; danger from colds; yellow fever not to be feared, 25; cases have occurred in barracks, prisons, and at the coast towns; it is unknown in the country; it is a disease of the night; sanitary suggestions, 26
Planters' hospitality, 54; their houses and surroundings, 55
Political methods—the laws meaningless vaporings, 238; the fact that there are no gold-mines on the island has saved the peons from much oppression; no government reports of receipts until the beginning of the present century; the government formerly supported by taxes levied in Mexico, until the rebellion in 1810;

INDEX

Political methods—*Continued* liberal terms to colonists, 239; the general laws exceedingly liberal to them; the inducements offered doubled the population in fifteen years; office-holders stole everything; Governor De la Torre works a change; under his administration the island was self-supporting for the first time in its history; gross peculations curtailed to limits of decency, 240; Governor-General the supreme power of the island; unjust discriminations; "Elduayen," another unjust law; effects of the Cuban scare, 241; no benefit from the new laws; members of the Autonomy Commission; no hope from the Canovas ministry, 242; division of the house into Liberals and Autonomista Puros; schemes of Lower House; autonomy granted, 243; peons selling themselves for office; the masses against the classes; "Glory Day," 245; greed for pecuniary aggrandizement; the landing of the Americans ended the faction fights, 246; conflict of authority; universal suffrage impossible at present, 247; eighty per cent. who can neither read nor write; one-eighth of the people own the island; urgent need for practical education; necessity for primary lessons in control of affairs; can Americans bring order out of chaos? 249

Ponce—its harbor and surroundings, 11; the population of, 188

Pork—quality of the native article; imported chiefly from the United States; raising of hogs a doubtful experiment, 75

Poultry—breeding game-cocks mainly; quality of the chickens, 75

Principal cities—the coast towns have less favorable climate than those on the hills; sanitary conditions generally bad, 180; San Juan, the leading city in population; the seat of the island government; immense sea-walls and massive fortifications, 181; narrow and dark streets, 182; the grand theater; clubs and casinos, 183; fine barracks; founded by Ponce de Leon in 1511; restricted area; sanitary conditions easily improved; the water-works just approaching completion; imperfect construction; quantity of the water-supply; precautions against trouble in the filter beds; planned by a Scotch engineer; plans stolen from the post-office under the direction of the Governor-General; cost of the plant, 187; Ponce, the population of; possibilities for expansion; well built and well paved; hospitals, schools, and clubs; the best cafés on the island, 189; no wharfage; commercially second in rank; good connections with the neighboring districts, 190; Mayaguez, one of the three large centers; the lightness and grace of its architecture; population about 12,000; the "white population" difficult to determine; easy to drain, 191; few evidences of poverty; big coffee-mills; large tannery, 192; small industries; ice- and elec-

INDEX

Principal cities—*Continued* tric-light plants; the only town on the island which has a street-railway; poor harbor; fine barracks, hospitals, and cathedral; a delightful little opera-house, 193; a charming park; Americans unwelcome at the Spanish club; Caguas, a large tobacco center; poor business methods of the Spaniards, 194; Cayey, another tobacco center; a good opening for Americans, 194; a most delightful climate; fine cigar factories; fine commercial possibilities, 195; Lares, only approach to, by execrable trails; a busy, thriving town; very hospitable to strangers; the very heart of the great coffee district; richest haciendas on the island; wanton destruction by native bandits; Yauco and Arecibo, coffee towns on the coast; Guayama and Humacoa, sugar towns on the southeast; Fajardo and Aguadilla, other small coast towns, 196

Provisional Minister of Justice, invested with supreme power, 234

Puerto Rico—first impressions of; "Isle of the Gate of Gold," 9; mountain-ranges, 10; scarcity of harbors; area of the island; remarkable fertility; mountain-ridges, 14; wonderful possibilities; a tropical Elysium; the "Mecca of America," 15; advantages over all the other West Indian islands, 21; a desert for a poor man; questionable employment, 65; expensive living; cheap clothing, 66; cost of ordinary luxuries; the native menu, cheap fruits, 67

R

Railroad construction, many difficulties offered, 71

Rainy seasons—spring rains, 17; yearly fall, 18; autumnal deluges, 20

Revengeful Puertoriqueños — destruction of property during the transition period, 53; a native's idea of the Spanish character, 54

Revenues and taxes — burden of taxation; money in circulation per capita; compared with the United States, 225; direct taxation; comparison with New York State, 226; a pitiable commercial and industrial condition; cost of the Army, Navy, and Church, 227; the "Ultra Mar"; sharing the expenses of the war with Cuba; taxes swallowed up by officials; customs and stamp duties, 228; sinecures for informers and spies; no real-estate transfers without a bribe to the recorder; the postal system; "Cedula Personal," a certificate of identity; "Arvitrios," license for dealers; "Octroi," duty paid on every article of food or fuel, 229; board of public works; government lottery scheme; cost of collecting the revenue; two sets of collectors; the police force, 230; taxation excessive; disproportionate civil list; every position a sinecure, 231

INDEX

Rice—the native product; importation of; immense quantities consumed, 76; possibilities of its successful cultivation, 77

Rio Piedras, suburban town of San Juan, 38

Rivers—deep and fast-flowing; dangerous character of, for navigation, 13; innumerable small streams the cause of exceptional fertility, 20; value as water power, 21

Road-houses—counters opening on the road; places for refreshment for the oxen-drivers, 39

Roof-tiles, made by hand, 81

S

San Juan—withdrawal of Spanish troops, 3; marriage between Spanish soldiers and Puerto Rican women, 4; massive fortifications, 6; extensive barracks; immense quantity of captured war material, 7; curious metamorphosis, 8; political discrimination in favor of, 11; picturesque approach to, 39; the seat of the island government; best harbor on the island; immense sea-walls and defensive structures, 181; direct tax on all the real estate on the island assessed here, 229; captured by the Earl of Cumberland in 1598; the Dutch repulsed in 1615; for three hundred years no flag floated over the town but the Spanish, 251

Schools, churches, and charitable institutions—bad administration; appropriation for public instruction, 198; proportion of children in the population; appropriation *pro rata* for educational purposes, 199; poor accommodations; salary list of teachers, 200; teaching considered a menial employment; attendance at the schools; oral system of teaching, 201; schools for grown-up poor; percentage of illiteracy; good natural ability of the peons, 202; America the ideal savior; the priests' opinion of the people; the people's opinion of the priests; no purity in the administration of the holy institutions, 203; seventy-one cathedrals on the island; salaries of the clergy; the life of, 204; church used to foster political ends; prospects as to the future support of the church; divorce impossible under the law; the basis for possible separation, 205; scant provision for the poor and sickly; lack of comforts in the homes for the destitute poor, 206; loathsome roadside beggars; the dying abandoned by their friends, 207; no money; no medicine; the inbred brutality of Spain, 208

Spices—raised in small quantities; soil and climate favorable for all varieties, 142

Springs, thermal, mineral, and medicinal, 83

Stamp duties, proportion of revenue from, 228

Starch, made from the yautia and cassava roots, 141

Straw-hat making—the variety of material for; rice-straw, scores of grasses, and tree barks, 80

INDEX

Sugar—the chief product of the island, in avoirdupois, 101; growth of the industry; money value of the crop, 102; the past and present conditions, 103; average number of pounds to the acre; methods of culture; transplanting the cane, 104; antiquated machinery; by-products, rum and alcohol, 105; wages of laborers; a problem for the planters, 106; the factor of transportation; process of manufacture, 107; abandoned mills, 108; prohibitory tariff on American machinery, 109; centralizing the industry; profits of, 110; insufficiency of cane; cost of cultivation of, 111; life of the root; plowing; manner of ditching and draining; contract farming, 112; transportation an important item; profit-sharing; profit of sugarlands, 113; crop double that of the United States, 114

T

Timber—scarcity of; cost at Lares, 78

Tobacco—the culture of; Cuba the largest customer, 115; sold in the United States with the Havana brand; methods of manufacture unskilled and slovenly, 116; soil and climate favorable to its culture; quality deteriorates when manufactured in the north, 117; variation of the exports of the leaf; estimated amount of quantity raised, 118; favorable lands for cultivation; preparation of; screens to protect the plant from the winds, 119; grown chiefly in small patches; draining and guttering; cutting time, 120; need for careful attention; imperfect method of curing; the weakest side of the culture; time required for curing, 121; sweating process; price of land; principal buyers, 122; the average quality of the cigars is vile; the price of, 123; bacteria-bearing cigars; lack of skilled workmen, 124; wages of; varieties of cigarettes; plug-tobacco ropes one hundred feet long, 125; not a desirable article; the better class of women not smokers; present price of the leaf, 126; fine quality of the wrapper; a bright future for the industry, 127

Tradesmen, chiefly Spanish, capable and polite, 84

Trail-riding — character of the roads, 41; from Ponce to Mayaguez; time of trip; market venders on the road; "Heart of the Black Hand" country, 42; modes of travel; suburban residences; home of the well-to-do, 43; a "camino reale"; picturesque scenery on the way; view from the mountain road toward Adjuntas, 44; a question of distance; a perilous path; harmless natives, 46; winding paths; insecure habitations, 47; an incident on the road; "no rest for the weary"; cross-purposes, 49; a beautiful panorama; hillside maize-fields; plowing on the hillside, 50; dangerous mudholes; castellated mountain farms, 51; lost on the trail, 52;

INDEX

Trail-riding—*Continued*
a perilous track; a change of steeds, 53; a coffee-planter on guard; plantation hospitality, 54
Tramway, from San Juan to Rio Piedras, 69
Trolley lines—great future for, 69; advantages over steam, 70

V

Vegetables—a great variety grown; sweet potatoes and yams reach a high degree of perfection; Irish potatoes grown on the hillside are fine, 140; yautia and cassava, starchy edible roots; gedianda, a weed bearing a narrow pod, a substitute for coffee, 141
Vieques—low in contour, but very fertile, 12; finest sugar-land in the province, 104

W

Wages—coffee-berry pickers, 92;
average of the peons, about fifty cents Spanish per day, 106; of cigar-makers, 125, 156
Winds, in October, north and northeast, 20
Woods, asoubo, capa blanca, capa prieta, capa de sabana, aceitillo, cedro, tachuelo, ciera, and others, 79

Y

Yauco, a coffee town on the south coast, 196
Yautia, a big lily, with edible tuber-like roots, much esteemed by the natives, 141
Yellow fever—not to be feared; has never been epidemic on the island, 25; confined chiefly to barracks and prisons; not heard of on the hills; is a disease of the night, 26

www.ingramcontent.com/pod-product-compliance
Lightning Source LLC
Chambersburg PA
CBHW032010220426
43664CB00006B/201